HAYNES **MAX** POWER

PERFORMANCE

HAYNES MAX POWER
PERFORMANCE

The definitive guide to **modifying**
by **Jay Storer** and **Bob Jex**

Acknowledgements

We are grateful for the help and cooperation of APC (American Products Company), 22324 Temescal Canyon Rd., Corona, CA 92883 (www.4apc.net), who supplied many of the modified car photographs used throughout this book, Steve Rothenbuehler at Dynamic Autosports, Inc., 23901 Remme Ridge, Lake Forest, CA 92630 (www.dynamicautosports.com), who provided valuable insight, and to the many hot hatch owners who offered their vehicles for photography at various shows and events during the winter and spring of 2003. Special thanks to Charles Gutmann and Team Speedtrix for making their cars available and assisting with research.

Cover photo: Photo used with permission by Lund International, Honda Civic project vehicle for Auto Vent Shade (www.autoventshade.com).

ISBN 1 84425 056 3

Printed by **J H Haynes & Co Ltd,**
Sparkford, Yeovil, Somerset BA22 7JJ, England.

Tel: 01963 442030 Fax: 01963 440001
Int. tel: +44 1963 442030 Fax: +44 1963 440001
E-mail: sales@haynes.co.uk
Web site: www.haynes.co.uk

Haynes Publishing
Sparkford, Yeovil, Somerset BA22 7JJ, England

Haynes North America, Inc
861 Lawrence Drive, Newbury Park, California 91320, USA

Editions Haynes
4, Rue de l'Abreuvoir
92415 COURBEVOIE CEDEX, France

Haynes Publishing Nordiska AB
Box 1504, 751 45 UPPSALA, Sweden

4056 - 200

It wasn't my idea guv'nor!

1 Advice on safety procedures and precautions is contained throughout this manual, and more specifically on page 196. You are strongly recommended to note these comments, and to pay close attention to any instructions that may be given by the parts supplier.

2 J H Haynes recommends that vehicle customisation should only be undertaken by individuals with experience of vehicle mechanics; if you are unsure as to how to go about the customisation, advice should be sought from a competent and experienced individual. Any queries regarding customisation should be addressed to the product manufacturer concerned, and not to J H Haynes, nor the vehicle manufacturer.

3 The instructions in this manual are followed at the risk of the reader who remains fully and solely responsible for the safety, roadworthiness and legality of his/her vehicle. Thus J H Haynes are giving only non-specific advice in this respect.

4 When modifying a car it is important to bear in mind the legal responsibilities placed on the owners, driver and modifiers of cars, including, but not limited to, the Road Traffic Act 1988. IN PARTICULAR, IT IS AN OFFENCE TO DRIVE ON A PUBLIC ROAD A VEHICLE WHICH IS NOT INSURED OR WHICH DOES NOT COMPLY WITH THE CONSTRUCTION AND USE REGULATIONS, OR WHICH IS DANGEROUS AND MAY CAUSE INJURY TO ANY PERSON, OR WHICH DOES NOT HOLD A CURRENT MOT CERTIFICATE OR DISPLAY A VALID TAX DISC.

5 The safety of any alteration and its compliance with construction and use regulations should be checked before a modified vehicle is sold as it may be an offence to sell a vehicle which is not roadworthy.

6 Any advice provided is correct to the best of our knowledge at the time of publication, but the reader should pay particular attention to any changes of specification to the vehicles, or parts, which can occur without notice.

7 Alterations to vehicles should be disclosed to insurers and licensing authorities, and legal advice taken from the police, vehicle testing centres, or appropriate regulatory bodies.

8 The vehicles chosen for this project are some of those most widely modified by their owners, and readers should not assume that the vehicle manufacturers have given their approval to the modifications.

9 Neither J H Haynes nor the manufacturers give any warranty as to the safety of a vehicle after alterations, such as those contained in this book, have been made. J H Haynes will not accept liability for any economic loss, damage to property or death and personal injury arising from use of this manual other than in respect of injury or death resulting directly from J H Haynes' negligence.

Contents

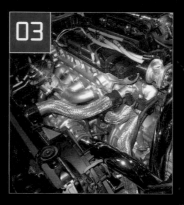

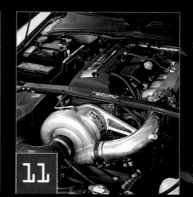

Engine performance

It's been said "speed is just a question of how much you want to spend." There's a lot of truth in this statement. People with big incomes and racers with sponsors can afford to build 7-second cars. But remember also that speed comes with compromise, and an engine built to make 600 horsepower at the track won't idle smoothly, get decent fuel economy or go 100,000 miles between major overhauls. Performance modifications are frequently called "upgrades," but we need to keep in mind that the *performance* is what's being upgraded, and often you'll have to give up some of the practical aspects, like the smooth, reliable and economical operation that modern cars are famous for.

So it's best to have a plan for your project, even if you don't have all the money to do everything right away. Perhaps the best compromise is a car that's fast enough to race when you feel like it, but still practical to drive to work every day. Many upgrades, such as a four-branch manifold, cat-back system, and induction kit give "free" horsepower, meaning the only downside is more engine noise (that's a downside?). These mods are also relatively inexpensive and are "no-brainers" for any modifier. When you get into nitrous, turbos and superchargers, you'll be spending more money, and also getting into more risk of engine damage. Camshafts and cylinder head work will reduce your car's low-speed driveability and frequently also hurt your fuel economy (bothered?). Generally, any mods designed to increase power at high revs will lose some at the bottom end. Sometimes you can't have everything.

Many mods work best only when combined with other upgrades. For example, fitting a high-performance ignition coil and HT leads to your otherwise stock engine will look nice, but probably won't add any power. These bits are designed to provide ultra-high voltage to overcome high cylinder pressures created by high-compression, turbocharging or supercharging. At the normal pressures created by your stock engine, your old gakky-looking ignition components were probably plenty adequate. Unless, of course, they were knackered anyway, in which case, go ahead.

So it's more than just whether or not the parts fit. It's also important to make sure that the upgrades are appropriate to your engine, and to your plans for it. Fitting a de-cat pipe or a cat-back exhaust system will surely get a performance increase, maybe even one that you can feel in the seat of your pants. But how much of an increase?

Magazine ads are very specific with horsepower numbers, but it's important to understand that these numbers may not always apply. Why? Because a new free-flowing exhaust system will do wonders for a car with some engine mods but still stuck with a restrictive standard exhaust. On the other hand, those same components might do little (apart from sound better) for a bog-standard engine with a decent factory exhaust system.

The mystery of how some components work together (and some don't) is why it's important to talk with a tuner or knowledgeable engine builder before you get out the tools (or your wad). Figure out how much power and performance you want, how important things like driveability and economy are to you, and how much you have to spend. A tuner who has experience on modern engines will guide you to the best answers for your needs.

So, what are you waiting for? There's plenty of horsepower out there, just waiting for a home under your bonnet.

Choosing a tuner

Who needs a tuner? Well, at some point, anyone interested in building a quality, reliable performance car will. There's always going to be someone out there who knows a little (or a lot) more than you do about transforming a standard motor into a tarmac-shredding missile. An experienced tuner fully grasps "The Big Picture," of how everything under the bonnet works as a complete system, not as individual items. All this complexity makes tuning a modern engine more challenging, especially when aftermarket high-performance parts are thrown into the mix.

If you've read this far, you've probably already started calling and e-mailing tuning firms with questions about the engine mods you want to make. Maybe you're still looking for a tuner. If so, this section will help you choose a good one. Even if you already have a tuner lined up for the job, this section will help you determine whether he's the right tuner for you. Is he a good technical consultant whose advice you can count on, a teacher from whom you can learn how to set up your car, and a businessman whom you can trust? Yeah? Cool.

First impressions can be misleading. Tuners have to make a living just like the rest of us, so at some point in their relationship with a customer they have to make some money. Many tuners don't just tune cars. They also sell high-performance products. So being a tuner is a balancing act: a good tuner dispenses advice about how to go faster, and he also sells the goods and services to make it happen. You're employing this guy to help you improve your car's performance. He's going to tell you how to get there, and much of his advice will be free. But he's a businessman, and he's in business to make money. Sure, he wants to have fun, and hang out with other enthusiasts, but he does have a bottom line. So keep this in mind when you're searching for the perfect tuner.

What should you look for in a tuner? Someone honest, knowledgeable and affordable, someone who will help you prioritise your modification plans, who will step up and do the job for you when it's over your head, but who'll also willingly step aside when he thinks you can handle the job yourself. Maybe you can't judge a book by its cover, but you can rate a prospective tuner by answering the following questions.

What kind of tuner are you looking for?

Tuners are not all the same. Some "tuners" are in business mainly to sell high-performance hardware. These guys often know something about the kit they sell (some actually know quite a lot), and some of them will even install the products you buy from them on your car. But they often don't provide tuning services such as flow bench and dyno work, custom machining, welding or fabricating. In the initial stages of a project (when you're upgrading the wheels, tyres, brakes, suspension and installing bolt-on performance mods) a guy like this might be perfectly satisfactory.

Other tuners are more "hands-on" - they don't just sell speed products, they act as technical consultants to their customers, sell them the products and/or services they need to improve their car's performance, and then install the product or make the necessary modifications. If you're not already blessed with mechanical ability and plenty of tools, get yourself a "full-service" tuner like this. What you need is someone who can serve you not only as your technical guru, but who can help you reach your performance goals by doing some or all of the work for you. Novices often waste thousands on inappropriate mods because they don't take into consideration how one mod affects another. The full-service tuner can save you a lot of aggravation and money in the early stages of designing and building your project vehicle because he'll help you make good decisions on expensive upgrades that require some planning.

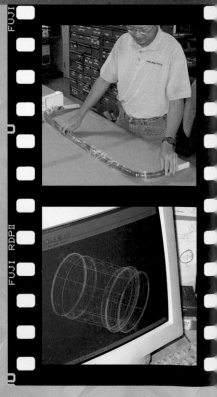

Does the tuner know what he's talking about?

There are no shortcuts to becoming a good tuner. The best ones are standing on top of the tallest piles of broken parts. Basically, all tuning knowledge comes from taking chances, trying out new ideas, adding what works to the performance repertoire and eliminating what doesn't. Don't let your car become just another rung on the learning ladder - in other words, make sure your tuner's broken-parts-phase is behind him.

To the real tuner, there are two kinds of experiences: good experiences and . . . learning experiences. When a modification works the way it's supposed to, that's a good experience. When it doesn't, that's a learning experience. A good tuner isn't afraid to make mistakes, but he doesn't repeat those mistakes. He learns from them and moves on. And good tuners use their own vehicles, not customers' cars, to research and develop new products and services. If you decide to work with a tuner who intends to use your car as a test-bed for new ideas and/or products, make sure you get paid for this service, perhaps in the form of free or discounted parts and labour.

When asked about his background, a novice tuner looking for new customers might fudge the truth a bit. An experienced tuner who's been in business for a while won't need to. If his workshop is neat, clean and filled with hand, power and machine tools and clean vehicles, and he's got an office full of trophies from the track and photos of smiling customers and their cars, then stick around.

Some of the best tuners gained their special knowledge and skills working for a car maker, garage or even a racing team. A former car factory employee might even still have some backdoor connection to the factory, to gain insights into the inner workings of, say, the latest engine management systems, unavailable to his rivals.

Some people will tell you that tuning is art; some will tell you that it's science; some will tell you it's both. But it's neither. Tuning is engineering. Good tuners may not be engineers, but they do have "engineering minds," i.e. they understand physics, mechanics, hydraulics, pneumatics, electronics, etc. enough to define a problem in engineering terms, and then solve it the way an engineer would.

Look for a tuner with experience not only with spanners but also in machining, welding and fabricating. Someone with these skills onsite won't be relying on subcontractors, or be sending you across town to another outfit you're not familiar with.

You'll also need a tuner with sharp analytical and diagnostic skills. Does he have an exhaust gas analyser, fault code reader, an oscilloscope, rolling road and a flow bench? If he doesn't, he shouldn't be tuning modern cars. Just having the gear is a good sign, because these tools are too expensive to buy just to impress customers. If things go wrong, knowing how the engine management system components interact with each other means he can approach problems systemically and solve them logically.

Look for a tuner with satisfied customers. Word-of-mouth advertising should be part of your search, but don't make it the only part. Remember, no-one actually wants to admit they've had a poor job done on their car.

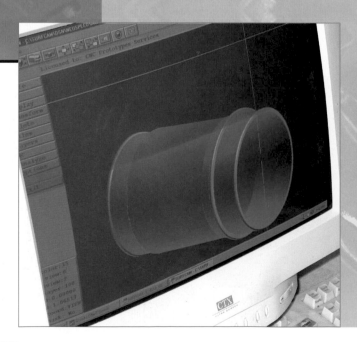

Can the tuner deliver what he's promising?

Most tuners start out as self-employed small businessmen who "do it all" themselves. As they become established, smart tuners hire skilled and knowledgeable technicians to fill any gaps in their abilities, enabling them to become "full-service" tuners, who can do everything for you. If possible, try to get to know some of the key people who work there. Are they happy working for this particular tuner? What's their speciality, and who have they worked for previously? A tuner who's really proud of his staff will probably brag a bit about them.

Good tuners get results; bad ones don't. So look at a prospective tuner's track record. If more straight-line performance is what you want (of course), look for a tuner with race track experience. Many tuners marketing themselves as horsepower specialists have a race or rally team (or they sponsor one) which they use to try out new ideas and develop new products in competition. If a tuner has achieved success here, what works for them will probably work for you.

Is the tuner local?

Most tuners are set up for mail order, and when you're buying wheels, tyres, suspension components, tune-up parts or bolt-on performance goodies, mail order prices can be hard to beat. But, if you're planning to do modifications that require precision machining, welding, fabrication or actual tuning, don't get into a long-distance relationship with a tuner unless absolutely necessary. Even if his reputation is sterling, you don't want to get involved in lengthy e-mails, phone calls and rewrapping and returning custom parts that don't fit or don't work.

Is the tuner affordable?

Ask yourself some questions here - your car's probably basically okay the way it is, so why do you want to spend money making it faster - to pose, make you feel better, or to seriously race? Things like this, coupled with how much dosh you've got in the first place, should tell you how much to blow on engine tuning. Some mods are more cost-effective than others. A pro may have upwards of twenty grand in his engine, but is a twenty-g motor twice as powerful as a ten-grand one? Er, no. You'd be amazed how many people spend megabucks on one part of their car, only to ignore the rest of it because they're broke! A good tuner will sit you down before you spend a penny, and have you do a "build sheet", which is an overview of what you want to do your car, and how much each mod's going to cost. The total cost gets into five figures pretty quickly, so shop hard when buying parts. Is your tuner ripping you off? Compare prices of everything you'll need on the internet, mail order, etc.

Always be straight with a tuner about how far you want to go, and what you can really, really afford. This is your hobby (okay, maybe it's your obsession!), so don't let it snowball to the point that it interferes with essential living expenses. Figure out how much money a month you can realistically afford to spend, then divide that into the total estimated cost of the project and you'll know roughly how long it's going to take to get there. You'll also know the true meaning of affordability!

Is the tuner easy to get along with?

Most tuners are helpful and supportive. But some are eccentrics or egomaniacs. This is probably unavoidable in a field that's filled with self-made, self-promoting small businessmen whose success is tied to their accomplishments. But - if you find your tuner is patronising you, lecturing you or grumbling about the stupidity of other customers and/or his competitors, get rid of him. You want results, not therapy. A truly hard-working professional doesn't have the time to talk trash about his customers or fellow tuners. He's too busy taking care of business.

Does the tuner do the work on time?

Project vehicles are like new buildings - work proceeds in spurts, with long intervals of waiting (for parts, rebuilds, custom fabrication, etc). So patience is a virtue you must have, or must learn, putting together a project vehicle with the help of a tuner.

Even so, nobody wants a tuner who's unable, or unwilling, to deliver goods or services on time, particularly if the car in question is also your daily driver. Be realistic. If you can't afford to be without a car for lengthy periods of time, either borrow something, or look for a tuner who'll work on your car when you don't need it, like evenings, or weekends, or holidays. Some projects are unavoidably time-consuming - don't hook up with an over-optimistic tuner who promises things he can't deliver.

The flowbench:
The tuner's wind tunnel

If you're looking for a tuner to re-work your cylinder head for optimum airflow, look for one who owns and knows how to use a flowbench.

Since the power output of an engine is directly proportional to the amount of air it can inhale, a good tuner will try to remove all resistance to airflow in the induction system, so the engine can pack as much mixture into the combustion chambers as possible. In order to do so, he must be able to measure the volume of air flowing through the intake manifold and the cylinder head to check that his modifications have done the business. The device he uses to measure airflow through the intake manifold and the cylinder head(s) is known as a flowbench. For tuners, the flowbench is an essential tool - without it, you're just guessing. Don't mod your head without one.

Superchips

Dynamometers

Horsepower talk is cheap when you're sitting around, kicking tyres and telling lies with your mates. If a friend claims a certain amount of horsepower for his car, can he prove it? Do you care? The only way to be sure is to subject it to the ultimate tuning tool: the dynamometer. A dynamometer is a device that can accurately measure horsepower. There are two kinds of automotive dynamometers: engine dynos and chassis dynos.

Engine dynamometer

Engine development work is easier with the engine removed from the vehicle and fitted to an engine dynamometer. An engine dyno is capable of "loading" the engine as if it were being run while installed in the vehicle. Engine dynos can provide a very accurate picture of an engine's power output because they measure power at the flywheel, with no power losses through the transmission/transaxle or driveline. This means, of course, that the engine must be removed from the vehicle and installed on the dyno. Then all the auxiliary systems - fuel supply, electrical supply, exhaust extraction, intake air for combustion, air flow for cooling, coolant temperature control, throttle actuation, etc - must be provided. Because of these requirements, engine dynos are usually installed in enclosed, soundproof "test cells" that can provide the engine with these auxiliary systems. Despite the complexity of setting up an engine dyno/test cell site, engine dynos are popular with car makers and engine developers because of the degree of control over the test parameters made possible by isolating the engine from the vehicle. Serious developers and researchers want repeatability (consistent results from test to test) unaffected by factors that can't be controlled by the tester. They also want the capability to install special testing sensors and to make easy adjustments and changes to the test engine. For these reasons, engine dynamometers are used extensively by car makers to develop new engines, and to test them for reliability and endurance. Engine dynos are not used much by aftermarket tuners because testing an engine out of the vehicle isn't practical, or affordable for most customers.

Chassis dynamometer (rolling road)

If a tuner proudly shows off his dynamometer when you "take the tour" of his shop, chances are it will be a chassis dyno (rolling road). The rolling road is the dyno of choice for most tuners because it allows them to test an engine's performance without removing it from the vehicle. A typical rolling road uses a series of big rollers that are connected to some type of power absorber capable of controlling the load that's applied to the rollers. To measure horsepower, you simply drive the car onto the dyno, position it so that the drive wheels are resting on top of the rollers, start the engine, put it in gear and record the data. The chassis dyno operator can dial a specific amount of load into the rollers to simulate acceleration, passing or going up a steep hill. Another advantage is that the chassis dyno delivers "real world" numbers, i.e. it gives the actual power at the drive wheels (bhp at the wheels), not the power at the flywheel. The flywheel figure's always more impressive, because you lose some power through the car's drivetrain (gearbox, driveshafts, tyres, etc). The disadvantage of a rolling road is that the results aren't that consistent or repeatable because of these driveline losses. Even things like tyre wear, pressures and temperatures can influence each dyno run.

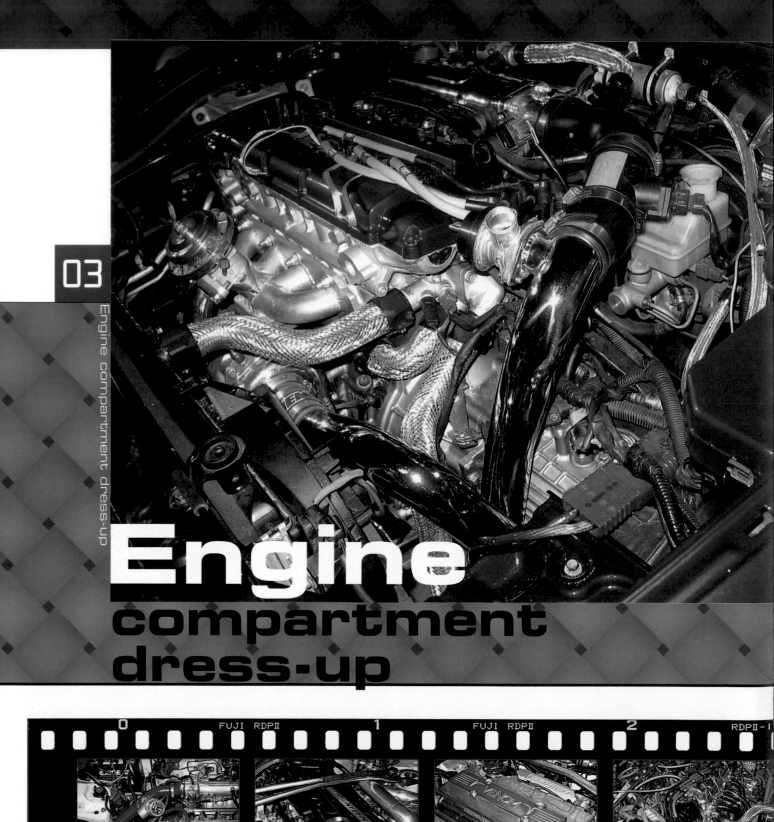

03

Engine
compartment
dress-up

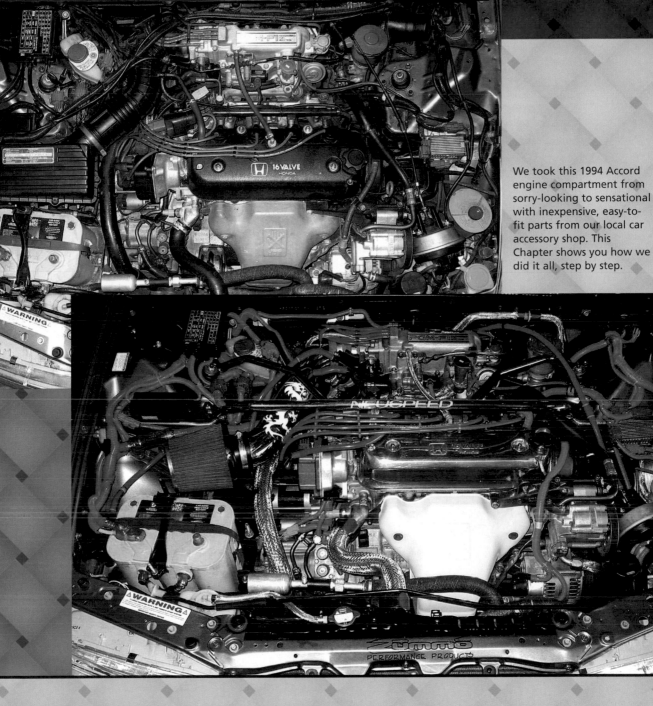

We took this 1994 Accord engine compartment from sorry-looking to sensational with inexpensive, easy-to-fit parts from our local car accessory shop. This Chapter shows you how we did it all, step by step.

Pop the bonnet on a typical modern hatchback, and what do you see? Black plastic air filter housing, black air intake duct, black battery, black radiator and heater hoses, black vacuum hoses, black fuse box, black electrical harnesses, black accelerator cable, black valve cover (with, of course, a black oil filler cap), black . . . A sea of black! Oh wait, hang on, there's a grey bit over there - phew. Is your engine compartment dressed for a funeral or something? Did the engine just die?

Show-car engine compartments don't look like midnight in a coal mine, so why should yours? Look how we transformed the engine compartment shown above - this only took a few hundred quid and a couple of weekends.

Detail your engine
compartment

before dressing it up

Before we talk about things you can do to dress up your engine compartment, let's take a few minutes to discuss detailing. This, in case you're wondering, is another word for cleaning, which is a good thing to do even if you never spend a penny to trick out the engine bay.

After 20,000 or 30,000 miles, an engine usually begins to leak a little coolant or engine oil. Brake fluid, power-steering fluid and transmission fluid leaks might also appear. As the miles build up, so does the mess - these little leaks slowly spread out, dirt and road grime start sticking to the areas covered by oil, and the engine gets dirty. Some of the leaking fluids, if they're not regularly removed, can attack paint, plastic and rubber. Batteries can also be messy. A duff voltage regulator (in your alternator) can result in the battery being overcharged, which can spit highly-corrosive battery acid onto painted surfaces. Dirty battery connections could mean that one day you'll hear the dreaded "click-click", which means that you're not playing with a full 12 volts.

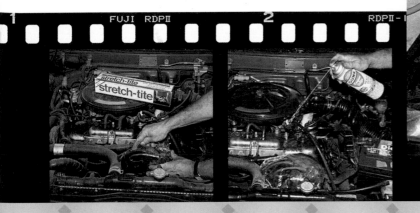

Engine washing

In a basic wash and detail, a clean engine might need nothing more than a simple soaping up and hosing down. If you can't remove the accumulated dirt and grime this easily, stronger measures are called for. Chemical cleaners for degreasing engines are available at your local car accessory shop, and there are even some effective household cleaners. Most oven cleaners work well on heavy grease deposits on your engine, and many household liquid or spray cleaners will also work in most cases. Observe all the cautions on the container, and wear rubber gloves and eye protection when hosing off this stuff - some of these cleaners are caustic, and most can damage your eyes and skin.

Proper engine cleaners are even more effective than household cleaning agents. Gunk is a widely-available brand that has been used for many years, but it's not the only option. Some of the engine cleaners are available in both spray and foam - the foam type is good at staying in place on vertical surfaces such as timing covers and the engine bulkhead.

Pressure washing

On engines with heavy grease deposits, it's helpful to have some kind of pressure to help loosen the deposits. Renting or buying a pressure-washer is the best solution if you're willing to spend the money.

The local coin-op carwash or supermarket jet wash is an ideal place to clean your engine. There's plenty of pressure, hot water and even soapy water to wash off the chemicals before rinsing with clear water. But don't forget your mobile - if your car won't start after a vigourous session with the jet wash, you'll be stuck (see 'moisture'). Some people favour spraying on the Gunk first, then driving to the jet wash - this is a good way to start dissolving the grot, but remember those cleaning solvents might have burnt off by the time you get there!

Steam cleaning

The third option is to take your car to a place that does engine steam cleaning. Before the general availability of good consumer engine cleaners in spray cans, this was the only option, and you had to "know where to go" to even find a carwash that did engine steam-cleaning. As its name implies, this process involves a pressure spray of really hot water and solvent. It does a superb job of removing baked-on grease and dirt from engines, gearboxes and running gear. Many professional modifiers and tuners make the steam-cleaner their first stop when starting a new project.

Steam cleaning, if you can find somewhere that still does it, cleans everything extensively. The only drawbacks are that it can remove paint from the engine or from painted accessories, especially if the paint is already beginning to flake or peel off from age, chemical exposure or heat, and can also damage rubber components if you're not careful. But if you're going to go all the way with engine compartment detailing, this shouldn't matter that much because you'll eventually repaint most components anyway.

Moisture

Another problem with pressure washing and steam cleaning is moisture, which isn't good for ignition and fuel system components. Keeping critical components dry during engine cleaning is a precaution that should be taken no matter what wash method you use - hose, pressure-wash or steam. Of course, the best plan is to avoid getting water on sensitive components in the first place, but with steam cleaning it's pretty much unavoidable! Steamy, pressurised water can get inside your distributor cap and other places that you think are completely sealed. Your engine might start but run poorly after a steam bath, or it might not start at all. So have some WD-40 and some clean rags handy. You might have to dry out the distributor cap or the boots at the ends of the coil king lead and each HT lead.

To keep them from getting wet in the first place, protect the coil, distributor carburettor or throttle body, and any car alarm modules. These can be effectively covered with household aluminium foil, plastic bags or "cling-film" plastic food wrap.

Remove the big chunks first

After bagging or otherwise protecting vital components, use a paint stirring stick or an old plastic scraper to shift the heavier concentrations of grease. Don't use a screwdriver for this, as anything sharp will scratch surfaces and remove paint.

Look in crevices and places where dirt collects easily. The more grot you can remove this way, the fewer applications of cleaner you'll have to make.

Not too hot!

In most cases it's not a good idea to try cleaning a hot engine. Some enthusiasts like to clean an engine while it's still hot because the heat makes the chemicals work faster at loosening dirt. But some normally-hot components such as the exhaust manifold (and turbocharger, if you have one) can crack if they're exposed to a sudden bath of cold water when the part is really hot. Like we said before, solvent-based cleaners will evaporate (or even catch fire) on a hot engine. If you're doing your clean-up at the jet wash, let the engine cool off before you start.

Use lots of cleaner

Begin your underbonnet cleanup by applying a liberal coat of cleaner everywhere, even on areas that you don't think are that dirty. Douse the bulkhead (back of the engine compartment), inner wings, radiator and all around the engine. Work your way down to the parts of the chassis that are exposed in the engine compartment. Most engine cleaning products work best if they are not allowed to dry out completely before rinsing. If you notice that warmer areas seem to be drying out, spray them again with cleaner and let it work for the required number of minutes. Use a brush with a long wooden handle and stiff bristles to scrub the cleaner into areas of baked-on grease. Remember, even the best cleaner probably won't do all the work for you.

Since you're probably using strong cleaners for your underbonnet session, either cover your wings and windscreen cowl panel, or wash down those areas right after the engine work. The cleaner and sludge you hose off can get on your paint and cause wax streaking, if not paint damage, when left on too long. It's also a bonus if you can still see through your windscreen - don't leave it to your wipers to get the muck off.

Inspect and clean rubber hoses, vacuum lines and cables

After a thorough cleaning, inspect all your engine compartment hoses and vacuum lines. If some of your hoses are noticeably spongy or soft, it's time to replace them. If all your rubber hoses are in good shape, they can be made to look like new very easily. Clean them with a rag and any tyre or rubber cleaner, then wipe them off with a silicone dash spray. You'll be amazed how fresh they look! Don't use cleaners or silicone products on drivebelts - it can cause them to slip and squeal. HT leads that have become greasy from handling during spark plug changes are also easily cleaned.

Braided hose covers

Braided covers are available in a variety of lengths and diameters. Typical cover kits include covers in all various diameters, to suit vacuum lines, fuel hoses or heater hoses. Radiator hoses are usually the largest under the bonnet (and they look the most impressive when they're done), so make sure your kit has enough to do all the hoses you'd like.

Most makers of stainless-look braided cover kits also include anodised aluminium "clamps" which look just like the more expensive fittings used on racecar plumbing. Except that they're just aluminium rings, machined to look like big nuts, which fit over a standard hose clip (which you can easily hide by putting it on the side of the hose that nobody will ever see).

Before heading for your accessory shop to buy braided hoses,

it's a good idea to measure the hoses and/or lines you plan to cover. How many feet of braiding do you need, and in what sort of sizes? The best answer to start with is to buy a kit, and take it from there. Some commonly-available kits come in two parts - i.e. the hose braiding and the end fittings are sold separately. Which is a bit strange, as you can't really fit one without the other, but there you go.

Before deciding that every black hose has to get the treatment, think about what's in those hoses. They have to come off, and that means losing whatever's inside - hot coolant and petrol are both dangerous, as is the refrigerant in air-con pipework. Have you got any antifreeze or power steering fluid, to top up the systems afterwards?

Installation on radiator hoses

01 First, unpack your kit and make sure that everything you'll need is included. Most of these kits don't include elaborate instructions, but after we walk you through some typical covering procedures, you'll wonder why you didn't tackle this job sooner!

02 Wait until the engine cools off completely. Drain the engine coolant (refer to your Haynes manual if necessary), then loosen the hose clamp at the radiator and slide it back . . .

03 . . . loosen the clamp at the thermostat housing and slide it back . . .

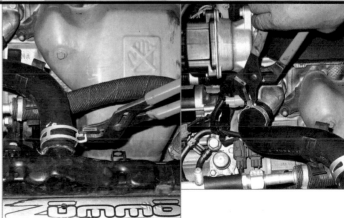

04 . . . then disconnect the upper radiator hose from the radiator and from the thermostat housing.

05 Insert the short section of PVC pipe (usually included in the kit) into one end of the braided cover to hold the cover in a rigid tubular shape, wrap the end of the cover with electrical tape . . .

06 . . . then remove the PVC pipe and cut off the frayed ends of the cover

07 Now run the upper radiator hose through the braided cover . . .

12 Unscrew the clamp . . .

13 . . . and then cut off the excess clamp at the mark you made. Okay? Now, go do the other clamp.

14 When both hose clamps are ready for installation, insert each clamp into its cover with the adjuster screw protruding through the slit in the cover. Then open or tighten the clamp so that it fits flush against the inside surface of the cover.

15 Install a hose clamp and clamp cover on each end of the radiator hose.

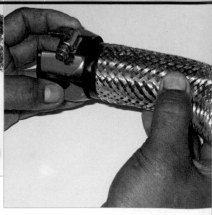

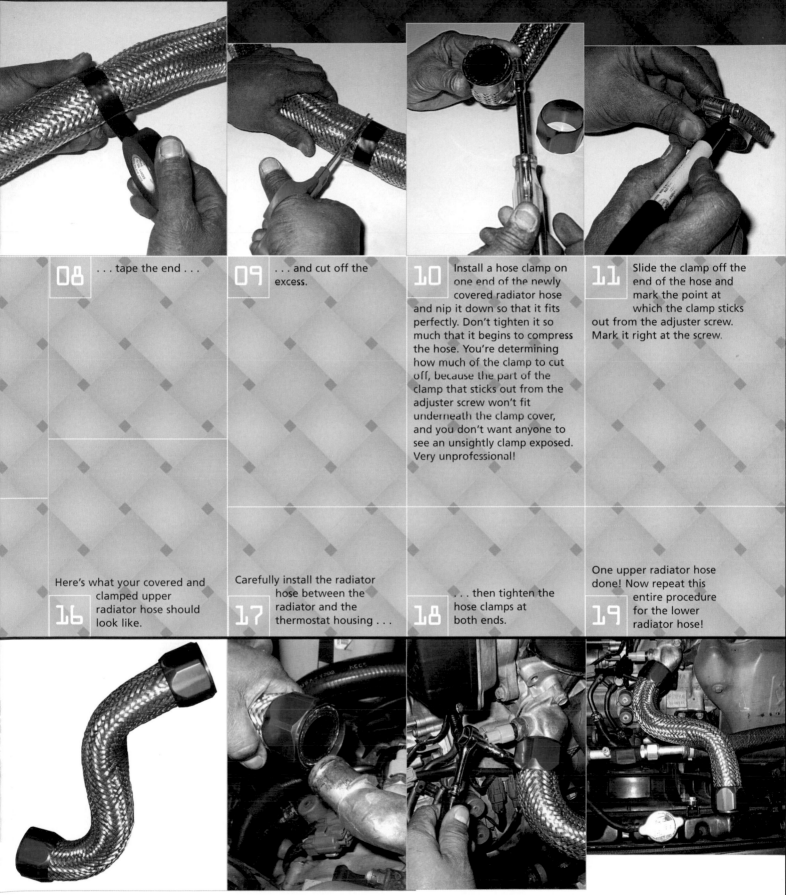

08 . . . tape the end . . .

09 . . . and cut off the excess.

10 Install a hose clamp on one end of the newly covered radiator hose and nip it down so that it fits perfectly. Don't tighten it so much that it begins to compress the hose. You're determining how much of the clamp to cut off, because the part of the clamp that sticks out from the adjuster screw won't fit underneath the clamp cover, and you don't want anyone to see an unsightly clamp exposed. Very unprofessional!

11 Slide the clamp off the end of the hose and mark the point at which the clamp sticks out from the adjuster screw. Mark it right at the screw.

16 Here's what your covered and clamped upper radiator hose should look like.

17 Carefully install the radiator hose between the radiator and the thermostat housing . . .

18 . . . then tighten the hose clamps at both ends.

19 One upper radiator hose done! Now repeat this entire procedure for the lower radiator hose!

Installation on breather (PCV) hoses

Engine compartment dress-up

01	Loosen the hose clamp and disconnect the PCV hose from the valve cover.
02	Loosen the clamp and disconnect the PCV hose from the intake manifold.
03	Disconnect and remove the PCV hose.

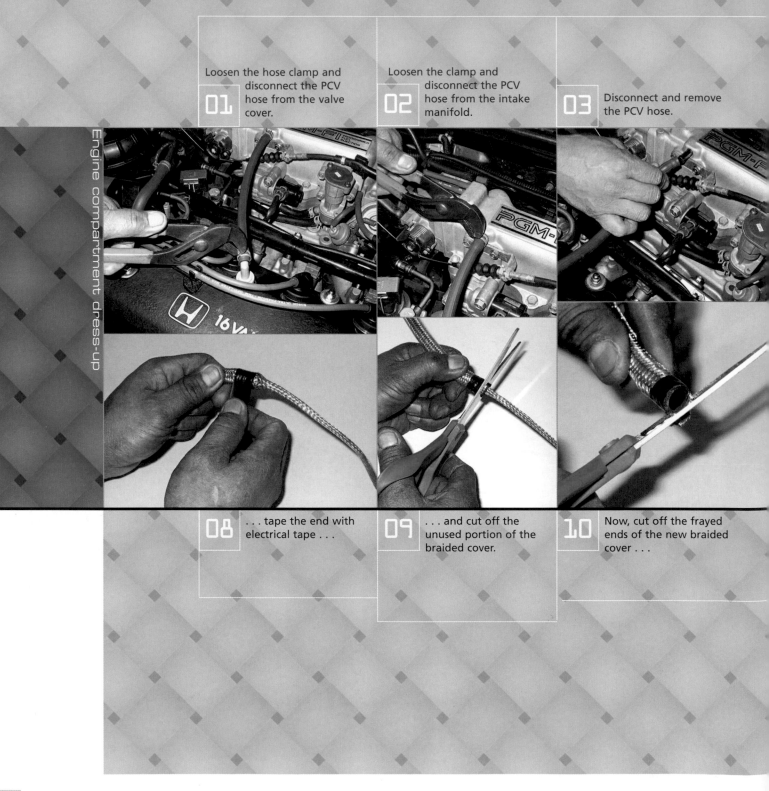

08	. . . tape the end with electrical tape . . .
09	. . . and cut off the unused portion of the braided cover.
10	Now, cut off the frayed ends of the new braided cover . . .

04 Insert one end of the PCV hose into the new braided metal cover . . .

05 Wrap a piece of electrical tape around the end of the braided metal cover . . .

06 . . . work the PCV hose through the braided cover until the hose is completely covered . . .

07 . . . pull on the braided cover to make sure that it's a tight fit over the PCV hose so that the braided cover won't bunch up later . . .

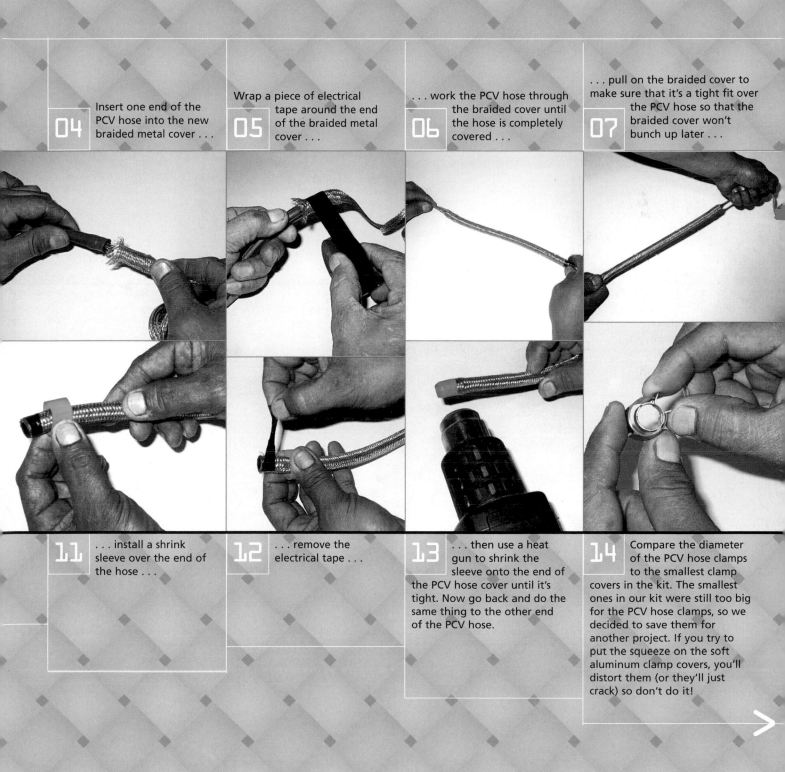

11 . . . install a shrink sleeve over the end of the hose . . .

12 . . . remove the electrical tape . . .

13 . . . then use a heat gun to shrink the sleeve onto the end of the PCV hose cover until it's tight. Now go back and do the same thing to the other end of the PCV hose.

14 Compare the diameter of the PCV hose clamps to the smallest clamp covers in the kit. The smallest ones in our kit were still too big for the PCV hose clamps, so we decided to save them for another project. If you try to put the squeeze on the soft aluminum clamp covers, you'll distort them (or they'll just crack) so don't do it!

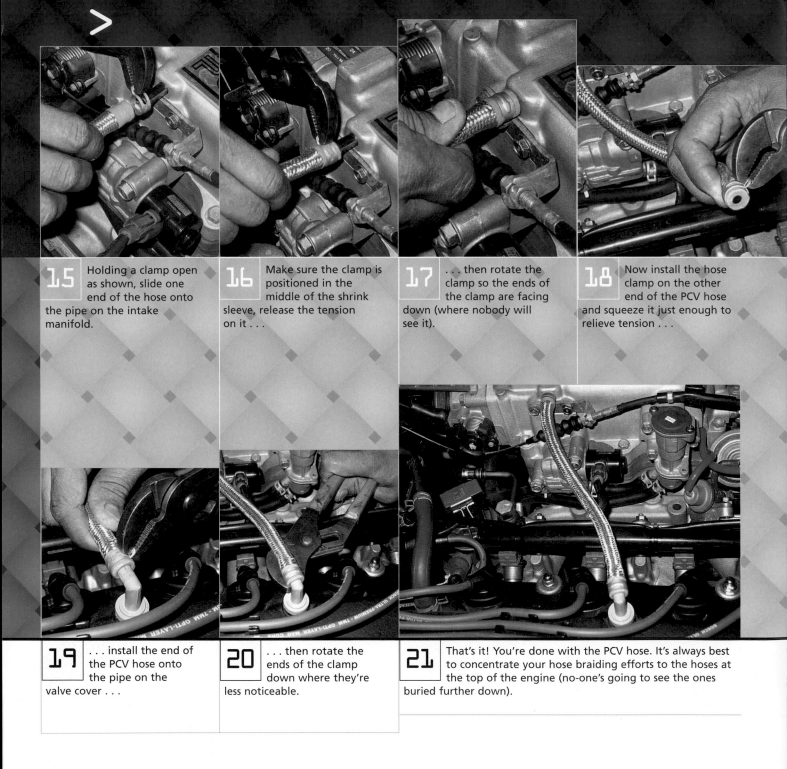

15 Holding a clamp open as shown, slide one end of the hose onto the pipe on the intake manifold.

16 Make sure the clamp is positioned in the middle of the shrink sleeve, release the tension on it . . .

17 . . . then rotate the clamp so the ends of the clamp are facing down (where nobody will see it).

18 Now install the hose clamp on the other end of the PCV hose and squeeze it just enough to relieve tension . . .

19 . . . install the end of the PCV hose onto the pipe on the valve cover . . .

20 . . . then rotate the ends of the clamp down where they're less noticeable.

21 That's it! You're done with the PCV hose. It's always best to concentrate your hose braiding efforts to the hoses at the top of the engine (no-one's going to see the ones buried further down).

Replace the dipstick and the oil filler cap

01 Remove the old oil filler cap. Hmm, this could be a tough job.

02 Install the new cap. You won't find too many engine dress-up swaps any easier than this!

Most replacement dipsticks look better than the stock unit, but the ones with billet handles are among the prettiest, so we selected a blue-anodised billet-handled dipstick for our engine compartment dress-up project.

And while you're at it, why not add a matching oil filler cap? Get a billet cap! Anodised in the color of your choice, of course. If you own a popular car, you may find someone who does chrome or stainless bottle caps (or cap covers) - go for it!

. . . then install the new dipstick. Check out this beautiful blue-anodised, billet handled model. A nice touch for any engine.

01 Yank out the old dipstick . . .

02 . . . make sure that the old unit and the new model are the same dimensions, and that the level marks are in the same places . . .

03

Wiring and small hoses

Wiring covers can protect your wiring from damage, in addition to making it look good. Replacing your old, rotting vacuum hoses with long-life silicone hoses may even fix a vacuum leak that's causing your engine to run poorly. And you've got to get some high-performance silicone HT leads in a matching color. You'll be enhancing your car's performance as well as giving it a cool look.

Installing silicone vacuum hoses

01 First, break out your new silicone hose kit(s). The owner of this project car wanted something blue, so we rounded up some popular kits in the various diameters we would need

02 Where to start? Well, if you're going to replace all the old vacuum hoses, just pick a hose! We started with some small vacuum hoses in the vicinity of the throttle body. Disconnect one hose at a time (so you don't get confused) from the throttle body . . .

03 . . . and from the metal pipe at the other end.

04 Compare the inside diameter (I.D.) of the new silicone hose to the I.D. of the old vacuum hose, and make sure they're the same. You can get away with using a slightly smaller I.D. than the one you're replacing because it produces an even tighter fit. But don't fit a bigger-diameter hose, unless you use hose clips either end - vacuum hoses have to be a good tight fit, or you'll have a major problem.

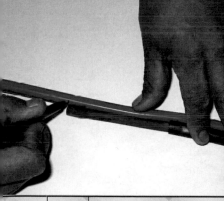

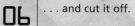

05 Using the old vacuum hose as a template, mark off a piece of the new silicone hose the same length . . .

06 . . . and cut it off.

07 Okay, push one end of the new silicone vacuum hose onto the pipe on the throttle body . . .

08 . . . and the other end on the pipe at, well, the other end. Check the new hose isn't kinked. If it is, air can't flow through it. If the new hose is the same length, all should be well.

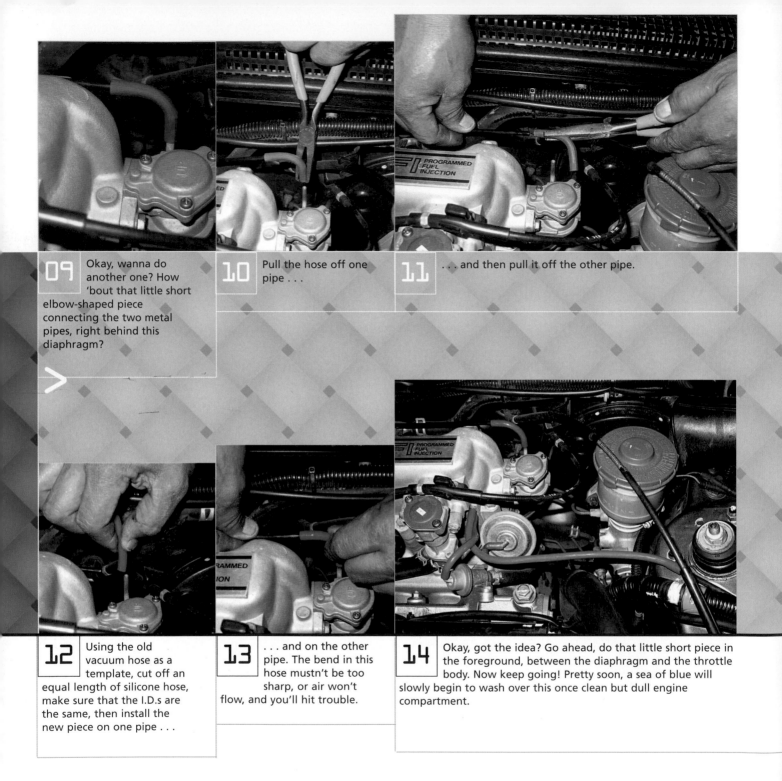

09 Okay, wanna do another one? How 'bout that little short elbow-shaped piece connecting the two metal pipes, right behind this diaphragm?

10 Pull the hose off one pipe . . .

11 . . . and then pull it off the other pipe.

12 Using the old vacuum hose as a template, cut off an equal length of silicone hose, make sure that the I.D.s are the same, then install the new piece on one pipe . . .

13 . . . and on the other pipe. The bend in this hose mustn't be too sharp, or air won't flow, and you'll hit trouble.

14 Okay, got the idea? Go ahead, do that little short piece in the foreground, between the diaphragm and the throttle body. Now keep going! Pretty soon, a sea of blue will slowly begin to wash over this once clean but dull engine compartment.

Installing silicone HT leads

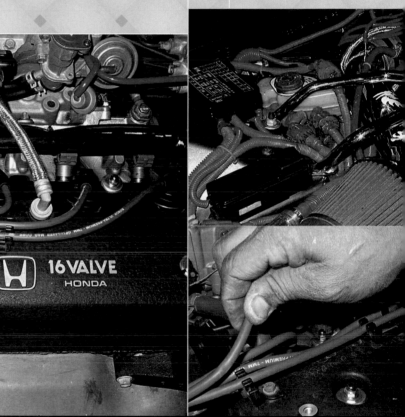

01 Before disconnecting the spark plug boots from the spark plugs, make sure that you can put them back on correctly. If in doubt, draw a diagram, or just work on one lead at a time (top idea).

02 Disconnect the first spark plug wire and boot from its corresponding spark plug. The boots on some vehicles are rather long, and sometimes difficult to disconnect. Do not pull on the wire itself; pull only on the boot. Car accessory shops sell special plier-like tools with plastic-coated tips that wrap around and grip the spark plug boot, making it easier to remove.

03 Disengage the first HT lead from any cable guides on the valve cover, or anywhere between the distributor and the spark plugs.

04 Carefully disconnect the HT lead from its tower on the distributor cap (this is where things can get really confusing, if you try to remove all the leads at once).

>

05 Each HT lead, whether original equipment or aftermarket, has to be a certain length because each spark plug is a different distance from the distributor. Before fitting each new lead, make sure that the lengths are similar and that the fittings at both ends are identical.

06 Plug in the new HT lead to the same distributor cap tower from which you just disconnected the old lead.

07 Thicker leads could mean you'll need thicker cable guides. So remove the old guides . . .

08 . . . and install the new guides in the same location.

09 Connect the new HT lead boot to the correct spark plug.

10 Doing one lead at a time (to prevent mix-ups), keep going until you have replaced the other HT leads and the cable guides. Your finished upgrade should look something like this.

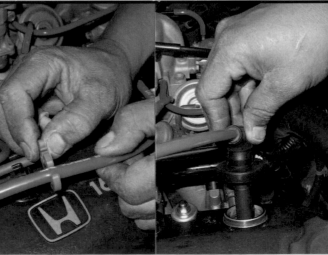

Replacing the breather hose with a filter

Another colourful upgrade is to eliminate that unsightly rubber breather hose and replace it with a trick baby air filter. Breather filters are available in blue, red, yellow and chrome, and look like miniature versions of the big K & N pancake filters. If you fit an induction kit (or even a pancake filter), you might find there's no provision for reconnecting the old breather hose. Leaving a breather hose hanging off is not acceptable (you'll fail the MoT), so fitting one of these little babies instead is a neat solution.

01 Loosen the hose clamp . . .

02 . . . and disconnect the breather hose from the pipe on the valve cover, or from the old air cleaner.

03 Fit the new breather filter . . .

04 . . . and tighten the hose clamp securely.

Covering wire harnesses with split loom

01 If the harness is already covered by the old black plastic stuff, remove it first.

02 Install the new split loom over the harness . . .

Plastic split-loom is easy to fit and looks great. It will help protect your wiring and is easy to remove for servicing. You'll never realise how many wires you have until you have to cover them - but don't worry, this one's easy!

. . . and tape the end (the end that you're not going to cut) with electrical tape.

03

Keep pushing the new split loom onto the harness until you reach an electrical connector or anything that serves as a natural stopping point for a continuous section of split loom. We stopped here because of a junction in the harness, at which point the harness splits off into two smaller sections. At this point, pull off the end of the split loom and cut it (but don't tape it yet).

04

Okay, now cover the two smaller sections with split loom, and then cut them to fit.

05

Now go back and wrap the junction for the three sections of split loom with electrical tape. That's all there is to it! Keep going until you've covered every harness in the engine compartment with new split loom!

06

Replacing the accelerator cable

The accelerator cable isn't something you'd normally think of replacing unless it breaks or is sticking. But take a minute to just look at this aftermarket cable, clad in genuine braided stainless steel. Are you going to sit around and wait until the stock cable breaks to install one just like it? Not! You're going to rush out, buy one and install it right now!

01 When you get home from your accessory shop, break out your new braided stainless steel accelerator cable kit, make sure everything's there, then read the instructions included with the kit.

02 Here's the standard accelerator cable setup. If you've never replaced an accelerator cable before, take a few minutes to study the cable installation on your car. Note the routing of the cable from the bulkhead to the throttle cam on the throttle body. Your new cable must be routed the same way, except that it'll look better. A lot better!

03 First, disengage the accelerator cable from any cable guides on the intake manifold or on the valve cover.

04 Using a pair of spanners, loosen the accelerator cable adjustment nut and the locknut at the cable bracket . . .

05 . . . then disengage the accelerator cable from the cable bracket. Your arrangement might be slightly different to this - your Haynes manual should get you out of trouble.

06 Disengage the plug on the forward end of the cable from its slot in the throttle cam.

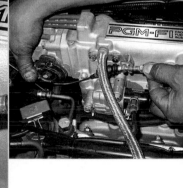

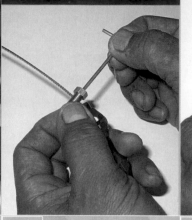

07 Now go inside the car, stick your head under the dash and, using a torch, locate the lower end of the accelerator cable, where it connects to the upper end of the accelerator pedal. Disengage the plug on the lower end of the cable from its slot in the accelerator pedal. Now, back in the engine compartment, pull the cable through the bulkhead grommet.

08 Okay, that takes care of the old accelerator cable. Now grab the new cable and, using an Allen key, loosen the set screw and remove the cable end plug from the end of the cable . . .

. . . but before cutting off the excess sheathing, make sure the sheathing is correctly routed, just like it will be routed when the cable is fitted and hooked up to the throttle body. Don't cut the sheathing too short, which will strain the cable if an engine mount starts to head south and allows the engine to move around. Instead, give yourself a little "wiggle room" by leaving a few inches of extra sheathing. If your guesstimate turns out to be a little too generous, you can always cut if off later.

09 . . . then pull the cable out of its braided steel covering . . .

10 . . . and remove the nut from the threaded fitting.

Hold up the forward end of the braided steel sheathing in its installed position, and mark the point on the sheathing which parallels the end of the threaded assembly you just installed . . .

15

After you have verified that your mark is more or less where it should be, wrap a little piece of tape around the braided sheathing at the mark, then cut off the excess sheathing.

17

Remove the tape from the sheathing, pull the little cable ferrule out of the threaded fitting at the cable bracket (the ferrule that you inserted into the big nut on the threaded fitting back in Step 14, remember?) and slide the little ferrule onto the sheathing.

18

16

11 Insert the threaded fitting through the hole for the accelerator cable in the bulkhead . . .

12 . . . then, working under the dash, fit the nut and tighten it securely.

13 Now go back to the engine compartment and insert the threaded fitting for the upper end of the braided steel sheathing into the cable bracket, and fit the locknut . . .

14 . . . then insert the cable ferrule into the big nut and leave it there for a minute while you mark and cut the excess cable sheathing. (You're not actually installing the ferrule just yet, but you need to put it in its installed position to help you figure out how much sheathing to cut off)

19 Re-insert the cable ferrule back into the big nut on the end of the threaded fitting at the cable bracket.

20 Okay. Insert the removable cable end plug (the one you removed from the cable back in Step 8) into its slot in the throttle cam. Position it so the hole that goes through the plug is more or less aligned with the cable (which isn't there yet, but - be patient - it soon will be).

21 Now go back inside the car and, using a torch, insert the plug at the end of the cable into its slot at the top of the accelerator pedal. Then insert the other end of the cable through the threaded cable fitting that you fitted in the bulkhead, and shove it all the way through the sheathing until it comes out the front end.

22 Pull the accelerator cable through the end plug . . .

>

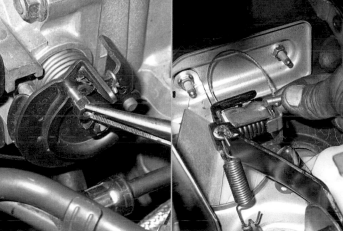

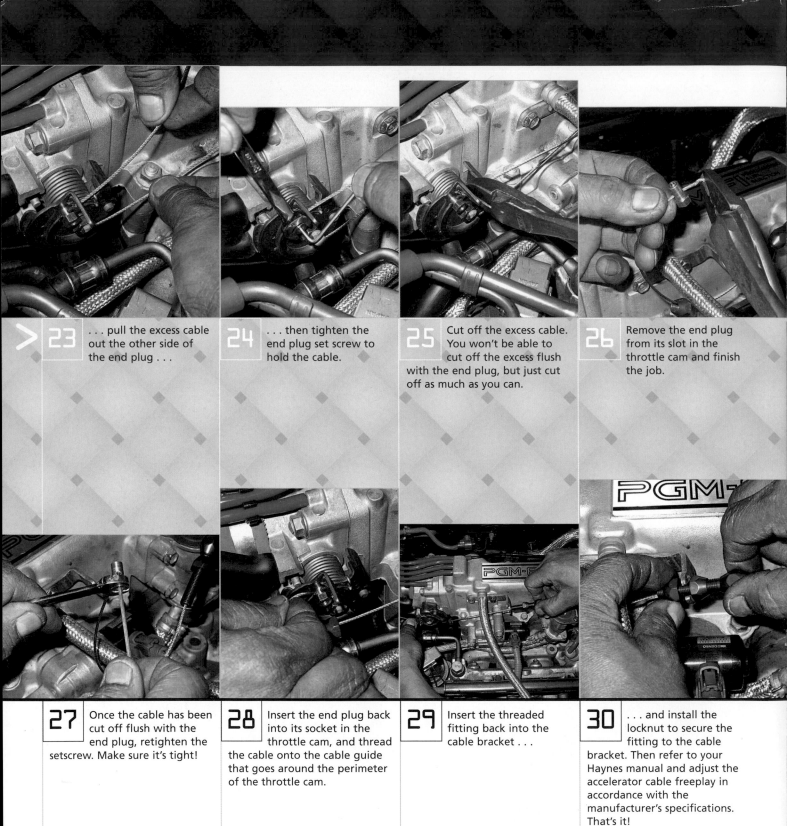

23 . . . pull the excess cable out the other side of the end plug . . .

24 . . . then tighten the end plug set screw to hold the cable.

25 Cut off the excess cable. You won't be able to cut off the excess flush with the end plug, but just cut off as much as you can.

26 Remove the end plug from its slot in the throttle cam and finish the job.

27 Once the cable has been cut off flush with the end plug, retighten the setscrew. Make sure it's tight!

28 Insert the end plug back into its socket in the throttle cam, and thread the cable onto the cable guide that goes around the perimeter of the throttle cam.

29 Insert the threaded fitting back into the cable bracket . . .

30 . . . and install the locknut to secure the fitting to the cable bracket. Then refer to your Haynes manual and adjust the accelerator cable freeplay in accordance with the manufacturer's specifications. That's it!

Polished valve covers

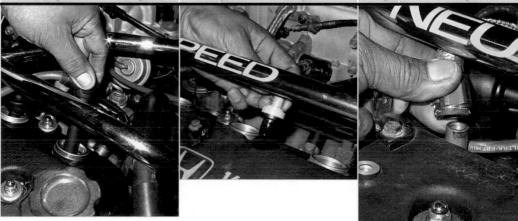

The traditional route for upgrading the appearance of your valve cover has always been to replace it. But that's because there wasn't much you could do with the typical stamped steel valve cover, usually painted in an exciting shade of . . . black (which inevitably wore off, leaving you with a rusty stamped steel valve cover). So you went out and bought a nice aluminium valve cover to replace the standard item.

   Nowadays, though, a lot of modern cars are already equipped with an aluminium valve cover. Trouble is, it's not polished, or anodised. It's often just painted in a crinkle-finish black paint. It won't rust like one of those cheap old steel valve covers, but it won't get any better looking with time, either. Which is why we decided that the black valve cover on this Honda had to go. But instead of replacing it, we simply removed the black paint and had it polished by a local specialist. The results speak for themselves.

| **01** Disconnect the HT leads, noting their positions. | **02** You might have a breather valve to pull out . . . | **03** . . . or more usually, a breather hose to disconnect. > |

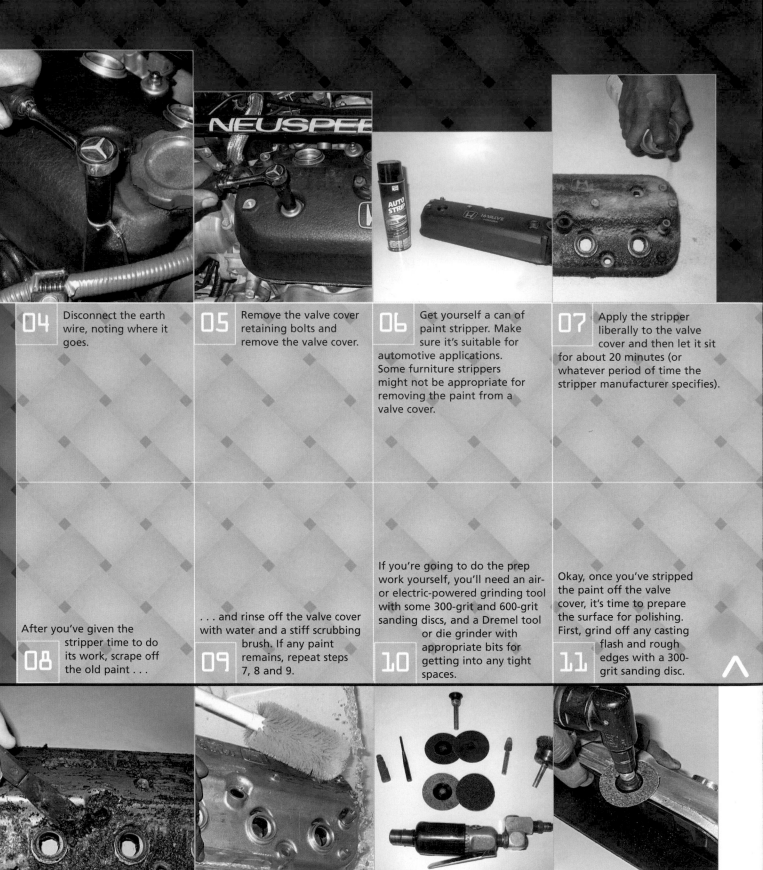

04 Disconnect the earth wire, noting where it goes.

05 Remove the valve cover retaining bolts and remove the valve cover.

06 Get yourself a can of paint stripper. Make sure it's suitable for automotive applications. Some furniture strippers might not be appropriate for removing the paint from a valve cover.

07 Apply the stripper liberally to the valve cover and then let it sit for about 20 minutes (or whatever period of time the stripper manufacturer specifies).

08 After you've given the stripper time to do its work, scrape off the old paint . . .

09 . . . and rinse off the valve cover with water and a stiff scrubbing brush. If any paint remains, repeat steps 7, 8 and 9.

10 If you're going to do the prep work yourself, you'll need an air- or electric-powered grinding tool with some 300-grit and 600-grit sanding discs, and a Dremel tool or die grinder with appropriate bits for getting into any tight spaces.

11 Okay, once you've stripped the paint off the valve cover, it's time to prepare the surface for polishing. First, grind off any casting flash and rough edges with a 300-grit sanding disc.

12 Then switch to a 600-grit sanding disc to produce a smoother finish.

13 Use a Dremel tool to get into any tight spots.

14 Here are some typical tools of the trade for polishing aluminium. You'll also need some metal polishing compound (available at most car accessory shops or DIY stores).

15 Switch to a 3M cutting pad and remove any scratches caused by the grinding discs.

16 We borrowed some typical blocks of polishing "rouge" (compound) from our local metal polishers to show you what the pros use. Each compound is different, and is designed to bring out the color or shine of certain metals. The black compound is for stainless steel surfaces; white is for "final finish" polishing; green is for chrome; and brown is for aluminium. (Of course, as a do-it-yourselfer, you won't need this many compounds, unless you plan to start polishing for a living!).

17 All right, enough talk. Let's get started. Add some (brown) polishing compound to the buffing pad . . .

18 . . . and start polishing the valve cover!

19 A big buffing wheel on a bench grinder will give you more polishing power (polishing power is like horsepower: you can't have too much!). At this point, you might consider subbing out the valve cover to a professional polisher, who can buff it to a mirror-like sheen. A professional will also be able to clean the finished valve cover better than you can, because he'll soak it in a hot parts-cleaner solution, then steam-clean it to remove any residue from the holes.

20 After polishing the valve cover, clean the gasket channel (or gasket face), the mounting bolt holes and the spark plug holes with cotton buds or clean rag. Don't leave any of the grease or residue from the polishing compound in any nooks or crannies. When the valve cover is spotless, fit the new gasket . . .

21 . . . and then (where applicable) fit the seals around the spark plug holes.

22 Apply some RTV silicone gasket sealant to any spots where the gasket has to negotiate a corner . . .

23 . . . such as this area, where the gasket has to clear a cam bearing cap.

24 Carefully - so as not to disturb the gasket or smear those little blobs of RTV sealant - place the polished valve cover in position.

25 Fit the washers for the valve cover mounting nuts . . .

26 . . . then fit the nuts . . .

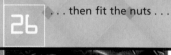

27 . . . and tighten them to the manufacturer's specifications. Refer to your Haynes manual if you don't know the correct torque. Don't guess at this torque. Too loose, and the gasket will leak. Too tight, the valve cover could crack or become warped.

28 Refit the earth wire, and securely tighten the bolt.

29 Fit the grommet for the breather valve (if you were smart, unlike us, you already fitted this grommet before fitting the valve cover!).

30 Fit the breather valve into the grommet . . .

31 . . . or connect the breather hose to the cover.

32 Refit the oil filler cap, and you're done. Is that valve cover shiny, or what? Shades are no longer an option.

33 Oops - almost forgot to mention this stuff. Get yourself a home metal polishing kit like this one to maintain a mirror-like finish on your newly polished valve cover.

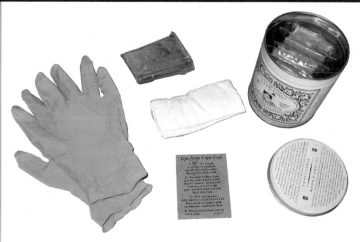

Painting an exhaust manifold heat shield

When you get enough dosh together for a chrome-plated four-branch manifold, you'll have the ultimate look. Until then, you can add some colour by painting the exhaust manifold heat shield. The only thing you'll need is a can of high-temperature paint in the colour of your choice. We chose white because it looks . . . well, it looks white hot!

01 First, remove the heat shield fasteners . . .

02 . . . then remove the heat shield. Did we ought to say this should only be done when the engine's stone cold, or is that stating the obvious?

Next, remove all grease and oil with a good solvent or degreaser. Then sand off all rust and any bugs or crud that's baked onto the shield. You're not trying to remove all the original paint, you're just trying to create a nice, roughed-up surface so the paint will adhere to it. **03**

The surface of the heat shield is one of the hottest places on the engine when it's running, so make sure that you use a **04** high-temperature paint.

05 Apply the high-temperature paint evenly to the heat shield surface.

06 Install the newly painted heat shield . . .

07 . . . and install and securely tighten the heat shield fasteners. Looks a bit better, doesn't it?

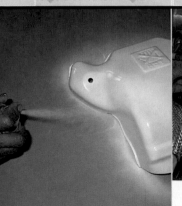

Painting brackets

No matter how pretty your engine bay might look by now, all those black cast-iron and stamped steel brackets for the engine, gearbox, radiator and other big or heavy components are always going to be an eyesore.

Of course, if you have access to a machine shop (or, better yet, own one!), you can swap the standard brackets for one-off pieces custom-machined from billet. But until then, why not simply paint some of the more prominent pieces to match your engine compartment colour scheme? The only things you'll need are some sandpaper and a can of spray paint. You'll be amazed at the transformation. We'll start with something easy like these two radiator brackets. Then we'll let you take it from there.

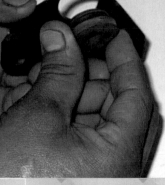

01 First, remove the radiator brackets.

02 Remove any rubber grommets or insulators from the brackets.

03 Sand off any rough edges or rust.

What paint to use? Broadly speaking, any paint designed for use on metals will do. Even ordinary car aerosols can be used, as long as you primer first. On metal subject to heat, make sure the paint's heat-resistant.

04

05 When the paint's dry, refit any rubber parts you removed.

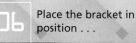

06 Place the bracket in position . . .

07 . . . then fit the bracket mounting bolts and tighten securely.

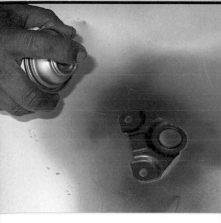

Adjustable bonnet prop

What happens every time you open the bonnet and want to keep it open? You grab the bonnet prop and swing it up into position, which prevents the bonnet from crashing down onto your tools (or, more importantly, your head!).

But what's wrong with this picture? Well, for starters, the bonnet can only be locked into one opening angle because the bonnet prop is a fixed length, and its upper end must be inserted into a specific hole in the bonnet that's there just for that purpose. Okay, fine. But have you ever wished that you could open the bonnet to the height that you want, and then just leave it there, at that height? Well now you can, with the addition of an adjustable bonnet prop. And in case the whole angle-of-opening thing passes you by - they look trick, too.

01 Mark the position of the holes you're going to drill in the bonnet for the prop upper mounting bracket.

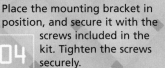

02 Drill the mounting bracket holes in the bonnet channel. Be careful - don't let the drill "pop" through and dimple the bonnet!

03 Clean up the edges of the holes with a reamer or round file.

04 Place the mounting bracket in position, and secure it with the screws included in the kit. Tighten the screws securely.

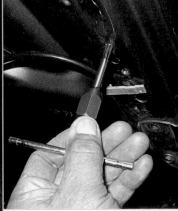

05 Now go down to the wing and mark the position of the holes you're going to drill in the wing for the prop lower bonnet bracket.

06 Drill the mounting bracket holes in the wing.

07 Clean up the edges of the hole with your reamer or round file.

08 Install the lower mounting bracket, and tighten the bolts.

09 Attach the lower end of the bonnet prop to the lower mounting bracket with the bolt and nut supplied with the kit. Tighten the fasteners securely.

10 Fit the spherical bearing stud in the upper bracket, secure it with the nut and . . .

11 . . . using a second spanner to prevent the bearing stud from turning, tighten the nut securely.

12 Pop the upper end of the bonnet prop onto the spherical bearing. Finished!

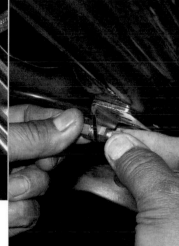

Computers
and chips

The condition of your spark plugs is a good indicator of conditions inside your engine - after each modification inspect the plugs with a magnifier to watch for signs of detonation, which might indicate changes needed in the fuel and/or ignition programming

Understanding your on-board computer means understanding how to get the most out of your engine

Engine management systems began as a means to reduce pollution by controlling numerous fuel and emission-control components. As the sophistication of fuel injection and information sensors increased, so did the power and reliability of the computer running things behind the scenes. In the world of cars, the computer has become a true boon now that the initial bugs have been sorted out.

As the engineers really got into it over the years, they kept finding new uses for computer control, taking into account seemingly non-emissions factors such as power steering, air conditioning and transmission performance. Where once there may have been crude information sampling, now cars have higher-performance computers, more sensors, more sensitive sensors, and impressive programming. Some cars have a main computer with one or more "sub-computers" that process data and transfer information between other on-board systems and the main computer. Automatic climate-control systems, where you set the temperature you want in the car and the system provides just the right level of heat or cooling to maintain that temperature, are a perfect application for a sub-computer.

If you're making some basic modifications, and not planning to go all out, a simple chip upgrade for your ECU can improve engine response with advanced ignition timing - to go along with this, you may have to start filling-up with higher-octane fuel, especially if your engine has a high compression ratio.

Not all ECUs have a customer-serviceable chip, but some companies offer "DIY" chips, or a postal service, where you send them your ECU for chipping.

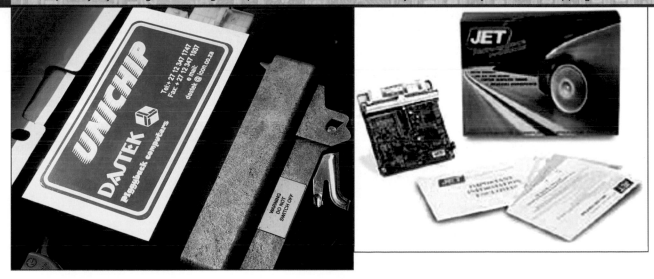

Use your Haynes repair manual to locate and safely remove your standard ECU before sending it off for an upgrade - the ECU may be located in the cowl (here on a German car) or under the dash. Many are hidden in the driver's or (especially) the passenger's footwell, behind the kick panel.

Computers and chips

By themselves, engine management changes can result in some improvement in power, but each different car will have varying levels of improvement, depending on how far off the factory programming was from a performance standpoint. As with any aftermarket product, be very careful of power improvement numbers quoted in advertisements and manufacturer literature. Exaggeration from the marketing department has been known to creep into print. In some cases, the power increase quoted may have been on a worse-case scenario, or on a modified engine that was still using the standard ECU. In that case, a modded engine would benefit more than a bog-standard engine would.

That's the thing about chip reprogramming - it makes only a small gain by itself, but should make more when other engine mods are made. Equally, some mechanical engine changes won't make their advertised power increases either, unless you do some reprogramming.

A standard car may only gain 7 or 8 brake when chipped, though it may affect torque enough at lower rpm to improve the "feel" of the car. Now take the same completely standard car, add an induction kit, manifold/exhaust, or a new camshaft. Have the ECU chipped now, and the gain could be worth 20 brake. The extra airflow and improved breathing all need more ignition timing advance to achieve their best numbers. If there's one lesson to learn about modifying modern engines, it's that all your mods must work together in a planned, integrated way to achieve the results you're looking for. Believe it or not, some mods done in isolation can actually make a car perform worse. It's a system we're dealing with here.

Engine management basics

The on-board computer is called the Powertrain Control Module (PCM), Engine Control Module (ECM) or Electronic Control Unit (ECU), depending on the manufacturer of you car. Apparently, everyone just calling it a "computer" would be too easy. For purposes of this Chapter, we'll use the term ECU. The other parts of this "engine management system" are the information sensors, which monitor various functions of the engine and send data to the ECU. Based on the data and the information programmed into the computer's memory, the ECU generates output signals to control various engine functions via control relays, solenoids and other output actuators.

The ECU is the "brain" of the electronically-controlled fuel, ignition and emissions system, and is specifically calibrated to optimise the performance, emissions, fuel economy and driveability of one specific car/engine/gearbox/accessories package in one make/model/year of vehicle.

Performance mods and the computer

The factory programming in your car's ECU is a highly-developed, extensively-tested system that works perfectly for your engine in standard condition. Remember that the goal of the factory engineers is maximum fuel economy, minimum emissions, driveability, longevity and efficiency. Our goal is performance - everything else takes a back seat - so our programming needs are slightly different.

Where the factory ECU programming needs some "help" for performance use is in the ignition timing and fuel curves. Virtually all new cars are designed to run on the lowest grade of unleaded fuel (in the UK, this is 95 RON unleaded, but you'll find 91 RON and lower in some parts of Europe). To get more performance, the ignition curve can be given more advanced timing and the fuel curve adjusted for more fuel at higher revs, but the fuel octane rating now becomes a problem. When timing is advanced, the engine may have more tendency to exhibit detonation or pinking (signs of improper burning in the combustion chamber) which is potentially dangerous to the lifespan of the engine. Thus, if you want to alter the timing "map" in your computer for more power, you'll probably have to go up a grade of petrol (assuming you can, of course - in the UK, 98 RON super unleaded continues to be available for now, but for how much longer?).

The need for higher-octane fuel isn't always due to increased ignition advance. While most bolt-on engine modifications will work well with increased timing, the serious "power adders" like nitrous oxide, superchargers, turbochargers and even high-compression pistons will require less ignition advance. The big gains in horsepower come from modifications that increase the cylinder pressure in the engine (the force pushing the pistons down). Increases in cylinder pressure really raise the fuel octane requirement in a hurry.

"Non-serviceable" chips must be carefully unsoldered from the board, which is why this is usually done by a specialized company or tuning shop with the proper tools and reprogramming equipment

The upgrade technicians will take into account the engine modifications you have made and "burn" the correct programming into your stock chip

If you have a number of engine mods and plan more over time, the S200 from Hondata can be installed in conjunction with your Honda ECU - it retains factory idle quality and fault code retrieval, but allows a Hondata dealer to tune for each mod you make any time, including control of the VTEC function.

In many new cars, the programming that affects the areas we want to modify is part of a "chip" on the motherboard of the ECU. The chip is a very small piece of silicon semiconductor material carrying many integrated circuits. These are usually called PROM chips, for Programmable Read Only Memory. In some cases, the chip is a "plug-in" which can be easily removed from the ECU and replaced with a custom chip, while other chips are factory-soldered to the board. Cars with plug-in chips are the easiest to modify, but unfortunately are pretty rare.

It isn't recommended to remove a soldered chip from the motherboard at home. Your factory ECU is very expensive to replace, and just a tiny mistake with the solder or the heat source could ruin it. Aftermarket companies offer reprogramming services for these kinds of ECUs, and some tuners also have equipment to do this.

Your car could be out of action for a few days, either parked at the tuner's doing the upgrade, or parked at home while you wait for your modified ECU to come back from a computer upgrade company. How it works in the latter case is that you order and pay for the upgrade service from a reputable company, and they send you instructions, forms to fill out, and special packaging for the ECU. You remove the factory ECU from your car (use your Haynes repair manual to locate and properly disconnect the ECU), and send it to the company. There, they will either replace the chip or reprogram it. Based on the information you have given them about your vehicle, driving needs, and modifications you have made to the engine, they will custom-programme the timing, fuelling and even the transmission shifting information on cars with ECU-controlled automatic gearboxes. They can also change (or remove) the factory-set rev limiter. They then post it back, and you refit it using their instructions.

The modified chip is resoldered to your car's motherboard with just the right amount of heat - too much and the board could be toast, so don't try this at home!

Technicians examine the chip reinstallation with a microscope to make sure it's right.

Information sensors

- **Oxygen sensors (O₂S)** - The O_2S generates a varying voltage signal which allows the ECU to monitor the oxygen content of the exhaust gas. Also known as a Lambda sensor.

- **Crankshaft Position (CKP) sensor** - The CKP sensor provides information on crankshaft position and the engine speed signal to the ECU.

- **Camshaft Position (CMP) sensor** - The CMP sensor produces a signal the ECU uses to identify number 1 cylinder and to time sequential fuel injection.

- **Air/Fuel Sensor** - Some models are equipped with an air/fuel ratio sensor mounted upstream of the catalytic converter. These sensors work similarly to the O_2 sensors.

- **Engine Coolant Temperature (ECT) sensor** - The ECT sensor monitors engine coolant temperature and sends the ECU a voltage signal that affects ECU control of the fuel mixture, ignition timing, and EGR operation.

- **Intake Air Temperature (IAT) sensor** - The IAT provides the ECU with intake air temperature information. The ECU uses this information to control fuel flow, ignition timing, and EGR system operation.

- **Throttle Position Sensor (TPS)** - The TPS senses throttle movement and position, then transmits a voltage signal to the ECU. This signal enables the ECU to determine when the throttle is closed, in a cruise position, or wide open.

- **Mass Airflow (MAF) sensor** - The MAF sensor measures the mass of the intake air by detecting volume and weight of the air from samples passing over a hot wire element.

- **Vehicle Speed Sensor (VSS)** - The vehicle speed sensor provides information to the ECU to indicate vehicle speed.

- **EGR valve position sensor** - The EGR valve position sensor monitors the position of the Exhaust Gas Recirculation pintle in relation to the operating conditions of the EGR system.

- **Vapour pressure sensor** - The fuel tank pressure sensor is part of the evaporative emission control system and is used to monitor vapour pressure in the fuel tank. The ECU uses this information to turn on and off the vacuum switching valves (VSV) of the evaporative emission system.

- **Power Steering Pressure (PSP) switch** - The PSP sensor is used to increase engine idle speed during low-speed vehicle manoeuvres.

- **Transmission sensors** - In addition to the vehicle speed sensor, the ECU on models with automatic transmission receives input signals from a direct clutch (or input shaft) speed sensor.

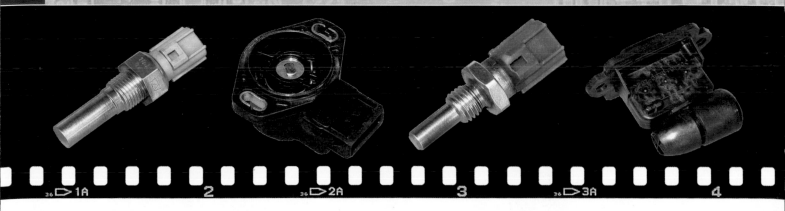

Output actuators

- **EFI main relay** - The EFI main relay activates power to the fuel pump relay (circuit opening relay). It is activated by the ignition switch and supplies battery power to the ECU and the EFI system when the switch is in the Start or Run position.

- **Fuel injectors** - The ECU opens the fuel injectors individually. On most modern engines, the system is called SFI (Sequential Fuel Injection), in which the injectors are fired sequentially according to the firing order of the cylinders. The ECU also controls the time the injector is open, called the "pulse width". The pulse width of the injector (measured in milliseconds) determines the amount of fuel delivered.

- **Igniter** - The igniter triggers the ignition coil, and determines proper spark advance based on inputs from the ECU.

- **Idle Air Control (IAC) valve** - The IAC valve controls the amount of air to bypass the throttle plate when the throttle valve is closed or at idle position. The IAC valve opening and the resulting airflow is controlled by the ECU.

- **EVAP vacuum switching valve (VSV)** - The EVAP vacuum switching valve is a solenoid valve, operated by the ECU to purge the fuel vapour canister and route fuel vapour to the intake manifold for combustion.

- **Vapour Pressure Sensor vacuum switching valve (VSV)** - The Vapour Pressure Sensor vacuum switching valve is operated by the ECU as part of the on-board diagnostic check, and during an emission test of the evaporative system.

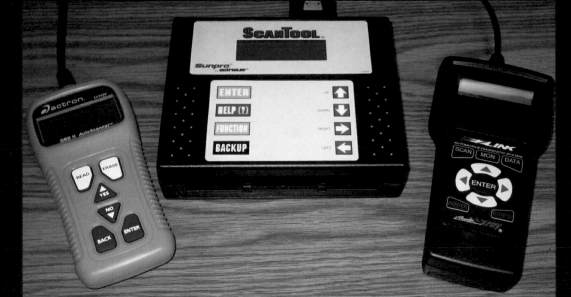

Cracking your computer codes

The ECUs in all vehicles manufactured since the early 80s have the ability to monitor the engine management system's input sensors and output actuators, and detect problems should they occur. This is called the On-board Diagnostic system, or simply OBD.

The diagnostic part of OBD refers to the ability to retrieve information from the ECU about the performance and running condition of all the sensors and actuators in the engine management system. This is invaluable information in diagnosing engine problems. The ECU puts on the CHECK ENGINE light (also called the Malfunction Indicator Light) on the dash if it recognises a component fault

The diagnostic codes for the OBD system can be extracted from the ECU by plugging a scan tool or fault code reader into the ECU's data link connector (DLC), which is usually located under the left end of the dash. Your Haynes repair manual will show you the location of the data connector (if your car has one) and tell you a lot more about the engine management system of your specific make and model.

On some models, the computer will spit out troubleshooting information by flashing lights on the computer itself or by having the Check Engine light blink out a numeric code. On some vehicles you can activate this process by simply jumping certain terminals with a small wire or paper clip (refer to the Haynes manual for your specific vehicle for the proper procedure)

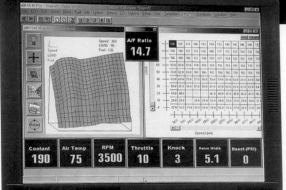

Programmable engine management systems like this one from AEM are ideal for fully-modified racers - the standard ECU is replaced by a "plug and play" computer that has tuneable fuel and timing maps that can be viewed with Windows®-based software on a laptop computer, and features on-board data-logging plus adjustable controls for boost and nitrous. We like.

High Performance electronic controls

In the case of some mods, particularly supercharging and turbocharging, you need a way to control ignition timing and fuel based on something the factory never considered: boost. Instead of the engine gulping fuel and air under atmospheric pressure like a normally-aspirated engine, a "blown" engine is being force-fed. The more pounds of boost applied to the engine, the more the ignition timing needs to be pulled back, and in some cases the more fuel needs to be injected. The aftermarket companies have a variety of add-on electronic controllers that connect to a manifold vacuum port on your engine, and send varying signals to the ECU based on how much boost is being applied. Some even have a dashboard control so that you can select the timing you need based on the quality of fuel available to you. When you have your engine set up for best results on 95-octane fuel, and you're stuck somewhere that only has 91 or 89-octane, you'll need to make a timing adjustment or risk engine damage.

If you have a piggyback fuel or timing box, or any other programmable management system, the dyno operator can spot any weaknesses in your overall engine operation much more easily than by unscientific, seat-of-the-pants driving, and he'll know right where your engine needs more/less fuel or spark.

When more control is needed, there are aftermarket computers that work in conjunction with the standard ECU. The factory ECU and its programming is retained to do all the closed-loop emissions and efficiency programming (closed-loop means that the ECU is in charge of all functions), while a secondary box attaches next to the ECU, and handles the functions of controlling timing, fuel and boost. Such boxes are called "piggyback" units. The beauty of these boxes is that they are user-programmable for the functions an enthusiast is interested in. They can be connected to a PC, which will display the fuel and timing maps and let you make changes to suit your level of modification. Some include a fall-back map of basically stock numbers. Once you have dialled-in exactly what you need, you save that map. If you make new mods to the engine, go back to that map and experiment some more. At least one aftermarket unit allows you to switch, at the dashboard, between any of four maps you have created. You could save your "street use with 95-octane" map, and your "race day with 100-octane" map.

Now for the boring bit. As you might expect, kit like this may or may not be legal for road use where you live. But they've gotta catch you first!

At the track, pit-tuning a race car is much easier when you can replay a run (from a system with data-logging capability), compare the results with your spark plug examination and make minor tweaks of the system before the next run. Serious stuff.

Ignition
Systems

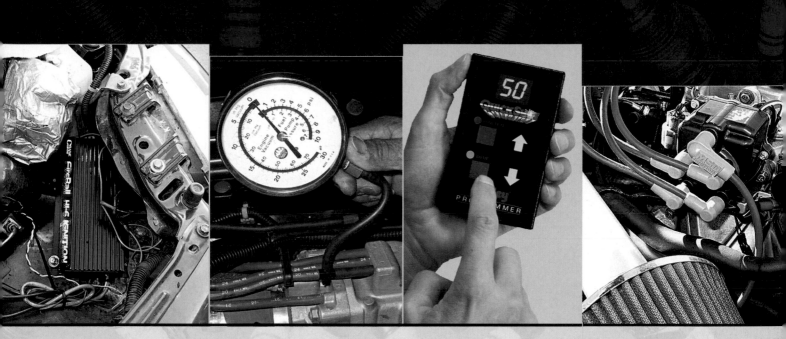

Ignition basics

Once you understand the basic principles of an internal combustion engine, it's easy to see why an ignition system plays a crucial role.

For those readers who might need a brief refresher on what happens inside their engine's cylinders, all modern engines run in a *four-cycle* (or four-stroke) mode. Let's start with the **intake** stroke. Here the piston is travelling down in the cylinder, creating a suction that draws the fuel/air mixture in through the open intake valve. When the piston reaches the bottom of its stroke, it starts back up again, starting the **compression** stroke, in which the valves close and the piston compresses the fuel/air mixture (which can't escape). This makes the fuel/air mixture very dense

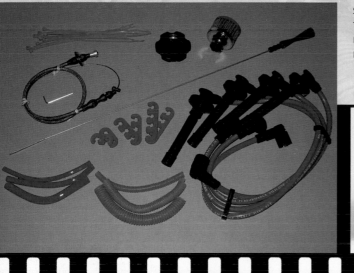

and capable of releasing a lot of energy when the mixture is ignited. Just before the piston reaches the top of its stroke, the spark plug ignites the mixture, beginning the **power** stroke, in which the rapidly-expanding gases from the burning mixture raise the cylinder pressure dramatically and this pushes the piston down the bore. The force on the crankshaft each time a power stroke pushes down is what makes the engine go. By the time the piston reaches the bottom of this stroke, the energy in the cylinder has gone and the piston starts back up again, on the **exhaust** stroke. The cylinder contains the mostly-inert residual gases left from combustion, and when the exhaust valve opens during this stroke, these gases are pushed out of the cylinder and past the exhaust valve (to the exhaust system) as the piston rises. This clears the cylinder in preparation for another intake stroke, beginning another intake-compression-power-exhaust four-stroke cycle. Or in pub language - "suck-squeeze-bang-blow". Ahem.

In a nutshell, that's how your engine works. You may be perceptive enough to guess that the exact timing of some of these events in a four-stroke cycle is critical. Chapter 8 will go into much greater detail about how the valves are operated and how valve timing is a major factor in increasing engine performance. This Chapter is concerned with requirements for making and timing that all-important spark that lights off the fireworks.

THE FOUR-STROKE CYCLE

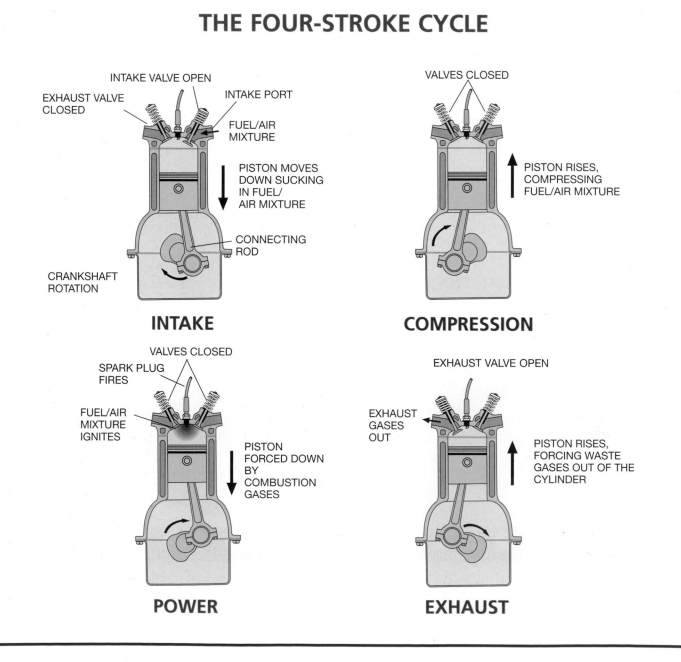

INTAKE

COMPRESSION

POWER

EXHAUST

Ignition by the numbers

- At 6,000 rpm in a four-cylinder engine, each spark plug is firing 3000 times per minute, or 50 times per second!

- In a basic ignition system, the juice-path starts with battery voltage, which is 12 volts. The ignition coil then steps-up this voltage to 10,000 or more volts.

- An aftermarket coil will typically step up the 12V battery voltage to as much as 60,000 volts.

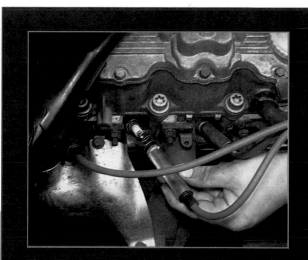

The voltages produced by modern ignition systems are very high, and are potentially lethal in some cases. Extreme care must be taken when working on or around ignition systems. Never disconnect or even touch an HT lead or ignition coil when the engine is running!

Computerised (electronic) ignition systems

What they are, and how to tell if you have one

On modern, fuel-injected and computer-controlled engines, the distributor only controls the sequence in which the cylinders are fired, while all other timing functions are handled by the computer.

In some modern cars, the distributor has been eliminated entirely. Called **DIS (Distributorless Ignition System)**, the distributor function is replaced by a **CPS (Crankshaft Position Sensor)** on the engine, giving the computer a reference to where the crankshaft is rotated in relation to **TDC (Top Dead Centre)** for number one cylinder. That's when the piston is at it highest point of travel in the cylinder. Based on this and other inputs, the computer makes all timing decisions, which are delivered to coilpacks that are in turn connected by HT leads to the spark plugs. On these systems, the plugs are fired in pairs (usually 1 and 4, 2 and 3). Since only one plug can actually ignite the mixture at any time, one of these sparks is wasted, which is why DIS systems are also known as "wasted spark" systems.

If you're not sure if you have a conventional or DIS system, follow your spark plug wires. If they end at a distributor driven by one of your camshafts, you have a distributor system. If the wires all go to a cluster of coils mounted on a plate somewhere in the engine compartment (and you don't see a distributor on your engine) then you have a DIS system.

Components of the DIS system include the camshaft position sensor, the crankshaft position sensor, coils (one coil for a cluster of cylinders), igniter and the **ECU (Electronic Control Unit)** or "computer".

A further development of the DIS ignition system is the coil-on-plug arrangement. On these models, each spark plug has its own small coil/igniter pack. The coil is mounted directly over the spark plug and bolted to the valve cover. These systems are easy to spot because there are no HT leads. The sensors generate signals that allow the ECU to trigger the correct coil/igniter assembly at the right time. Such systems offer the most complete control of spark ignition to date.

High performance ignition

Your factory ignition system does a perfectly adequate job on a completely standard engine. In standard tune, the engine runs smooth, has good economy and the spark plugs last a long time. These are all signs of an efficient engine with the right combination of parts and all parts working properly, but factory ignitions aren't well suited for high-rpm driving or engines modified to create increased cylinder pressure.

Higher revs put an increased load on standard ignition systems, and modifications that lead to increased cylinder pressure can really put out the fire. If you fit higher-compression pistons, the spark plugs need a lot more zap to light up a mixture that is packed-in tighter than ever. The denser the mixture, the harder it is for a spark to jump the plug's electrodes, like swimming through wet concrete. Other major power-boosters such as nitrous oxide, supercharging or turbocharging also create much high cylinder pressures and require several ignition improvements.

Check it out first!

Before splashing your cash on high-performance kit, make sure every part of your engine's up for modifying

Use a Haynes Repair Manual for your make and model and follow the simple, step-by-step procedures to test engine compression, vacuum readings, ignition performance, fuel pressure, etc. If anything's suspect, take care of it now, before you modify the engine. If the car's not had a service for a while, now would be a good time - especially an oil change, new plugs and a new cambelt (depending on what work you're planning).

It makes no sense to add performance equipment to a knackered or sick engine, though there is a temptation to do so. If your valves or rings are leaking under normal driving conditions and engine speed, just imagine how less effective they will be with an engine putting out more horsepower. The modifications will make the car seem faster, but you're only going to kill the engine faster, very likely doing more damage than if you'd corrected the problems first. Read the information about engine management systems and the retrieval of computer "fault codes" from your car. Have someone with a fault code reader check for any existing fault codes. It would also be great to have your car run on a rolling road to check for problems that may only show up under load. This would also be the best time to establish the "before" horsepower and torque figures, which you can compare to later tests after you've had all the engine work done.

To use a compression gauge, you must have a gauge with an adapter long enough to reach down the spark plug holes - be sure to disable the fuel pump and ignition system, and open the throttle as far as possible during the compression check.

A simple vacuum gauge can be very handy in diagnosing engine condition and performance.

Aftermarket ignition coils

This aftermarket coil can produce up to 44,000 volts; some can put out upwards of 60,000 volts!

One of the reasons standard ignition doesn't handle high revs well is that the standard coil doesn't have time to build the necessary spark energy because of the short time between ignition firings (remember, it's trying to fire 50 times per second). Imagine holding your thumb over the end of a slow-running garden hose, blocking the flow of water. You release the water and it blasts out at first, then settles down to a slow flow. If you keep your thumb in place long enough the water pressure builds up, but if you open and close it too often, the pressure never has a chance to build between events.

The typical aftermarket coil is capable of making more secondary voltage than standard, and that's about it. It won't add any horsepower and won't improve fuel economy (what's that then?), but it could eliminate some misfire problems in the upper rpm range, and that will become more important as you add other modifications to your engine. On most engines with a distributor and separate coil, replacing your standard coil with an aftermarket unit is as simple as modifications get, and it's not expensive, either. Bonus.

Your basic distributor will work fine with a mildly modified engine. On Hondas, the ignition is somewhat limited by the small coil inside the normal distributor as shown here. Most original caps are made for small HT leads, and haven't enough room for the larger aftermarket ones.

An aftermarket cap like this MSD "Power Cap" can be used on a Honda to accept an external performance coil, and the posts are made for large silicone-jacketed HT leads.

The standard coil inside a Honda distributor can be removed and an aftermarket external coil utilised, with a modification to the cap.

This standard Honda cap has been modified for an external coil by drilling out the coil post and attaching this post adapter to accept an external coil.

Timing controls

A multi-spark capacitive-discharge (CD) ignition like the Holley "Quick Strip Annihilator" is especially useful for modified engines - the box is fitted with EEPROM microprocessors that can be overwritten many times and adjust the spark output based on engine rpm.

Exactly when your spark ignites the cylinder's fuel mix is critical; this is called ignition timing. The mix doesn't explode in an instantaneous flash; it actually takes a period of time. The flame front from the point of ignition travels through the mixture, slowly at first and then building speed. This is good, because what is needed is a gradual build of pressure, not a sharp spike, which can be destructive to pistons, con-rods and crankshafts. Since the mixture takes time to burn, the spark is timed to trigger sometime before the piston reaches the top of its stroke (Top Dead Centre). So the initial timing is a number of degrees BTDC, or Before Top Dead Centre. Firing with too much advance (too far before the piston reaches the top) can cause too much pressure to build in the cylinder before the piston reaches TDC, so that the piston and the rising pressure are fighting each other. On the other hand, if the timing is too late (not enough in advance), the engine can't make the most of the gas expansion, so power and economy are wasted.

To complicate the timing discussion even further, the spark event must have a different timing at different engine speeds. As engine speed goes up, there is less time available for the combustion event, so the spark must occur sooner. Other factors also influence the correct ignition timing, such as engine load, temperature and fuel mixture. If you map out the amount of ignition advance on a graph related to rpm, you have what's called an advance curve, an important factor in performance tuning.

Luckily, your factory ignition takes in information from its sensors to provide the optimum ignition timing under all conditions. The system however, is designed for normal driving and standard components. Once you start modding the engine, you've moved the goalposts, and you now need to adjust the timing with something other than the factory ECU. Chapter 4 covers modifications to your standard ECU that change the timing parameters. That will help some in power, as long as you use higher-octane fuel to compensate for the increased timing, but installing a chip or reprogramming your ECU will not increase the energy level of the spark. For that you need a CD (Capacitive Discharge) aftermarket ignition system.

For racing applications, the ignition system can utilise a "soft-touch" keypad to make instant changes to the ignition programming - it's called the Quickshot Programmer, and can change rev limits and has a built-in LED tachometer.

MSD's street-and-strip SCI-Plus (Sport Compact Ignition) is a digital ignition control that has dial-in controls for rev-limit and retard functions for single-stage nitrous applications.

Jacobs Electronics makes the "Energy Pak" ignition system, which can be set up either with the factory coil used as a trigger or with an external coil - features include spark output adjusted for engine load (more spark under acceleration) and a 10-degree start-retard that works well for engines with high compression - an optional add-on is a nitrous control.

The CD ignition usually consists of an electronic box you mount in the engine compartment, and the wiring harness to connect to your vehicle. Your ECU still does the triggering and controls the advance, but in the CD box is a large capacitor, which is an electronic storage device. Juice usually comes into the coil or coilpack as battery voltage (12V) and is bumped up from there to 5,000, 10,000 or 40,000 volts of secondary current. In the CD ignition, the capacitor stores incoming juice until there is more like 450 volts to go to the coil. Now the coil has a much easier time of quickly building up to the required voltage for good spark, regardless of the engine speed.

There are different models of CD ignitions, with varying "bells & whistles", but one of the most common side benefits is a "rev limiter." A single-step limiter will allow you to set a specific rpm that you don't want the engine to exceed, to prevent engine damage from over-revving during a missed gearchange or a blown clutch, for instance (such events do happen, even if they're not planned!). Some units are capable of programming-in an adjustable rate of spark retard at high revs, which is ideal for supercharged or turbocharged applications. Because of the increased cylinder pressure with boosted engines, it is common to retard the spark progressively as the boost level increases. CD ignition systems are available for both distributor engines and DIS engines.

For vehicles that have distributorless ignition systems with coilpacks, MSD makes this digital ignition box that features two-step rev-limit controls and an adjustable high-rpm retard function for boosted engines.

HT leads

Aside from making your engine compartment look cool, high-performance HT (high tension) leads serve a very useful purpose. If you fit a high-voltage coil and keep your standard leads, you're asking for voltage to "leak" from the leads under load, at high engine speeds, or boosted (blown or turbocharged) conditions. Voltage will try to find the "path of least resistance" and that could be any engine earth close to one of your plug leads.

The typical factory plug lead has a core of carbon-impregnated material surrounded by fibreglass and rubber insulation, which is fine for stock engines.

Most aftermarket performance leads use a very fine spiral wire wound around a magnetic core and wrapped in silicone jacketing, and are available in thicker-than-stock diameters to handle more current flow. Some cars have standard plug leads as skinny as 5 or 6 mm, while aftermarket leads come in 8 mm, 8.5 mm and even 9 mm for racing applications. Good aftermarket leads also come with thicker boots, which is important, since the boot-to-plug contact area is a frequent source of voltage leaking to earth. Leads in the 8mm range are big enough to handle the spark of most modified cars, and the bigger leads are good for racing, but there's no such thing as having too much insulation on your plug leads.

If you want to check for leaking voltage on your plug leads, just watch the engine running at night with the bonnet open (do this outdoors). If there are breaks in the leads or boots, you'll probably be able to see the voltage leaking like tiny bolts of lightning. If the air is damp, the voltage is even more likely to show up. If you look for it while your car's on a rolling road (in the dark) you can check for voltage leaks with the engine under load. This is where your standard ignition is most likely to break down.

Spark

The final link in the ignition system's chain-of-command is the spark plug. We may have mentioned this before but, as with other ignition modifications, don't expect to make big gains in power by switching spark plugs. Despite the wild claims dreamed up by advertising copywriters over the last fifty years, the only time spark plugs will make much difference on a road car is when the engine's really in need of a service and you fit fresh plugs. In that case, the spark plugs could bring back 5 or 10 lost horsepower, but most aftermarket plugs can't really make new horsepower the engine didn't have before.

Nonetheless, there are a wide variety of spark plugs out there to choose from. If your engine is only mildly modified, stick with the factory-recommended spark plugs, gapped to factory specs. If you add an increasing number of performance modifications to your engine, you may have to reconsider what type of plugs to run, and even what size electrode gap is best.

Your first key to choosing the right plug is to examine the ones you're running currently. Close examination of spark plugs is the way professional racers fine-tune their engines and detect engine problems in their early stages, before serious damage is done. Even engine builders with sophisticated and fully-instrumented dyno facilities still read the plugs with a magnifying glass.

You can read your plugs with an inexpensive tool from a car accessory shop. It's like a small torch with a magnifying glass on the end. We've included a colour-photo chart of spark plug conditions and what they indicate about the state of the engine - compare your plugs to the ones on the chart. The first thing to check is that they all look the same. Any variation in the plug reading indicates a problem specific to that cylinder, and the engine will need a compression test and mechanical examination to find out what's wrong.

Spark plugs play an important role in a performance ignition system, and modified engines need better plugs - on the left are NGK BCPR7ES-11 plugs, just one range colder than stock Honda plugs, and a good choice for this car, if the engine's been "breathed-on". On the right are competition plugs that feature a very fine center electrode; these are really expensive, but are often required for highly-boosted race engines.

plugs

Assuming you have made modifications, the most common spark plug conditions you might see would indicate them being either too cold or too hot. Each plug design is made to operate at a certain temperature, and the final choice is a compromise meant to work well in most operating conditions. In a standard engine, the proper plug has been tested to give good results for many miles. However, once you start modifying an engine and running at higher revs, with modified ignition timing and perhaps more fuel and more cylinder pressure, that plug is no longer the right choice.

Spark plugs are described as being "hot" or "cold", referring to their heat range. High revs, high engine temperatures and increased ignition timing or fuel flow can all cause a plug to run hotter. When a spark plug runs too hot, detonation can occur, risking serious damage to the engine.

The compromise in spark plug heat range is bigger with a modified engine than something standard. Doing everything we can to make more power at high revs, we need a colder plug to handle this, but at lower speeds our fuel mixture may be a little richer than standard, and the colder plugs may get soot fouling on them that interferes with driveability. A few simple mods such as a manifold/back box, camshaft and induction kit will probably require a plug that is one range colder than the standard plug.

One way to keep the plug compromise of a modified engine less of a problem is to run a performance ignition system, with a better coil and CD box, plus improved plug leads. This should allow the engine to run well at higher revs, and still have enough spark energy to keep the colder plug firing cleanly at the bottom end. It's just another reason the modification of your standard ignition system has to be a "complete-package" approach, with no weak links.

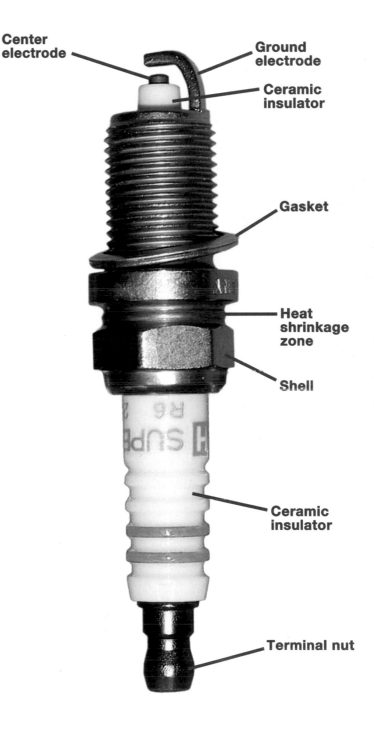

Center electrode

Ground electrode

Ceramic insulator

Gasket

Heat shrinkage zone

Shell

Ceramic insulator

Terminal nut

Common spark plug conditions

Your spark plugs can tell you a story about how your engine is running

Worn

Symptoms: Rounded electrodes with a small amount of deposits on the firing end. Normal colour. Causes hard starting in damp or cold weather and poor fuel economy.

Recommendation: Plugs have been left in the engine too long. Replace with new plugs of the same heat range. Follow the recommended maintenance schedule.

Normal

Symptoms: Brown to greyish-brown colour and slight electrode wear. Correct heat range for engine and operating conditions.

Recommendation: When new spark plugs are needed, replace with plugs of the same heat range.

Too hot

Symptoms: Blistered, white insulator, eroded electrode and absence of deposits. Results in shortened plug life.

Recommendation: Check for the correct plug heat range, over-advanced ignition timing, lean fuel mixture, intake manifold vacuum leaks, sticking valves and insufficient engine cooling.

Carbon deposits

Symptoms: Dry sooty deposits indicate a rich mixture or weak ignition. Causes misfiring, hard starting and hesitation.

Recommendation: Check the plug has the correct heat range. Check for a clogged air filter or problem in the fuel system or engine management system. Also check for ignition system problems.

Ash deposits

Symptoms: Light brown deposits encrusted on the side or centre electrodes or both. Derived from oil and/or fuel additives. Excessive amounts may mask the spark, causing misfiring and hesitation during acceleration.

Recommendation: If excessive deposits accumulate over a short time or low mileage, fit new valve guide seals to prevent seepage of oil into the combustion chambers. Also try changing fuel brands.

Oil deposits

Symptoms: Oily coating caused by poor oil control. Oil is leaking past worn valve guides or piston rings into the combustion chamber. Causes hard starting, misfiring and hesitation.

Recommendation: Correct the mechanical condition with necessary repairs, and fit new plugs.

Gap bridging

Symptoms: Combustion deposits lodge between the electrodes. Heavy deposits accumulate and bridge the electrode gap. The plug ceases to fire, resulting in a dead cylinder.

Recommendation: Locate the faulty plug and remove the deposits from between the electrodes.

Pre-ignition (pinking)

Symptoms: Melted electrodes. Insulators are white, but may be dirty due to misfiring or flying debris in the combustion chamber. Can lead to engine damage.

Recommendation: Check for the correct plug heat range, over-advanced ignition timing, lean fuel mixture, insufficient engine cooling and lack of lubrication.

High-speed glazing

Symptoms: Insulator has yellowish, glazed appearance. Indicates that combustion chamber temperatures have risen suddenly during hard acceleration. Normal deposits melt to form a conductive coating. Causes misfiring at high speeds.

Recommendation: Fit new plugs. Consider using a colder plug if driving habits warrant.

Detonation

Symptoms: Insulators may be cracked or chipped. Improper gap setting techniques can also result in a fractured insulator tip. Can lead to piston damage.

Recommendation: Make sure the fuel anti-knock values meet engine requirements. Use care when setting the gaps on new plugs. Avoid labouring the engine.

Mechanical damage

Symptoms: May be caused by a foreign object in the combustion chamber or the piston striking an incorrect reach (too long) plug. Causes a dead cylinder and could result in piston damage.

Recommendation: Repair the mechanical damage. Remove the foreign object from the engine and/or install the correct reach plug.

Induction
systems

Your standard intake system is like going through life with a head cold

. . . Let it breathe!

Induction basics

Your engine needs air to mix with the fuel coming into the cylinders. At high revs, when it's making the most horsepower, it wants more air. If you start adding performance mods, it wants even more air. And if that's not being greedy enough, it would like that air to be as cold as possible, please.

Your standard air filter box is designed for smoothing and quietening the airflow (who wants a quiet engine?), and it represents a considerable restriction, especially at high revs.

Induction systems

If you take a close look at most standard air intake systems, it's a wonder the engine gets enough fresh air to run at all! In the intake tract, the engineers have their first priority to develop smooth, reliable power with maximum fuel economy and driveability. Performance is far from their minds.

A further priority faced by factory engineers, and this applies to engineering on all aspects of production car design, is NVH, which stands for Noise, Vibration and Harshness. As most owners want their cars to be as quiet and smooth as possible, the engineers are increasingly challenged. How does this affect our induction system? Take a look at the standard induction path. If you follow the airflow from outside the car to where the intake manifold bolts to the cylinder head, you'll see a tortuous roadmap with more twists and turns than a rat maze experiment at the school science fair.

One step further away from basic induction would be to eliminate the standard air filter box and flexible hose, then attach an aftermarket cone filter right to the throttle body - in the case of this model, there's no room for an aftermarket intake pipe unless the battery is relocated to the boot. Best place for it...

The standard inlet bringing air into the air filter housing (the beginning of the air intake system) usually attempts to get some sort of cool air in, but the factory plays it very safe in locating this pipe, hoping to fend off customer problems if any dirt or water were to get into the airbox. Once inside the air filter housing, the air may have to pass by plastic baffles and other devices designed to limit the noise produced by air rushing into the engine. Once past the air filter, the airflow usually goes through a "corrugated" flexible tube and connects to the throttle body. If you're lucky, that tube has only one bend in it on your car, but some vehicles have several. The flexible tubing used is designed more for noise-reduction than smooth, unrestricted airflow. The ribs inside the plastic tubing may dampen noise, but they restrict high-revs airflow.

To improve the air intake for your engine, you have basically three options.

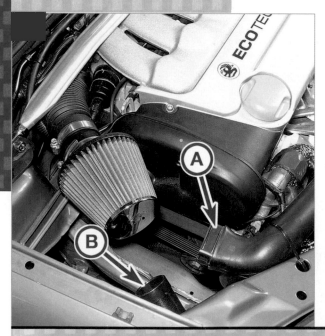

- Your first and simplest improvement to your induction is to step up and pay the price for a panel air filter, to go inside the standard airbox. If the car has a decent filter box design, just changing to a quality aftermarket air filter can be worth a few horsepower.

- The next step is a performance induction kit that will replace the stock plastic tubing and air filter housing. This kit will come with its own pleated-cotton, high-flow filter. So if you're serious about adding power to your engine, go for the induction kit option straight away. They also sound superb. Which is nice.

- Step three would involve more serious modifications, in addition to the induction kit. If you really need some air, look to improvements in the throttle body and intake manifold on the engine.

On this Corsa engine, the standard airbox has gone, replaced by an induction kit. Ingeniously, the standard inlet air pipe (A) has been retained, only now it's used to aim cooler air at the filter, as well as another flexible pipe (B) that picks up even cooler air below the bumper. Since the pipes aren't connected directly to the filter, there's no danger of water even getting into the engine from driving through flood water.

The easiest power mod you can make

01 The simplest modification you can make to your standard air induction system is to open the factory airbox, lift out the original paper air filter, then drop in a high-flow aftermarket panel filter - these can be reused over and over by washing them, then treating them with a special oil.

02 A replacement air filter is dead easy to fit - release the clips securing the air cleaner top cover . . .

03 . . . then lift the cover enough to lift out the old element. Take care not to strain the wiring from the airflow meter as the air cleaner cover is lifted up.

04 Before you fit the new element, if you can, clean out the inside of the filter housing. Use a damp cloth, and make sure that none of the dust and muck goes into the engine.

A typical aftermarket bolt on induction mod is to install a short ram, which is a new, large diameter pipe with an aftermarket filter - these flow much better than standard, and make a great noise. This engine installation doesn't allow the best design, since there is a sharp bend near the throttle body that could slow down the airflow.

Short ram intakes

Performance air intakes are generally available in two basic forms, the "short ram" induction kit and the "cold-air" intake. In each type, the aftermarket manufacturer has tried to design a free-flowing intake without any regard to engine noise. Virtually all are made of metal tubing, generally aluminum, with the smoothest possible bends and an interior that has a larger cross-section than the stock system. All types are fitted with a high-flow filter, usually in a conical configuration. The best designs are not only capable of flowing more air volume, but maintain a higher air velocity than a stock system.

The least expensive and easiest intakes to install are the short ram types. You'll spend longer getting the stock air filter box and inlet tube out than installing the short ram. If you have any

>

Some kits come with a trick-looking sheetmetal "dam" - this can keep the hot air radiating from the engine away from the filter.

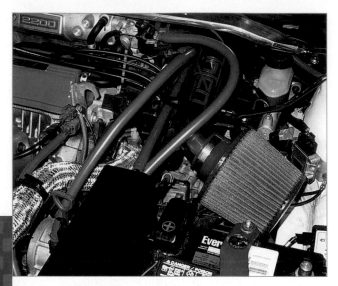

The Injen short ram on this Toyota is good - although not picking up cold air, at least it's away from the hot radiator, and there's no chance it could suck up water.

doubts about removing the standard bits, consult the Haynes repair manual for your car. On some cars, the airflow sensor is located on the air intake, and must be removed, then refitted on the aftermarket intake. Most cars also have a hose connecting the crankcase (usually at the valve cover) to the air intake, and the standard hose may need to be shortened to connect to the aftermarket pipe, or a new, longer hose must be used. Induction kits place the new filter relatively close to the engine, and modifications to the engine or body are rarely necessary. Most induction kit installs take only a half-hour and may be good for 4 to 8 horsepower, depending on the application - and they sound excellent.

Because of the upright mounting of the throttle body on this single-cam application, even a "long" ram pipe stills mounts the filter inside the engine compartment - the sharp bend near the throttle body is the only detriment to airflow here.

01 Our kit came with all the necessary hardware for installation. Looks great - nothing standard-looking about this.

05 Fit the silicone step hose and hose clamps onto the throttle body . . .

06 . . . then fit the intake hose to the silicone step hose.

an induction kit

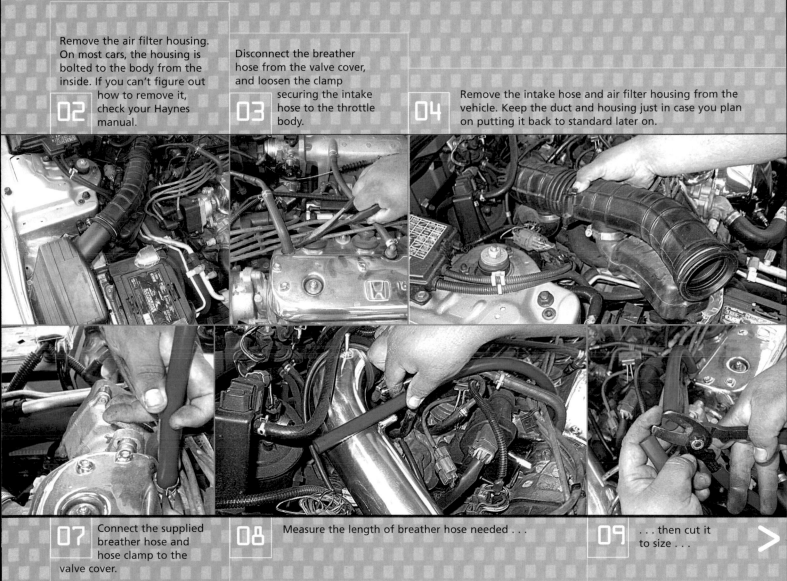

02 Remove the air filter housing. On most cars, the housing is bolted to the body from the inside. If you can't figure out how to remove it, check your Haynes manual.

03 Disconnect the breather hose from the valve cover, and loosen the clamp securing the intake hose to the throttle body.

04 Remove the intake hose and air filter housing from the vehicle. Keep the duct and housing just in case you plan on putting it back to standard later on.

07 Connect the supplied breather hose and hose clamp to the valve cover.

08 Measure the length of breather hose needed . . .

09 . . . then cut it to size . . .

>

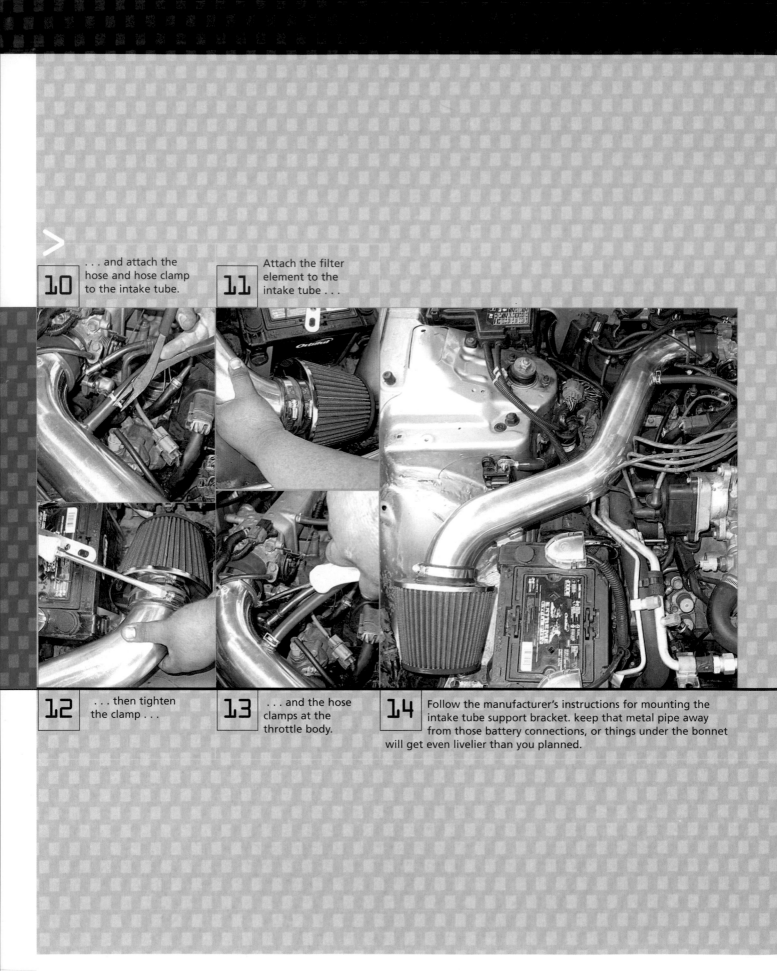

10 . . . and attach the hose and hose clamp to the intake tube.

11 Attach the filter element to the intake tube . . .

12 . . . then tighten the clamp . . .

13 . . . and the hose clamps at the throttle body.

14 Follow the manufacturer's instructions for mounting the intake tube support bracket. keep that metal pipe away from those battery connections, or things under the bonnet will get even livelier than you planned.

Longer rams can pick up colder under-car air - this installation on a Ford Focus looks like a short ram, but the pipe ducks down under the battery box and gets air from under the bumper.

Not all cold air intakes are polished metal - this unique system is roto-molded plastic and features a radiused entry at the bottom and a quiet filter box that uses a high-flow foam element.

When at the track for dragstrip runs, the filter can be removed and a pipe run out to the front of the car to pick up high-speed air - on most Hondas, this means temporarily removing the right headlight, such as on this car where the owner taped a plastic funnel onto the pipe to hopefully pick up even more air.

Cold-air intakes

Did we say colder air was important? In performance terms, the colder the air, the more power you make. For every drop of 10-degrees in the intake air fed to your engine, your power goes up about 1%. That may not sound like much, but if you have a 150 hp engine now, and you manage to reduce your intake air temperature by 100 degrees, you could gain 15 brake! Air gets denser as it gets colder, so more air is packed into the engine, even with the same volume of airflow.

Aside from the power boost, aftermarket intakes just look cool! Available anodised in blue, red, or purple, a chrome-like high-temperature coating, or a polished finish on the metal tube, they make the most powerful statement that your engine is modified. That "wow" factor when you pop the bonnet is something you've just gotta have.

The cold-air package is important because the intake pipe's longer, reaching down to pick up colder air from below the grille or in the car's front wheelarch, rather than the hotter engine compartment air. Typical engine compartment air temperature could be 30 to 50 degrees higher than the ambient outside air, even when the vehicle is at speed and cooler ambient air is presumably flowing through the engine compartment.

Aftermarket cold air intake systems can be worth 8 to 20 horsepower, depending on the design and the quality of the air filter included with it. Obviously, a cold air intake is going to need some bends in order to reach the cold air, but if there are too many bends, the horsepower gain from the colder air could be offset by a reduction in airflow. The longer the pipe, the more friction there will be for the incoming air, even on a straight length of pipe. Add a few bends and the air is further restricted.

One additional note about aftermarket air intakes - they're noisier (but you already knew that, didn't you?). You're eliminating the carefully-engineered sound baffles and plastic dams in the standard intake, so you're going to be much more aware of the sound of air rushing through to feed your engine - this is the sound of increased engine power, and that's no bad thing.

A straight end on a pipe doesn't pick up air well, even out in front of the car, because the pipe entry is too sharp - a funnel is good, but a tapered round entry like this is much better.

This Typhoon kit from K&N is typical of cold-air induction systems, shown here with a "rain hood" that slips over the filter for wet weather - the junction of the two pipes is a spot where the lower pipe can be removed to attach the filter there inside the engine compartment, making a short ram out of a long ram, another way of preparing for winter driving.

When a gulp of water can be a very bad thing

Don't get too cute about where you put the air filter

Of course, we want it to be in the cold air stream, but this is usually where the filter can be at the mercy of dirt and water. In some weather conditions, the filter could become blocked by snow or mud, or water could actually be sucked in by the engine. If it happens it could spell the end of your engine! The condition is called hydraulic-lock - when water gets into the cylinder(s), it doesn't compress like a gas. Instead, the pistons are pushing up against something virtually solid, so the result is often bent con-rods and crankshaft.

There are several ways to avoid the hydraulic-lock disadvantage of the cold-air intake. First, don't mount the end of the pipe too low! The intake and filter companies have wraps and protective plastic or sheetmetal pieces that protect the filter from most water and dirt. Lots of enthusiasts take the front pipe off their cold-air intake off during the winter. There are some models of two-piece cold-air intakes where the wheelarch pipe can be removed, and the filter attached to the pipe still on the engine, effectively making a long-ram into a short-ram. Perhaps the best solution if you want to keep the cold-air intake on all year is an air bypass valve. The bypass valve opens if the air filter is submerged in or blocked by water, and temporarily lets engine compartment air (filtered by a foam element) feed the engine.

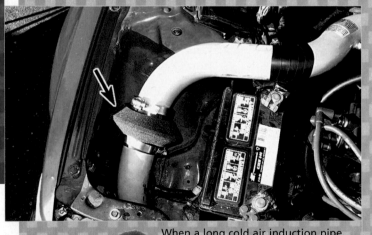

When a long cold air induction pipe mounts the filter down low on the car, there's possibility water could get into the airflow when driving through a big puddle, causing engine damage - an air bypass valve (arrow) can be installed in the piping to prevent hydraulic-lock.

The AEM bypass valve reroutes air through an external diaphragm to keep dry air flowing, even if the filter is clogged with water - such valves can generally be used only on normally-aspirated (not supercharged or turbocharged) applications.

Wicked air

Throttle bodies

Once you have an improved intake system fitted, there are other improvements you can make to the intake system to flow more air. Everything that's between the cold air pipe and the intake port on your cylinder head also controls the airflow - once you start modding your engine and need more airflow, these other parts become the still-restricted limitation on how much air you can get into the engine.

If you've changed cams or ported the head, etc, then you may need to increase the airflow allowed by your standard throttle body. As we mentioned in previous chapters, all your engine modifications have to be chosen to work with each other as a system. You don't want only one or two parts making high-rpm power if the rest of the components are going to restrict that effort. Mind you, it does no good to

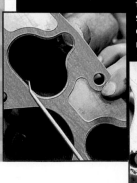

If you've modified the engine enough, you might need a larger-than-stock throttle body - carefully measure the inside diameter of the old throttle bore before shopping for a new one, and don't make a big leap in bore size unless the manufacturer of your turbo or nitrous kit, etc, recommends it.

Free horsepower

An old trick is to "port-match" the manifold to the cylinder head. If you look at the cylinder head mounting surface of the manifold and compare its ports to that of the intake manifold gasket, you'll invariably see that the ports in the gasket are slightly bigger than the ports in the manifold or the head. Remove your intake manifold and mount it in a vice with the ports facing up. Clamp a new gasket on the manifold, with the gasket perfectly aligned over the mounting bolt holes. Now scribe a line inside the gasket ports onto the manifold.

Take the gasket off and use a small electric or air-powered die grinder (eg a Dremel) to grind out the manifold ports to the scribed line. Take your time and don't go beyond the scribed line or you could hinder the gasket's job of making a good seal. Try to gently blend the new port size back up into the ports on the manifold as far as you can, to improve the transition for the incoming air. Ideally, the cylinder head should be treated similarly to match the gasket, but you can wait until you have some other reason to pull off the head.

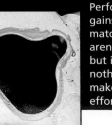

Performance gains in port-matching aren't large, but it costs you nothing to make the effort.

install a high-flow component in one area of the engine, such as a big throttle body, unless you can run at higher revs. Don't even think about changing throttle bodies until you've removed all restrictions in the exhaust side of the engine.

Throttle bodies are available in various sizes, usually only differing from the standard units in the main throttle bore diameter.

If yours is a mild engine and there are several steps in throttle body size available, don't just buy the biggest one made, even if it is super-trick red-anodised aluminium. Play it safe and buy the smallest increase over standard, unless you install a big throttle body at the same time that you make other major engine changes. If you fit a too-big throttle body now, and don't make your other modifications until much later, the interim period will find you with a low-rpm dog (and we don't mean that in a good way).

If you do fit a larger throttle body, remove your intake manifold and have the throttle body opening in the manifold enlarged to the same size. For instance, on a Honda, It does no good to install an expensive "Type R" throttle body if it's restricted by a smaller, standard-sized hole at the manifold.

Fitting a throttle body isn't too complicated. A good aftermarket unit will come with clear instructions. Carefully mark all the hoses and wires on your standard throttle body with masking tape and a marking pen so you can connect them all to the right places on the new throttle body. Some cars have hot water hoses connected to the throttle body, in which case you must wait until the engine is completely cool and clamp-off those hoses before disconnecting them. You also have to disconnect the throttle linkage, and on some cars, the cruise control or transmission linkage as well. On most cars, the throttle body is attached to the intake manifold with four bolts, and sometimes it isn't easy to get at all the bolts. Take your time, and if necessary, follow a Haynes repair manual for your car.

Here's a billet-aluminium aftermarket throttle body fitted on a thoroughly-modified Honda VTEC application.

This Holley billet aluminium throttle body for Hondas accepts all the standard wiring and plumbing, and is available in 62mm and 68mm bores, said to be good for 5 to 10 brake.

If you've modded the fuel system or added nitrous, you might need more volume in your intake plenum - for some applications, AEM makes these spacers that mount between the throttle body and the intake manifold, to add a little more plenum volume without having to buy a new manifold.

This serious aftermarket Honda intake manifold from Edelbrock has a larger plenum (the bit with "performer" on it), nine-inch-long passages, and mountings for extra injectors. It's not for girls, then...

Intake manifolds

The final component in your intake system is the intake manifold that connects the throttle body to the cylinder head. This is that last section of the exterior intake path. If you've made the kind of mods that necessitate a larger throttle body, then an improved intake is probably on the agenda too.

Intake manifolds are designed for specific levels of engine performance and rpm range. Your standard manifold was probably a good design for normal driving. To design a performance intake manifold, increased airflow volume and velocity are the goals, just as with the big throttle bodies. The perfect manifold would be one that combined the right size ports, the right length of runners and the internal shapes to make maximum power. As with throttle bodies, the best manifold for pure high-rpm power is going to be unsuited to normal road use.

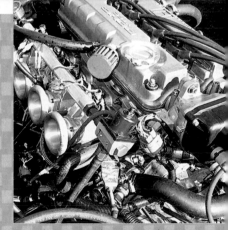

Another race-only setup is this engine with individual throttle bodies for each cylinder, and tuned-entry velocity stacks on each throttle body - when ready to make a run, an airbox mounts over these stacks to feed them cold air. Who's yer daddy?

Fuel system

It's all about getting the right amount of fuel, at the right time, into your engine

With a stock engine, or one that's only mildly modified, the ECU/computer that came with your car will work with your engine management system and fuel system components to do an adequate job of delivering fuel to the engine. But if you become a bit more aggressive with your modifications, your engine will begin starving for more fuel to keep it happy.

This can be achieved in several ways. If you add more pressure, each time the injector opens, more fuel will be delivered (but not much). If you control the length of time that the injector stays open, you have also added more fuel, even at the same pressure. The final way to inject more is to install fuel system components (injectors, fuel pump, etc.) that physically flow more fuel.

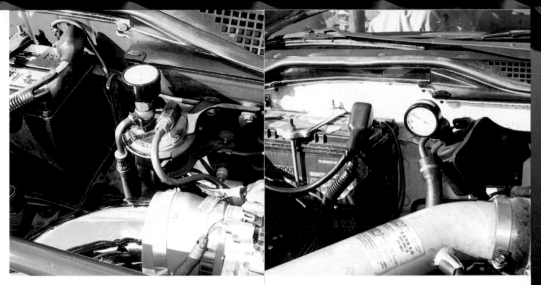

If you're adjusting fuel pressure, you need a convenient gauge to monitor the pressure - many enthusiasts mount theirs on top of the standard fuel filter at the bulkhead, where possible.

On this drag racing engine, the gauge is on the fuel filter assembly, but mounted so that it faces the tuner when he's working on the engine.

Fuel pressure

An adjustable fuel pressure regulator is probably the first modification for your fuel system. The aftermarket units are a direct bolt-on for the standard regulator, with the same vacuum connection, but feature an adjuster screw on top. Loosening or tightening the adjuster will change the fuel system pressure. Once you start playing with your fuel system, you must have a reliable way to measure the fuel pressure, which usually means installing a quality fuel pressure gauge. Most enthusiasts mount theirs in the engine compartment, where they do most of their tuning work. Some aftermarket gauges are designed to be screwed right into the fuel rail in place of the Schrader valve. An aftermarket fuel rail will usually have a threaded hole just for adding a gauge. It would be nice to have the gauge inside the car to watch it under different driving conditions without having to use a dyno, but a fuel gauge and fuel line inside the cockpit is potentially dangerous. A problem with the gauge or the pressurised line supplying it could leave you with a faceful of fuel.

When you increase the fuel pressure in your fuel injection system, you're putting a greater load on the injectors themselves. Too much fuel pressure will shorten the life of the injectors. Experts tell us that for road cars with mild bolt-on modifications, you shouldn't raise the factory fuel pressure much more than 10%. On a vehicle with 45 psi as the standard pressure, you could safely raise it with an adjustable regulator to 49.5 psi, assuming that your modifications require an increase.

If you assemble a high-pressure fuel system for a boosted or nitrous application, you must use a bypass-type fuel-pressure regulator with a separate return line back to the fuel tank. Too much pressure without a bypass regulator could cause the pump(s) to fail. Also, use only high-pressure-rated metal or decent braided hoses in a high-pressure system to avoid possible fuel line rupture.

Without your own rolling road to examine your engine under all conditions, especially under load at full-throttle, you have to tune fuelling by feel and by ear. If you have an experienced tuner near you, they can help a lot because they know what's worked on engines like yours. If you have too much fuel, your engine will be "doggy" at the bottom end, and you'll be bogging down every time you pull away with less than 6000 rpm showing. With a minor increase in fuel system pressure, you can have your standard ECU or chip reprogrammed to handle higher fuel pressure, and this is recommended, but there is a limit to how much the standard ECU can handle. An exhaust gas analyser is a big help, especially if you can run the car on a rolling road (driven by the car's wheels under load). You can also learn something from your friends - see what they've done and learn from their mistakes.

Working with fuel can be a dangerous thing!

- Don't smoke or allow open flames or bare light bulbs near the work area, and don't work in a garage where a gas-type appliance (such as a water heater or a clothes dryer) is present.

- Since petrol is carcinogenic, wear fuel-resistant gloves when there's a possibility of being exposed to fuel, and, if you spill any fuel on your skin, rinse it off immediately with soap and water.

- Mop up any spills immediately and don't store fuel-soaked rags where they could ignite.

- The fuel system on fuel injected vehicles is under constant pressure, so, if any fuel lines are to be disconnected, the fuel pressure in the system must be relieved first.

- When you perform any kind of work on the fuel system, wear safety glasses and have a Class B type fire extinguisher on hand.

About relieving fuel pressure

- One method is to pull the fuse that controls your fuel pump and run the engine until it cuts out for lack of fuel.

- After relieving the fuel pressure, be sure to disconnect the cable from the negative terminal of the battery.

- Purchase a Haynes Repair Manual for your specific model to get important information on safely relieving fuel pressure and working on fuel system components.

01 On our Honda we relieved fuel pressure by loosening this small bolt on the fuel filter. Each model is a little different, so buy a manual to do it right.

02 Mark and disconnect the vacuum line and fuel hoses from the stock regulator – on this Honda, the regulator is attached to the fuel rail with two bolts.

03 We're using a B&M kit that modifies the standard regulator - carefully cut off the top of the regulator "can" with a hacksaw, then remove the stock spring and file the edges of the regulator body smooth.

Fuel pressure regulator modification

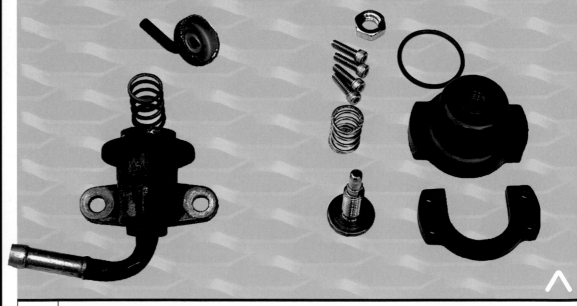

04 Here the cut-apart standard regulator and spring (left) is compared to the pieces in the B&M kit, which includes a new spring, adjuster screw, anodised aluminium housing and an O-ring

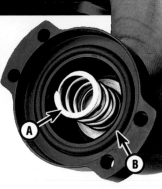

05 Put the adjuster screw into the housing and thread it in so about half its length is on the outside, then put on the adjuster locknut finger-tight over the exposed (outside the housing) threads of the adjuster screw.

06 Place the new spring (A) onto the adjuster screw, and fit the O-ring into the groove in the regulator body (B).

07 Push the new assembly onto the bottom section from the stock regulator and hold it tightly in place . . .

08 . . . until you can slip the anodised aluminium bottom piece under the top and start the two screws – Loctite is provided with the kit to use on the screws, which are tightened with an Allen key.

09 Before fully tightening the screws, make sure the two flat sections of the aluminium bottom piece align with the mounting flange of the regulator, otherwise the assembly won't bolt up to your fuel rail.

10 You now have a complete fuel pressure regulator that is both good-looking and adjustable – make sure you use a new factory O-ring at the fuel rail side when refitting the regulator.

For engines with 400 or more horsepower, you'll need a large fuel pump and fuel filter with large lines, preferably in braided-stainless-covered hose that can take plenty of pressure.

Your boring black fuel filter can be replaced with a more attractive anodised aluminium filter housing like this one from AEM, which accepts a standard filter element (available at motor factors) and has enough fuel flow for mega-horsepower engines.

Fuel system volume

If you make more serious engine modifications, either internal mods like a ported head and bigger cams, or install a nitrous system, supercharger or turbocharger, you will have to address the fuel volume needs of your engine. This is where fuel system tuning can get tricky, but remember that you're not a pioneer here - many other enthusiasts have done just what you're doing, probably to the exact same vehicle. The manufacturer of the power-adding kit you buy should be able to tell pretty much just what is needed to compensate for the extra fuel needs of the nitrous, turbo or supercharger. How much boost or nitrous you employ has a lot to do with it.

For the typical engine modified with bolt-on equipment, your standard fuel pump should be able to handle the fuel supply. Where you might want to make a change is the fuel rail that holds all your injectors. An aftermarket fuel rail is usually machined of billet aluminium, and available polished or anodised in cool colors. They look great sitting on your engine as a visual signal that you have a modified engine, even if your particular combination doesn't really need a bigger fuel rail yet.

There is a practical reason to install a fuel rail, especially if you contemplate more modifications in the future. Horsepower can be addictive! The typical aftermarket fuel rail is machined to bolt onto your standard engine with minimal trouble. The main advantage, beside looks, is that it can deliver a greater volume of fuel because the main internal passage is bigger.

An aftermarket rail such as on this race engine can carry the fuel volume to steadily feed larger injectors, and is more easily adapted to braided stainless hoses than a standard fuel rail.

Holley offers billet fuel rails in four colours – they are available for either standard injectors or larger performance injectors.

Another feature of a custom fuel rail is an extra pressure port that can be used to fit a fuel pressure gauge. The port can also be used as a convenient source of pressurised fuel if you install a nitrous system and add a separate fuel/nitrous nozzle to your intake tract. The fuel rail is also adaptable to accept aftermarket AN fittings (sometimes called "aircraft" fittings) for tuners who want to plumb their fuel system with colorful, custom lines. For bigger modifications, this will become important, because you may need to increase the fuel line diameter all the way back to the fuel tank to ensure adequate supply, and the billet fuel rail accepts bigger-than-standard fuel lines easily.

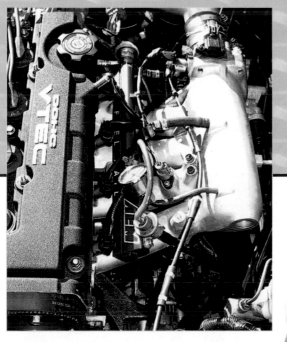

An aftermarket fuel rail is a common fuel system modification, for good looks and the ability to flow more fuel volume for modified engines – the typical billet-aluminium rail accepts a fuel gauge and a range of fuel pressure regulators.

Fuel pumps

With the bigger engine modifications, your standard fuel pump may not be able to supply enough volume or pressure. In most modern cars, the electric fuel pump is mounted in the fuel tank, usually in an assembly that includes a filter and the fuel level sending unit. With these other components connected to the fuel pump, and the number of hoses and electrical connectors attached there at the top of the tank, not everyone wants to substitute another pump for the in-tank unit.

Most tuners in need of extra fuel pressure use an extra fuel pump as a booster, leaving the stock pump in the tank. Racers often use two big aftermarket electric pumps just outside the fuel tank. Electric fuel pumps are designed to push fuel rather than pull it, so generally they should be mounted near the rear of the car, close to the fuel tank, but as long as your in-tank pump is in good shape, an aftermarket booster pump can be installed almost anywhere in the line up to the engine, and is more than enough fuel supply for a road car. It can be fitted under the car, as long as it's safely away from hot exhaust components or moving suspension parts, and is tucked up high enough that it can't be damaged by road debris. Some modified applications have the extra pump in the engine compartment.

When you have fuel pressure needs that go up with high revs and boost, you can increase flow with MSD's fuel pump booster – it adds more voltage to your in-tank pump as needed, and can be varied from 1.5 to 22 extra volts over a range of 5 to 30 psi.

For higher horsepower engines with power adders, Holley's line of direct-replacement high-flow fuel pumps are available from 190 litres-per-hour to 255 lph (enough to supply an 800 bhp engine).

Electric pumps are noisy, another reason car makers stick them down in the fuel tank where the sound is dampened. Wherever you mount the pump, make sure you use the rubber isolation mounts that should come with the pump. A chassis-mounted pump without rubber mounts can make an annoying hum, audible inside the car if you don't have your stereo on.

01 On most vehicles, the in-tank fuel pump is accessible once the rear seat base or boot floor mat is removed, then an access plate is unbolted and removed. Consult a Haynes Manual for specifics on your car. Higher-flowing fuel pumps can be exchanged for the standard pump when fitting a supercharger or turbocharger.

02 Relieve the fuel system pressure, mark and disconnect the fuel lines, wires and hoses, then remove the fuel pump assembly mounting screws or nuts.

If you don't want to replace the in-tank pump, extra fuel volume can be added with an aftermarket performance pump like this one from MSD added in-line to your fuel system.

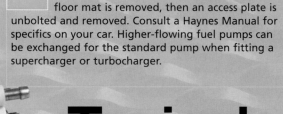

Typical fuel pump replacement

03 Lift the pump/fuel level sending unit assembly from the tank and use a large rag to catch any fuel drips.

04 Pull the "sock" filter from the bottom of the pump, then release the protective cover over the main electrical connector at the pump and pull the pump out of the assembly. Fit the high-flow replacement pump and replace the sock filter.

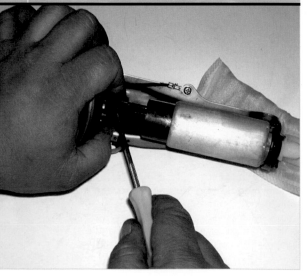

Test and tune

The oxygen sensor in your cat-equipped car has a limited range of air/fuel ratios it can act upon, since it's designed to be sensitive only in the range of the standard car, with all original equipment in place. Once you start modifying your engine, especially the fuel system, the oxygen sensor isn't going to be able to act properly and keep the engine in the "normal" air/fuel ratio range.

Highly accurate air/fuel meters are used by pro racers, but are extremely expensive. A few more-affordable aftermarket sensors and dash-mounted meters are available that can be used to study your fuel needs. They feature a row of LED lights that correspond to different air/fuel ratios, and while you drive you can see what range you're in under different conditions.

If you do go to a piggyback engine-management box added to your standard ECU, or go all the way and have a stand-alone aftermarket system, a laptop PC can be used to monitor your engine as you drive (with a mate along to hold and watch the computer while you focus on driving - of course), and you can make changes to various parts of the fuel curve.

As mentioned in previous Chapters, you have to learn to "read" your car's driveability and performance. When you know your engine inside and out, you can better evaluate each new modification and how the car behaves differently than before the modification. We always recommend keeping track of your engine by checking the spark plugs as an indication of what's going on inside the combustion chamber. Compare your plugs with the spark plug condition chart in the *Ignition systems* Chapter to evaluate your engine conditions. It's vitally important to catch the early signs of detonation before engine internal parts are damaged.

An air/fuel ratio monitor can tell you what's going on inside your engine in both economy and power modes - this one from K&N has ten LED lights in different colours that correspond to different A/F ratios. It comes with its own oxygen sensor that can be used with almost any fuel (including alcohol) except diesel, nitromethane or leaded fuels.

A fuel computer can be added to your system to display air/fuel ratios and make adjustments - the VAFC fuel computer from A'PEXi can adjust fuel ratio for both the low-lobe and high-lobe modes of a Honda VTEC engine.

Fuel injectors

Telling you how to choose a set of higher-flow fuel injectors could take up a huge chunk of this book by itself. There's a lot of science to choosing the right set, and a little bit of mystery as well. We'll give you some of the basics, but don't expect all of your questions to be answered here. It'll take an experienced tuner working with a dyno and plenty of instrumentation to really make a good selection for you.

An electronic fuel injector performs an amazing job when you think about it. Under considerable fuel pressure, it must open, squirt and close in a matter of milliseconds. At high revs, the injector's working overtime to keep up with the engine's demands. How much fuel gets into the engine depends on the physical size of the injector, how quick it can respond, and how long it stays open. Big injectors obviously flow more fuel, and an injector that is told to stay open longer will also flow more fuel.

The parts of your engine management system that control the injector operation are called "drivers". Your standard drivers are designed for the normal fuel system, and raising the fuel pressure or changing to larger injectors can leave the computer out of calibration. You car may have the top-end power you need, but fuel economy is going to go down and the air/fuel ratio at lower speeds is going to be too rich, causing sluggish performance. Injector selection is always a compromise, unless it's a perfectly standard car, or a perfectly race-only machine that's been tuned and tested with a stand-alone fuel management system for high-rpm operation only. In some ways, it's easier to find the combination for a race engine, because idling, cold-starts and low/mid-range performance or efficiency aren't important.

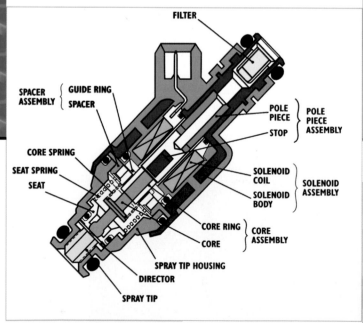

FILTER

SPACER ASSEMBLY { GUIDE RING / SPACER

POLE PIECE / STOP } POLE PIECE ASSEMBLY

CORE SPRING

SEAT SPRING

SEAT

SOLENOID COIL / SOLENOID BODY } SOLENOID ASSEMBLY

CORE RING / CORE } CORE ASSEMBLY

SPRAY TIP HOUSING

DIRECTOR

SPRAY TIP

An electronic fuel injector is more complicated than you might think, so aftermarket performance injectors can be expensive - if you know you don't actually need bigger injectors, you can have your standard injectors flow-tested and balanced, restoring the spray pattern, and protecting your engine from a burned piston due to one bad injector.

Fuel injector replacement

After relieving the fuel pressure and disconnecting the battery, disconnect the electrical connectors from the injectors. Most cars use connectors like these, with a wire locking clip that you slide out to release and unplug the connector. Don't just pull on the plug - this stuff's a bit delicate.

01

02 Detach the fuel return line from the pressure regulator.

03 Unscrew the banjo bolt fitting, and detach the fuel feed line from the fuel rail.

Whether you're simply fitting your standard injectors with new seals, or fitting high-flow performance items, the procedure is essentially the same. Injector removal and refitting is very similar from one car to the next, though there's no harm in having the right Haynes manual for your car.

> **04** Remove the fuel rail mounting nuts or bolts . . .

05 . . . then carefully wiggle and pull on the rail until the injectors are freed. No great force should be needed for this.

06 Remove the injectors from the fuel rail - on most cars they pull straight out, but on some they are secured by clips.

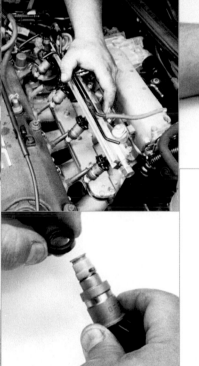

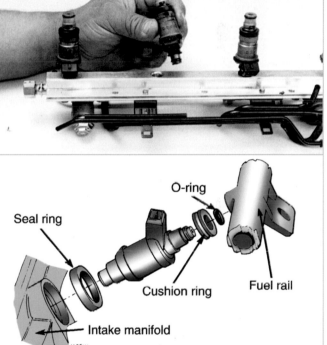

O-ring

Seal ring

Cushion ring

Fuel rail

Intake manifold

H 25111

07 Remove the injector O-ring seals. Don't re-use these - always fit new ones.

08 Some injectors have a seal ring and cushion ring - remove these, too. Fit new if they're worn.

09 Fit new O-rings (and seal/cushion rings, if fitted), then reverse the procedure to refit the injectors. Lubricate the O-rings with a light film of engine oil before inserting the injectors into the fuel rail or manifold.

Valvetrain

Deep breathing

When you run fast, you breathe harder - so does your engine. To make more power, an engine must "inhale" more air and "exhale" more exhaust. To make this happen, you can open the intake and exhaust valves more, leave them open longer and enlarge the "ports" (passages in the cylinder head where the air and exhaust flow). These cylinder head and valvetrain modifications can seem complicated, but understanding them is essential. Mistakes here can cost you power or even an engine overhaul.

Adjustable cam gears ("vernier pulleys") like these from AEM allow you to adjust camshaft timing to suit the other tuning modifications you have made or plan to - SOHC engines would use one gear, most DOHC'ers use a pair (some DOHC engines have only one gear - the other cam being driven by a gear or chain from the camshaft with the sprocket).

Cam gears (a.k.a. cam *sprockets*)

Aftermarket cam gears are generally made of aluminium, with colour anodising in red, blue, purple or silver, and can certainly add to the show-worthiness of an engine compartment, especially when you're going for a "theme" of co-ordinated colours. Unfortunately, in order for anyone to see your cool cam gears you have to leave off the timing belt cover (at least the upper cover). With the wraps off, people can not only see the gears, but, when the engine is running and you see them spinning, it gives the impression of an extra 30 horsepower!

The only problem with leaving the timing belt cover off is that stuff can get into the "beltway" and cause serious problems. If you happen to drop a socket or something else down there when working on the engine and then start the engine up, you could toast the whole motor. Oops.

Anything that gets caught up in the belt can cause it to shred or come off the sprockets or tensioner, and either situation on a running engine means that some of the valves are going to be open when the piston comes up. When this happens in a split second, valves and/or pistons are going to be destroyed. But we know you'll leave the cover off anyway. Just be careful.

Aftermarket cam gears look cool and racy, but the only potential power gain by fitting them is if an adjustment in cam timing is necessary on your engine. The mounting holes for the gears are slotted on the aftermarket units, and a scale is usually engraved there to indicate whether the timing is straight up (normal), advanced or retarded. The range of adjustment is usually 5 to 10 degrees. Engines with forced induction (supercharger or turbocharger), high-compression pistons or aftermarket camshafts are obvious candidates for vernier cam gears, although almost any engine can benefit from a little cam tuning. If your cylinder head has been milled at a machine shop, either to gain extra

You'll find that cam gears are one of the most popular engine modifications there is.

The adjustable gear is two-piece, so the bolts can be loosened and the relationship between the inner section on the camshaft and the outer section connected to the timing belt can be advanced or retarded. Good ones like this AEM "Tru-Time" gear are machined of billet aluminium and feature very clearly engraved timing marks.

compression or because the head was warped from overheating, you may need adjustable cam gears because milling the head brings the camshafts closer to the crankshaft and retards the cam timing slightly.

If you have a single overhead cam engine (SOHC), you'll only need one cam gear, and on SOHC engines, the phasing between the exhaust and intake lobes can't be adjusted, since exhaust and intake lobes are all on one hunk of iron. You can experiment with your camshaft advanced two degrees and see how it performs, then try it with two degrees retarded. You may find that advancing the cam helps top-end performance but hurts low-end, and vice-versa. You can't get improvement at both ends.

On DOHC (double overhead cam) engines that utilise a separate gear for each camshaft, you have more to play with. By adjusting the intake and exhaust camshafts separately, you are in effect altering the overlap (the period where both valves are open at the same time on the exhaust stroke). This is one of the factors that makes

a cam design "road" or "rally/race." The more overlap there is, the better the engine will run at higher rpm, but the bottom-end will suffer some. Most twin-cam Honda owners, for example, start out with their exhaust camshaft retarded a few degrees and the intake camshaft advanced a few degrees, which is like having a slightly hotter camshaft. On DOHC engines that only have one cam gear, you can't do this (it's the same situation that was described for SOHC engines).

The exact amount of camshaft advance or retard that's best depends on a host of factors, including the efficiency of the intake and exhaust systems you're using. What works for your mate's car isn't necessarily what your engine needs. Follow the instructions that come with your aftermarket cam gears and/or camshaft to determine how to set your camshaft timing to "straight-up," then test or drive the car before making any further adjustments to advance or retard.

Most tuners like to show off their modifications, and that means leaving off the upper timing belt cover to show the anodised cam gears - this makes them easy to access for making timing changes, but be careful nothing drops down behind the lower belt cover - it could cost you an engine.

Probably no valvetrain modification is as important as good aftermarket valve springs that are strong enough not to "float" or "bounce" the valves at high engine speeds - these "Ultra-Rev" springs are designed specifically for high-rpm and high-boost forced-induction engines.

Valve springs

As mentioned before, proper aftermarket valve springs are a critical component of your modified engine if you hope to run higher revs and have the engine survive. The valve springs themselves don't make any horsepower, but can be considered insurance. At high revs, the camshafts are spinning at a high speed, forcing the valves to open really fast. The only things that keep the valves following the camshaft are the springs.

Valves: more is better

To oversimplify, more valves mean more usable power. The standard for modern high-performance engines is four valves per cylinder. But why can't you just use two valves per cylinder, and make them really big? This is where nerds will tell you about fluid dynamics and port velocity. Boiling it down, small ports and valves keep air flowing faster through the heads at low engine speeds, which makes a road car drive smoothly. Many super-fast drag-race engines use only two (huge) valves per cylinder - on these cars, low-rpm driveability isn't very important!

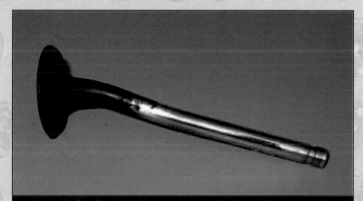

Valve float/bounce

Valve float or bounce occurs when, at high revs, the valves are trying to move so fast that they momentarily "float" away from the camshaft or rocker arm lobes. If they float away when the piston is up, damage to something is inevitable. Two factors can keep the valves from floating - the strength of the valve springs and the weight of items in the valvetrain, such as the valves, keepers and retainers. Stronger, aftermarket valve springs are an important upgrade for any engine. The stronger springs keep the valves following the camshaft, even at high rpm.

Reducing the weight of the valve train items (such as with titanium retainers) is another way to lessen the onset of valve float.

You could fit new springs in your engine and use the standard valve spring retainers, but most tuners fit new lightweight retainers at the same time as the springs - these titanium alloy retainers are stronger than standard, and their lighter weight allows the engine to rev quicker. Okay, we're convinced.

Everything we do to make power in an engine is eventually limited by the camshaft(s) - aftermarket profiles are available from mild to wild, but the bigger you go, the more the low-end performance may suffer, which is why cams are offered in "stages" so you can pick the design that suits your driving style.

Camshafts

The camshaft is one of the key players in the operation of an engine, It determines the what, when and how much of anything that goes into and out of the engine. This is another subject a great deal can and has been written about, and we're not going to bore you with heavy theory and formulas. What you need to know for now is that a standard camshaft is designed as a compromise to consider economy, emissions, low-end torque and good idling and driveability. The performance camshaft lifts the valves higher (lift), keeps them open longer (duration) and is designed mainly to produce more horsepower. A performance camshaft usually makes its gains at mid-to-higher rpm and sacrifices some low-rpm torque. The hotter the cam, the more pronounced these attributes become. A really strong cam may not be suitable for the road at all, exhibiting really low engine vacuum and not idling below 1000 rpm.

When you do get the camshaft specs right for your engine and your kind of driving, it's a thrill to hear and feel the engine get up "on the cam" and just take off. A cam design that's advertised for power between 3000 and 8000 rpm won't start feeling really good until that band is

One cam or two?

All e ngines have at least one camshaft to actuate the valves. On Single Overhead Camshaft (SOHC) engines, the camshaft does double-duty in opening both the intake and exhaust valves. Double OverHead Camshaft (DOHC) engines use one camshaft for the intake valves and one for the exhaust valves. The general rule is that SOHC engines use two valves per cylinder (one intake, one exhaust) and DOHC engines have four valves per cylinder (two of each). There are many exceptions to this rule, and some modern engines have four valves per cylinder with only one camshaft.

reached. Aftermarket cams are usually offered in "Stages" of performance. A typical Stage 1 cam might have a little higher valve lift than standard, a little longer duration, and perhaps slightly more overlap. It should retain an excellent idle and work from idle or 1000 rpm up. A Stage 2 cam would be hotter in all specs (with a band from 3000 to 7000 rpm) and have a slightly rough idle (maybe at 750 rpm), while a Stage 3 cam would feature serious lift,

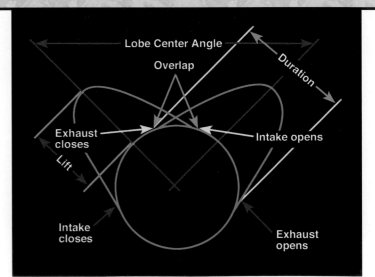

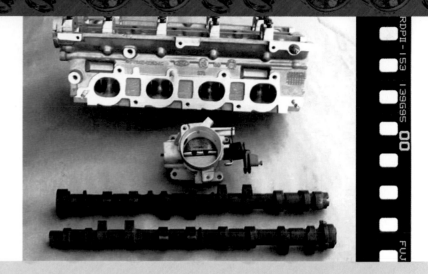

A valvetrain package from Gude that the manufacturer calls the "turbo beater at half the price" includes a ported cylinder head with performance cam(s) - this kit for the Ford Focus also includes a tweaked ECU and a bigger throttle body.

duration and overlap and make its power from 5000 to 8000 rpm. The hotter the cam specs, the worse the idle, low-end performance and fuel economy is going to be, but the more top-end horsepower you'll make. After the Stage 3 cam, which is usually a serious race/rally item, the cam profiles are strictly for racing.

One exception to the "can't have your cake and eat it too" philosophy is the VTEC system offered by Honda. Ideally, an engine would have a continuously variable valvetrain, always with the exact right profile for the rpm range. Someday, engines will have such a system, but Honda was on the right track. Basically, the VTEC valvetrain is like three cam profiles in one. There are three lobes on the cam for each cylinder's intake or exhaust: primary, secondary and the "mid" or middle lobe. These lobes with different profiles are actuated at different rpm ranges to provide the cam profile that's best for the engine speed.

When tuners tell you they have put in a "VTEC controller," they mean they have an electronic box that alters the signal to the factory ECU, to allow the VTEC high-rpm profile to come in sooner. You can watch your dyno sheets and if there's a lull at 5000 rpm, it may be that you could use slightly quicker engagement of the VTEC to take a soft spot out of your modified engine.

When buying a performance camshaft and kit, there is always a tendency to think "bigger is better," since the hotter cam doesn't necessarily cost any more. Look at the technical literature provided by the camshaft manufacturers, in their brochures and on their websites, and compare the specs of the cams and the comments that describe the cam's idle, driving and power characteristics. Going overboard can mean you have a miserable car to drive in normal traffic. Relate the cam choice to the modifications you've made. Some profiles are designed specifically to work well with nitrous, turbocharging or high compression.

Another consideration in choosing a camshaft profile is will it physically work in your engine. With a certain amount of lift, there can be interference between the valve and the pistons, especially if you've skimmed the cylinder head or fitted aftermarket pistons. Usually the Stage 1 or 2 cams are OK for a standard engine, but check the manufacturer's recommendations. If there's any doubt, have your tuner check the valve-to-piston clearance.

The breathing package for the Mitsubishi Eclipse includes a ported head, performance cams, bigger throttle body and a matched intake manifold.

Your engine should be in good shape before doing any modifications, so if you pull off the car's head, check it carefully before reassembling the engine - this engine's tuner didn't monitor his engine, and heat and detonation have taken their toll - you can see where the spark plug hole threads are starting to erode (A), and between the two valves at the right there are two expensive-to-repair cracks in the head (B).

Cylinder heads and pistons

With the intake and exhaust system modified and a performance camshaft in place, your next step in improving your engine's breathing should be the cylinder head. Except for port-matching, most cylinder head work is not for the do-it-yourself modifier. Too much experience and expensive equipment is required, so find a well-recommended machine shop in your area that has experience with cylinder heads for road and racing use.

What you should do, especially if the head's off anyway for a camshaft fitting, is to have a performance valve job done. In the performance valve job, the valve face and valve seat angles in the head are changed from just one angle to three or more. In a three-angle valve job, the centre angle is the one where the valve meets the seat, and the upper and lower angles are designed to smooth the flow path from the port, around the valve head, and into the combustion chamber. This improves the flow at low-lift and is not as expensive as porting.

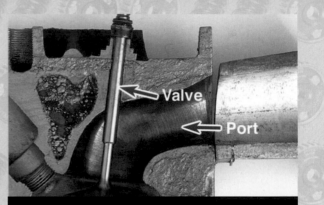

What's a head?

The cylinder head, or simply "head", is on top of the engine. The head seals the area above the pistons so that compression is created when the pistons travel up. The head is also where the air/fuel mixture enters the engine and exhaust exits. To do this, the intake and exhaust valves in the head open at precise times, controlled by the camshaft(s).

If your engine has 130,000 miles on it, chances are your valve guides are worn and you can't get a good tight valve seal if the guide allows the valve to wobble. When your head is rebuilt at the machine shop, they may suggest installing bronze-alloy guides that keep the valves cooler and reduce valve-to-guide friction.

When you're rebuilding your cylinder head, if you discover some bad valves, why not replace the whole set with performance valves like these. They're lightweight and made of high-temp alloys to handle boosted and nitrous-equipped applications.

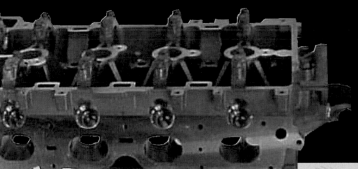

GM Performance Parts has quite a list of go-fast equipment for the ECOTEC four-cylinder engines, including this cylinder head that is CNC (computer) ported, has a three-angle performance valve job and comes with a flowbench tech sheet - the head accepts standard or aftermarket valvetrain parts.

Back to basics

If your car's got some miles on it, your valves are probably not operating as well as they should. On a worn engine, the valves don't "seat" properly because they wobble in their guides and don't sit properly against their seats in the head. Worn valve parts cost you power and can cause engine damage, since they are more likely to hit a piston. Any valvetrain rebuild should include a good valve job to re-seat the valves, and a thorough check of the valve guides and springs.

Notice the "eyebrow" looking recesses in these pistons. They allow more clearance for the valves to open more. Sometimes special pistons are necessary for your hopped-up valvetrain.

Bigger changes to the cylinder head may be detrimental to on-road performance, though they would be critical to a racer. If you're planning headwork, talk to the machinist first and thoroughly explain everything you've done to the engine so far, and any future mods you plan. He'll make specific recommendations for your particular set-up.

Sometimes swapping cylinder heads is the path to more power - the most common swap in Honda circles is the B16 VTEC head onto a larger-displacement non-VTEC block - when pros prepare the head, some holes in the head have to be modified by TIG-welding, then the head is surfaced.

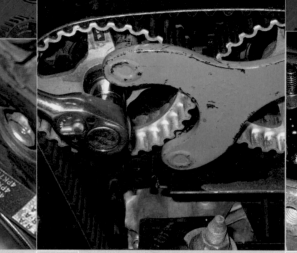

01 Start by turning the engine to TDC for the number 1 piston, aligning the mark on the crankshaft pulley with the mark on the timing cover.

02 With the timing belt upper cover removed, hold the camshaft sprocket with a two-pin spanner like this or with a large screwdriver jammed in one of the sprocket holes, while you use a spanner or socket to remove the camshaft sprocket bolt.

03 Use a pair of pliers to remove the Woodruff key from the slot in each standard camshaft - save them to re-use on the new cams.

HOW-TO: Camshafts, valve springs and timing gears

Our Haynes repair manual for your particular car covers the removal and installation of camshafts and the alignment of timing marks, but this procedure includes some details that are different in performance tuning applications. Our subject car was a typical Honda with a B16 DOHC VTEC engine, already kitted with a manifold and induction kit. We fitted a pair of Crane cams along with their performance valve springs, spring seats and lightweight spring retainers, all very important for keeping the valves from floating at high revs.

Two procedures used here are not covered in the repair manuals - finding true Top Dead Centre (TDC) for an engine, and "degreeing-in" the camshaft. For all ordinary purposes, the factory timing marks are valid, but in a performance application, precision is important. If your head has been skimmed, your camshaft timing may be off slightly, or your crankshaft pulley may be off a degree or so. So we check with a dial indicator.

To find true TDC, we use the dial indicator on the top of the piston, with the engine at the standard TDC marks and the indicator reading zero. Rotate the engine 10 degrees or so clockwise from TDC and read the indicator. Now rotate the engine counterclockwise the other direction until the pointer on the crank pulley is 10 degrees the other side of TDC and read the indicator again. Take the range of movement on the indicator and divide it by half, then rotate the engine clockwise until the indicator shows that exact amount, which puts the engine at true TDC. Now you can make the temporary timing pointer and marks we illustrate in the photos.

The point of degreeing the camshafts is to find where they are in relation to the crankshaft. Aftermarket cams come with a card that indicates the opening and closing times of the valves. There can be variations in your timing due to skimming the head or other tolerances in the engine. Tuners use adjustable cam gears ("vernier pulleys") to try different timing settings to seek out a few more horsepower.

In degreeing, you set the number 1 cylinder at TDC on our "new" temporary marks, then attach a dial indicator to rest on the rocker tip (or retainer or cam follower, whatever the case may be) of the number 1 intake valve, and zero the indicator at TDC. The timing card for the Stage 1 cams said the intake valve starts to open at 8 degrees after TDC. We rotated the engine very slowly past TDC while someone watched the dial indicator. When the indicator said the valve had opened 0.050-inch, we stopped.

When a cam "starts to open" is a relative thing to describe, so most cam manufacturers use the figure of 0.050-inch as a standard point of reference. Our timing marks showed we were at 6 degrees, which means that our intake cam was advanced slightly, which is what we wanted. If you wanted to advance it more, or have it "straight-up" to be exactly as the card described, you can adjust the timing gears to get what you want. On the alignment marks on most two-piece adjustable cam gears, one mark equals two degrees at the crankshaft, and the gears should have markings that indicate which direction is advance and which is retard. Once you have degreed-in your cams, you won't have to go through this procedure again, you just go by the marks on your adjustable gears. When you have the settings that seem to make the most power, leave it there and enjoy!

04 Loosen all of the bolts for the camshaft caps and the reinforcement plates, in the opposite of the tightening sequence (see Step 31) - loosen all bolts a quarter-turn first, then loosen again in sequence and remove the bolts.

05 Use a plastic-faced hammer to lightly tap the sides of the camshaft caps to separate them from the cylinder head. Make sure the caps are numbered from front-to-rear, and have an I for the intake cam caps and an E for the exhaust cam caps. If there aren't any marks, make your own.

06 Lift out both of the camshafts, taking the front seals with them.

> **Note:**
> The procedure shown here was performed on a Honda with a B16 DOHC VTEC engine. If you're working on something different you can use this as a guide, but be sure to consult your Haynes manual for the specifics.

07 Loosen the locknuts at each rocker arm, then use a screwdriver to back off the valve adjustments all the way, then tilt the rocker arms up for access to the valve springs and retainers.

08 The valve spring tool is a pair of stands that mount each end of the cylinder head and a shaft that runs between the two brackets - when you push down on the lever the spring is compressed at the retainer - you can hire one these tools.

09 To hold the valves in place while the springs are compressed, put the cylinder you're working on at TDC and insert an air hose that has a spark-plug threaded adapter at one end into the spark plug hole for that cylinder.

>

10 Connect an air-pressure regulator to the quick-connect from the spark plug hose . . .

11 . . . then connect an air line from your compressor to the regulator - when the cylinder is pressurised, the valves will be held in place - take care that the air pressure doesn't surprise you by pushing the piston down and turning the crankshaft, or secure the flywheel by jamming the ring gear if necessary.

12 With the cylinder pressurised, hold down the spring compressor while you extract the keepers at the spring retainer with a small magnetic tool, then slowly release the spring tension.

To remove the standard spring seat, which will be replaced with the new part, the seal must be pulled off, being careful not to scratch the valve stem in the process.

13 Remove the standard retainer from the spring . . .

14 . . . and the valve spring.

15

> **16** Remove the standard spring seat from the pocket in the cylinder head.

17 Clean the valve spring pocket in the head with a degreaser, then lubricate the new spring seat with engine oil and set it in place, making sure it is located properly.

18 Lubricate the valve stem with engine oil, then push a new valve seal onto the valve - push down evenly and no further than the standard seal went - the seal should hit a machined stop near the bottom of the valve guide. The seal package in your gasket set should say if the seal is for the intake or exhaust, which are different on some engines.

19 Place the new high-performance spring in, making sure that it sits flat and is centred on the new spring seat.

20 Now you can install the lightweight retainer - notice the stepped area on the underside of the retainer; this self-centres the retainer and spring.

21 Apply a little white grease to one of the valve keepers and insert it while you have the retainer and spring held down with the valve spring compressor - the grease will hold it in place. >

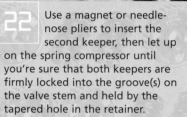

Valvetrain

22 Use a magnet or needle-nose pliers to insert the second keeper, then let up on the spring compressor until you're sure that both keepers are firmly locked into the groove(s) on the valve stem and held by the tapered hole in the retainer.

23 That completes the procedure for this first valve spring, seat, seal and retainer - when all have been replaced, remember to apply a little camshaft lube to the tops of each valve stem.

24 Clean all of the camshaft bearing saddles with lacquer thinner, then apply the camshaft lube supplied with the cams; coat the saddles and each camshaft lobe and bearing journal.

25 Lay out all the camshaft caps you removed from the head and clean them thoroughly - they are numbered from front to back - then apply a small amount of camshaft lube to the saddles of each one (the lube has been applied to these saddles, but still needs to be spread out over the bearing surfaces).

26 Make sure that the O-ring and dowel are in the cylinder head in the centre camshaft cap position.

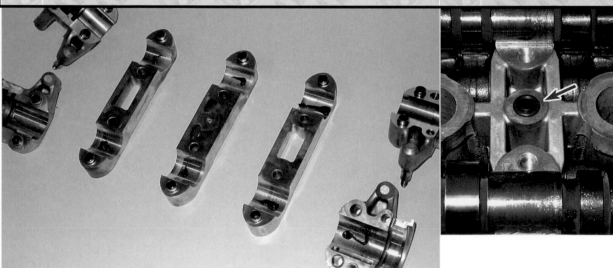

27 Grease the inner lip of the camshaft seals with white grease, then carefully push them squarely over the end of each camshaft.

28 Apply a small bead of RTV sealant to the areas indicated, just before placing the camshaft caps back onto the cylinder head.

29 Install all of the caps in their proper positions, tapping them squarely and lightly to seat them.

30 With all the camshaft caps in place, lay the two camshaft cap stiffener plates in position and hand-tighten all the bolts.

31 Torque all of the bolts in several stages and in the proper sequence, with the engine at TDC. See the Haynes manual for the correct specification and sequence (this is the proper sequence for our Honda B16 VTEC).

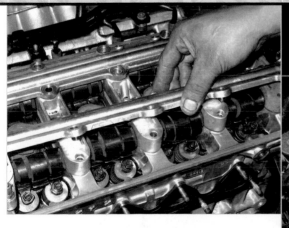

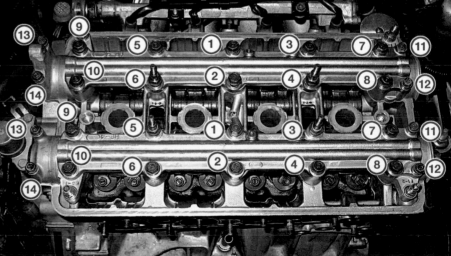

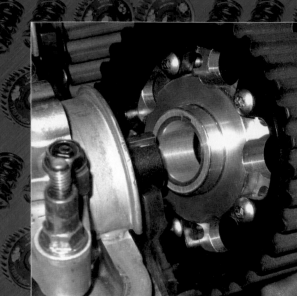

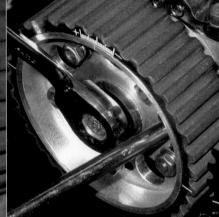

32 With the Woodruff keys tapped all the way into the keyways on the new cams, you can now fit the cam gears (technically they're "sprockets") - we're using a pair of adjustable gears.

33 With a tool through one of the holes in the cam gear, tighten the gear-to-camshaft bolt - note that all of the adjuster nuts on the gear must be tight before using this method to install the gear - the nuts can be loosened later if your need to advance or retard the cam timing.

34 With the crankshaft at TDC for number 1 cylinder, all the timing marks must align properly. Now fit the belt and release the belt tensioner - rotate the engine a few times by hand and check that the gear marks still line up at TDC - now follow the valve adjustment procedure in your Haynes repair manual, and fit the distributor at TDC.

If you don't have a degree wheel to attach to the crank, measure the circumference of the puller and divide by 360 (as in 360 degrees in a rotation) - in our case, this worked out to 1/16-inch for each degree of crank rotation - we glued a temporary pointer to the pan rail and made tiny punch marks on either side of the "new" TDC mark at 1/16-inch intervals (see intro text for procedure to find true TDC) - this location was used because it's much easier to see than where the standard marks line up at the timing belt cover.

For precise performance, we'll check to see if the TDC mark at the crankshaft pulley is accurate enough for us - we bent a large washer, drilled a hole in it and bolted it to the head as a stand for the magnetic-base dial indicator.

35

36 With an extension, we have the dial indicator on the top of the No 1 piston.

37

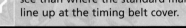

38 Set the engine to the new TDC mark, and position the dial indicator on the top of the rocker adjuster on the number 1 intake valve (either one of the two in this case), then zero the indicator (see text for explanation of degreeing the cams).

39 When we rotate the crank and watch the dial indicator, we stop just as the indicator shows the valve has moved 0.050-inch, which is the point most cam manufacturers give you a timing spec for - our cam timing card said we should be at 8 degrees ATDC (after TDC) at the crank with the valve down 0.050-inch.

40 If you look at your "new" timing marks at the crank, it should show the 8-degree ATDC mark lined up, this means our cam is "straight-up" to the engine - if it isn't, or we want to experiment with advancing or retarding the cams, we loosen the nuts on the gear, rotate the alignment marks the direction we want, and tighten the nuts again.

41 All timed and ready to go, we couldn't wait to put the valve cover and other pieces back on - our engine already had a manifold and induction kit, so the new cams were just what we need to add a little more "bite to our bark" - midrange was good, and the VTEC was even better.

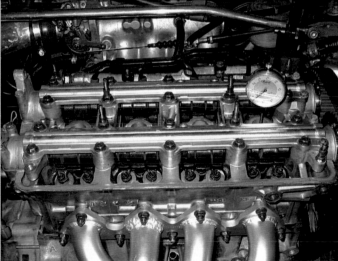

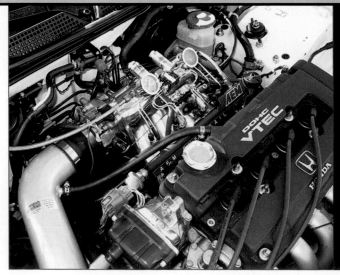

Nitrous oxide

Nitrous oxide as a horsepower source can appear to be a miracle or a curse, depending on your experience. It's a fact that nitrous oxide (N_2O) is the simplest, quickest and cheapest way to gain serious horsepower boost in your car. But, just like in children's fairy tales, you court disaster if you don't follow the rules that come with the magic potion.

Carefully used and tuned, a nitrous oxide system is the biggest bhp-per-pound boost you can make.

Nitrous oxide is an odourless, colourless gas that doesn't actually burn. It carries oxygen that allows your engine to burn extra fuel. When you inject nitrous oxide and petrol at the same time and in the proper proportions at full throttle, you'll get a kick in the butt as if you were instantly driving a car with an engine twice as big!

Nitrous kits

Done right, a nitrous kit is one of the best horsepower-per-pound investments you can make, and is the most popular power-adder for small engines. The smallest nitrous kits offer at least a 50-horsepower shot for an investment of £300. In other engine bolt-on speed budgeting, that same £300 wouldn't even cover a really nice cat-back exhaust system that may only net you 15 horsepower.

Kits are available that add up to 300hp, because the more nitrous and fuel you add, the more power the engine makes, right up to the point where the engine comes apart. And that's the other side of adding nitrous. In the end, it is the durability of the engine itself, that determines how much nitrous you can run. As tempting as it is to just keep putting bigger nitrous jets in your engine for more power, you need to do your research first to see what are the limits of your engine and what can be done to protect against damage done by detonation. You may have heard horror stories about engine disasters caused by nitrous oxide, but in most cases the cause is usually a fault in tuning the application. Serious racers have done everything possible to their engines to strengthen them to handle big loads of nitrous.

The basic road-use nitrous kit consists of: a nitrous bottle, usually one that holds 10 pounds of liquid nitrous oxide; bottle mounting brackets and hardware; fuel and nitrous jets; high pressure lines, usually braided stainless covered AN-type with a Teflon inner liner for the high nitrous pressure; nitrous filter; solenoids, switch and electrical connectors. Kits are always sold with empty bottles, but whoever sold you the kit should be able to get the bottle filled.

There are two basic types of nitrous kits that differ in how the nitrous and fuel are delivered. The "dry" system has a nozzle and solenoid only for the nitrous, and this nozzle may be almost anywhere in the intake system; behind the airflow sensor (if equipped) and ahead of the throttle body is typical. The dry systems are designed for factory fuel-injected engines. To deliver the extra

The basic nitrous oxide kit contains all you'll need, including the 10-pound bottle to hold the N$_2$O - this kit from NOS includes brackets to mount the bottle at the proper angle.

fuel to go with the nitrous, the standard system fuel pressure is raised during the full-throttle period of nitrous usage, and reverts back to the standard fuel pressure in all other driving conditions.

The "wet" system of nitrous will have solenoids for nitrous and fuel, both of which are turned on when the nitrous system is activated. The fuel and nitrous in a simple system are plumbed into a single injector that merges the two, the fuel and its oxidiser, as they enter the engine. More sophisticated wet systems may have an N_2O nozzle for each cylinder of the engine, and one or more fuel nozzles mounted separately. In high-output racing applications, individually feeding each

cylinder allows for tuning each cylinder separately for fine control. The extra nozzles also mean there is ample supply of nitrous and fuel for very high-horsepower installations.

There are all sorts of "bells and whistles" available as extra features on most of the nitrous kits on the market today. There are varying designs of nozzles, different electronic controls that work with your factory ECU to control timing and fuel delivery, optional bottle covers, bottle warmers, remote shut-off valves for the bottle, ECU piggybacks (see Chapters 4 and 5) that pull back the ignition timing under nitrous use, and "staged" nitrous kits that deliver a certain amount during initial take-off, then a little more, and the full blast for the top end.

On this Nitrous Express setup, there's an in-line filter in both the fuel (A) and nitrous (B) lines leading to the solenoids, a good idea to prevent clogged injectors or N_2O nozzles.

In "wet" systems, the nitrous nozzle (arrow) can mix and spray both fuel and nitrous into the intake.

No laughing matter

Nitrous can be intoxicating, but confine your high to the feeling you get from gobs of extra horsepower, not from inhaling the nitrous. Yes, it was once called "laughing gas" and used by dentists as an anaesthetic, but that is medical-grade nitrous, which is a controlled substance. The stuff you're going to buy is industrial-grade nitrous, which has a serious irritant added to it. If you try to inhale this stuff, you'll be sorry. Your engine, on the other hand, will love it.

The N_2O solenoids and controls should be mounted in the engine compartment, close to the intake system - this Zex installation is "dry", meaning that only nitrous is injected through the intake nozzle (the extra fuel comes through the standard injectors, based on an altered vacuum signal to the fuel pressure regulator under "juice").

Model-specific kits are available in addition to the more universal nitrous packages - NOS offers this kit for the Ford Focus with a unique plate-style injection and an rpm "window" switch to prevent rpm-induced backfires from the factory rev-limiter.

The two-piece construction of the Focus intake manifold lends itself to the plate system; the plate sandwiches between the two manifold sections.

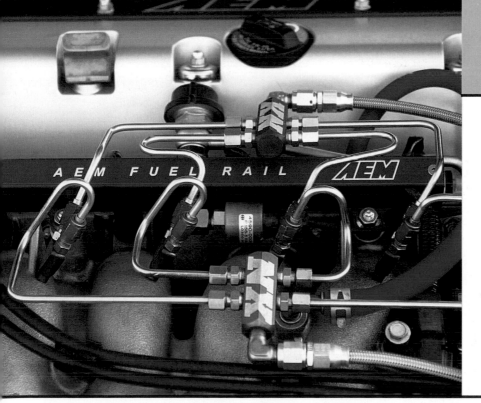

The most universal kit from Nitrous Express is this one that is adjustable from 35-50-75 horsepower levels - this wet-style kit needs no electronics for timing retard and uses the standard fuel pump.

In the really 'serious' nitrous installations, there may be a nozzle for each cylinder, installed in the intake runners - this clean setup uses fuel (blue) and nitrous (red) distribution blocks, and individual stainless-steel hard lines to connect to the four nozzles.

How does it work?

In basic terms for a simple nitrous system, the tank or bottle of nitrous oxide is mounted in the boot, and plumbed up to the engine compartment with a high-pressure line. This is connected to an electric solenoid, from which nitrous (still a liquid at this point) can flow to the nozzle attached to your intake system. If you turn on an "arming" switch in the car, battery voltage is available to another switch that is a button-type located on the steering wheel, dashboard or gear lever. Push that button when you're hard on the throttle and the solenoid releases nitrous oxide which passes through a sized jet or orifice and turns into a vapour, to mix with your vapourised fuel in the engine. The extra fuel admitted at the same time as the N_2O is easily burnt, and creates enough cylinder pressure to add 50, 75, 100 or more horsepower in an instant.

That's the basics, but there's a lot more to the science that's behind having this much fun. To start with, most systems today are not activated by a hand button. There are dangers associated with having the nitrous come on at any time other than full-throttle, not the least of which is the chance of a puddle left in the manifold. Anytime there is nitrous hanging around in the intake tract at other than full-throttle, a backfire could cause an explosion that could violently separate the intake system from the engine. Not a good thing. Thus, since you can't always trust yourself as the driver to only push a button during full-throttle, manufacturers have several methods to ensure that nitrous is delivered only at the right time. The most common system uses a momentary-contact electrical switch mounted to your throttle body, turned on only when the throttle is wide open. Other nitrous kits use a controller that taps into the signal wire from your standard throttle position sensor (which changes voltage with the amount of throttle opening).

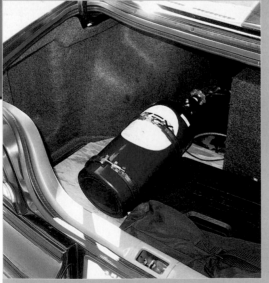

Your nitrous is generally stored in a 10-pound metal bottle mounted in the boot - it should be kept out of direct sun and mounted with the control knob forward, the label up and the bottle tilted slightly up at the front - like this.

Adjustable kits can vary the horsepower levels through small jets that control just how much fuel and nitrous are delivered to the engine - here's a handy kit that stores jets and a spare nozzle, and comes with a jet spanner.

Installations
Balancing function with style

Here are some of the things you'll be doing in a typical installation. Obviously, you should follow the instructions that came with the kit for specific steps. The bottle of nitrous oxide is usually mounted in the boot of the car as the first step. Your kit manufacturer's instructions will tell you how to mount the bottle, which must be oriented a certain way to supply nitrous under acceleration. The high-pressure hose is run from the bottle up to the engine compartment, either through the interior under the carpeting and through a hole (always have a grommet around the hose) in the bulkhead, or routed under the car. If you take the latter route, secure the hose all the way along with cable-ties, keeping the nitrous line away from hot or moving components and where it won't be subject to abrasion or rock damage. Whatever the route, tape off both ends of the hose before routing it through the car, and if you have any nitrous-related wires (such as for a bottle warmer, remote gauge or remote bottle opener), route them along with the hose.

Next, the solenoid(s) are mounted to the bulkhead, then the nitrous line for the tank is connected to the nitrous solenoid. If it is a "wet" system, the standard high-pressure fuel line must be tapped with a I-piece, and a fuel line run to the fuel solenoid. Remember, never disconnect any fuel line without first relieving the system pressure safely (see a Haynes repair manual for your car, and Chapter 7).

Your kit's instructions will be very specific about these safety-related connections. Now find the manufacturer-recommended location for the nozzle and install it (usually on the intake tube) with the nozzle oriented towards the throttle body, and install the jet(s) for the

On a cool day at the track, competitors often remove the bottle and keep it in the sun until it's warmed up enough to provide the necessary pressure, too low a pressure and you'll run rich and not make as much power - too much pressure and you run lean and perhaps hurt the engine.

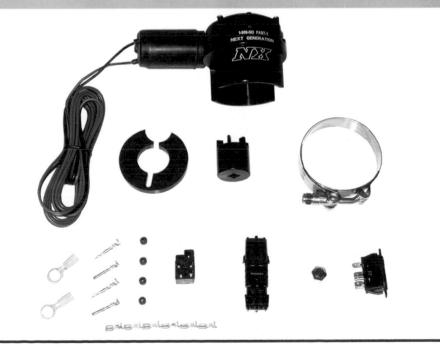

You have to open the bottle before you can use your nitrous, and you should shut the bottle off after use - a convenient way to do that without going to the trunk every time is a remote bottle opener like this Nitrous Express Next Generation kit.

A more dependable and civilised way to keep your baby's bottle warm on a cold day is an electrically-heated warmer like this Zex unit - it wraps around the tank, and you can turn it on at the dash.

horsepower level you've selected. If have an adjustable system, like 55-65-75 horsepower, start your first usage with the jets for the lowest bhp level until you've learned more about how it works on your particular engine. Connect a nitrous line from the solenoid to the nozzle, then do the same with the fuel (if yours is a wet system) from the fuel solenoid to the nozzle. Wet system kits generally have different-coloured hose for the fuel and nitrous lines so there is no mix-up.

Follow your kit's instructions carefully about wiring the solenoid(s) and switch(es), and about purging the fuel and nitrous lines. Having the fuel line empty on your first shot of nitrous will get you off to a bad start. When everything checks out, take your car out to a track or safe location and put "the squeeze" on your engine (give it N$_2$O)! Sweet!

If everything's working well, you'll soon discover your nitrous addiction will be cured when you realise that "horsepower isn't free". The cost of a nitrous oxide refill varies in different areas, but ranges from £20 to £30 to fill a standard 10-pound bottle. Just as an example of how long this can last you, a "100 hp" system will use 0.8 pounds in a ten-second blast. Actually, you may find that ten seconds is a long time at full-throttle, unless you're on a dragstrip with no other traffic. One final tip: when you're not using your nitrous, you should shut off the bottle, just in case there's a tiny leak somewhere in the system.

Detonation

If a detective were investigating all the horror stories about engine damage when using nitrous, he'd find that detonation was the culprit in almost every case. Detonation is when the pressure and temperature in the combustion chamber spike up enough to create uncontrolled burning of the fuel/air mix.

More than one flame front causes the detonation that burns up valves and pistons, and hammers at the rods and bearings. The use of nitrous oxide does not automatically mean you'll experience detonation, but even when using reasonable amounts of "juice" all conditions in the engine must be right to take full advantage of this power-adder without engine damage.

Improper setup of a nitrous system (otherwise known as "pilot error"), is one of the leading causes of detonation damage. Even mild road kits require the highest-octane pump fuel you can get. If you're in a situation where you're forced to buy lower-octane stuff, either don't use your nitrous until you use the cheaper fuel up and get some good stuff again, or carry a few bottles of octane booster in your boot. Just make sure the booster doesn't contain lead.

Octane requirement is critical to successfully using "laughing gas". For those of you lucky enough to be running Jap-import machines, remember that in Japan, pump fuel has much higher octane, and their engines have higher compression than ours. With a 10:1 compression ratio or higher, you can get by on the road with 95 octane, but if you add a nitrous kit on top of that compression, you should be using the absolute best you can get, plus an octane booster. In this country, the best you'll find is Super unleaded, at 98 octane - but it's not available everywhere, and there's increasing pressure for it to be phased out completely.

And what will we lovers of nitrous do then?

Prepping for nitrous

The ignition system is vitally important in a juiced engine. The mega cylinder pressure created when nitrous and extra fuel are ignited in the combustion chamber make it more difficult for the spark to jump the electrodes in your spark plugs, and misfiring is like throwing out an anchor behind you. In a typical 50 bhp road kit, standard ignition is probably all right as long as all components are in perfect shape. You'll need good HT leads, a good cap and rotor arm (where used), and the best spark plugs. For most road-use applications, you should go one range colder on the plugs. In setups using more than 50 bhp jets, plugs two steps colder may be required, and an aftermarket ignition with high-output coil, phat HT leads and ignition amplifier box will be helpful, as will a manifold and cat-back exhaust system.

If you've previously added a chip or had your ECU reprogrammed to make a few more horsepower, you should revert back to standard specs, since most computer "upgrades" increase ignition timing. The nitrous more than makes up for the few horsepower you might lose through "un-chipping", and going back to standard specs can help avoid detonation. In engines running 10:1 compression or using higher doses of nitrous, you'll want to fit an aftermarket timing control that will actually retard the timing while the juice is on. Some companies include with their N_2O kits an electronic controller that gives you two programs - one for standard performance with increased timing for normal driving, and another that retards timing and automatically switches on when the nitrous is engaged.

Your engine should be in top condition before adding a nitrous kit. The extra cylinder pressure can cause blow-by on worn piston rings, and any oil that sneaks into the combustion chamber can create immediate detonation. Even in a good engine, you should change the engine oil and filter after using a lot of nitrous, because some fuel may be forced past the rings and into your oil. Other engine conditions that could induce detonation under nitrous use include a partly-blocked or poor-performing cooling system, fuel pump not up to spec, restricted exhaust system, or dirty fuel injector(s).

Running the engine lean (not enough fuel going in with the nitrous), is one of the biggest tuning mistakes that results in detonation. After you've made your first few runs on your newly-installed nitrous system, you should do what any good race tuner would do, pull all of your spark plugs for a very close examination. Refer to Chapter 5 for inspection of spark plugs, looking for discoloration or any of the other signs of overheating that signal detonation. When you make any other modifications or changes to your engine, you should do another plug reading. When you see the early signs of detonation on the spark plugs, you have time to examine the engine and find the cause before any parts are destroyed. If you have a factory or aftermarket rev limiter and it interrupts the ignition system as a way to limit the revs, you may want to invest in an aftermarket "window switch" that can disengage the nitrous system just before your rev limiter cuts in.

The pressure in your N_2O bottle has a definite effect on the richness/leanness of your combination on nitrous. Consistent bottle pressure is important. Your kit manufacturer will probably give you a recommended bottle pressure, or a range to work within. Below this pressure will induce a rich condition, which will hurt power slightly, but won't damage the engine. Too high a bottle pressure will cause a lean condition, and we've established by now what *that* means.

If it's inconvenient to always have to open the boot to read the pressure gauge on the nitrous tank, you can use this remote electronic gauge from Nitrous Express and mount it in your dash or windscreen pillar pod.

When you see the radical purple components. You know you're looking at something from Zex Nitrous systems - their bulkhead-mounted box is unique because it puts the solenoid, throttle switch and nitrous manifold all inside for a clean look.

Here's a "pilot-friendly" location, and the angle of the bottle is good, but any bottle in the cockpit should have its relief valve hard-plumbed to the floor so that in case of a high-pressure blow-off (oo-er), the driver isn't in danger.

The temperature of the bottle has a lot to do with the internal pressure, which is why on a cold day at the races, you may see people in the pits with their nitrous bottle out of the car, trying to warm it in the sun. To raise the pressure in a bottle, many tuners use an electric bottle warmer, which is a plastic wrap that goes around the bottle and has a heating element in it. When the tank pressure is right, you can turn off the warmer, and a bottle cover (like an insulated blanket) can be put over the bottle to retain the warmth.

An additional option to avoid detonation is an adjustable low-fuel-pressure switch, which taps into your fuel system. If your fuel pump slows down or there's a leak that cause the fuel pressure to fall below a set level, the nitrous is shut off to save the engine from a lean burndown. That's good insurance.

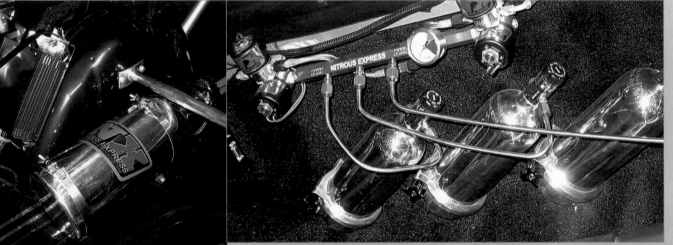

You've seen the pro racers squirting a blast of fog from the engine just before takeoff? - it's called purging, and it ensures the solenoid gets only liquid nitrous, no spots of gaseous N_2O - this is a NOS purge kit operated by a dash button.

On a show car, there's nothing like the appeal of a nitrous bottle, especially when it's a polished one.

In an unusual mid-engined application, this one gets the nod for "most interesting nitrous layout" - three bottles feed into a Nitrous Express rail with a single gauge, while two solenoids at each end of the rail feed the engine.

On a race car, every pound counts. And this bottle really shows you're serious about nitrous - it's made of composite, it's half the weight of a metal bottle, and it holds two extra pounds of N_2O, for 12 in total.

Sometimes the boot becomes the scene of a competition for space between two passions, music and performance - this owner laid things out right . . .

The bottom line for avoiding detonation is regular checks of your spark plugs. If you start to see any signs of detonation, then use a slightly smaller jet in your nitrous nozzle to richen up the fuel/nitrous ratio. Most systems are set up rich to start with to be safe, but once you're more familiar with the use of nitrous and you're brave enough to try leaning it out a little for more power, make sure you jet in tiny increments and keep checking those plugs!

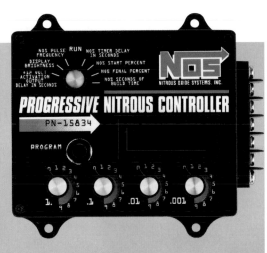

Nitrous controls have become very sophisticated compared to controls of even five years ago - this box from NOS can set a variety of tasks, especially multi-stage application of the nitrous for drag racing.

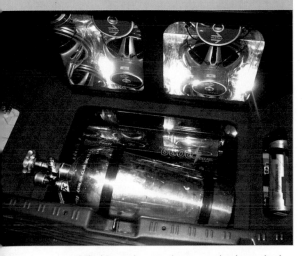

. . . while here, the speakers got the best deal, and the bottle's mounted all wrong - sideways-on locations means the system could go way rich under acceleration (not enough nitrous).

Nitrous and turbocharging

As we'll discuss in the next Chapter, turbocharging and nitrous can work well together, especially on a race car. Turbos can add tremendous horsepower to an engine, but it's not a simple bolt-on. The turbocharger itself must be sized exactly right for the application to work well in a variety of conditions. When a turbo is large enough to flow really well at high revs, it'll usually be too big to spin up quickly at the low end, thus exhibiting what most enthusiasts call "turbo lag."

Racers have found that they can have the best of both worlds by using nitrous and turbocharging together. They design a turbo system that works great at the top end for maximum horsepower, but add a carefully calculated dose of nitrous, which is just what is needed down at the low end. When it's coordinated properly, the car has a great launch from the nitrous, but the juice is cut off just when the boost is up and the turbo takes over for the rest of the ride, with no lag! Some nitrous kits can be specified with a controller that shuts off the "go-juice" when a preset level of boost is achieved.

Obviously, when you have two such amazing power-adders on your engine at once, there's a giant step up in the cylinder pressures. Some of the things we may have mentioned as "options" for a mild N_2O system are suddenly not options any more, like free-flowing intake and exhaust components, an all-out ignition system with racing plugs, a pumped-up fuel system with an extra pump, bigger injectors and a fuel management box, and a few items to prolong the life of the engine. Forged pistons, good connecting rods, strong crankshaft and cylinder head studs may all be necessary. Your car's going to have a serious problem getting all this new-found power to the ground, so you might even need to look at aftermarket driveshafts. If you put on the slicks you need to get traction, the high loads are going to take their toll on your economy-car driveline components.

One final note on nitrous oxide; you'll start off your "adventure in chemistry" with a manufactured kit for your car, designed for safe operation when installed and used as directed. If you start altering the engine in other ways or you're having some problems, contact the tech people at your kit's manufacturer. A few minutes on the phone getting their advice could save you an engine!

A number of companies offer a switch that cuts off the nitrous system in the event of the car's fuel pressure running low, and also prevents nitrous application if you operate the throttle when the engine's not running.

Turbochargers

Show, go, race, road, aftermarket or factory-installed, there's something special about a turbo car - equipped with all the right goodies, its like having a big monster motor under the bonnet, just waiting to come out and play.

Left - This layout of Edelbrock's 1996 to 2000 Civic SOHC VTEC turbo kit shows the kinds of components to expect in a good kit - there should be good instructions, turbo, turbo manifold, pipes hoses, hardware, oiling components and air filter - the Edelbrock kit makes 5-7 psi of boost with a Garrett T28 turbo, and includes an intercooler and their Performer-X intake manifold.

Below - If you're planning on making a show-and-go ride out of your Ford Focus, Gude has this turbo kit with intercooler and all the other hardware you need, plus the pipes are all chromed.

Boost, the increased pressure inside your engine when the turbocharger is working, pumps up both the engine and your heart rate. Unlike nitrous oxide, which only comes on when you arm a switch and hit full throttle, the turbocharger lies under your bonnet ready and waiting for any opportunity to rocket you forward with a smooth whoosh and a high-speed whine like a small jet engine. The sound and the performance are both addictive. You find yourself looking for opportunities to see some psi on your gauge, and let the guy you passed know what kind of magic science gave you that mid-range/top-end advantage.

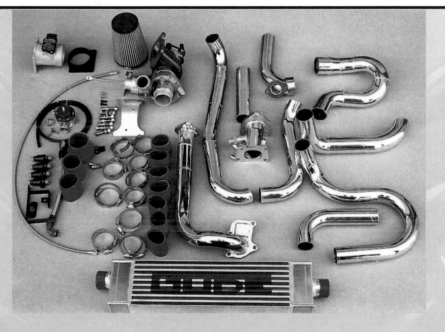

In a typical turbo installation, in this case a GReddy kit on a Honda Prelude, the main components of a non-intercooled system include: the exhaust-driven turbocharger (1); the exhaust downpipe from the turbine to the exhaust system (2); the compressor side of the turbo (3); the piping to duct the pressurised air to the intake manifold (4); and the intake piping that brings air into the compressor (5)

How it works

There are basically three main elements to a turbocharger - the exhaust turbine; the intake air compressor; and the housing/shaft/bearing assembly that ties the two pressure-related sections together. The job of the turbine is to spin the shaft of the turbocharger. The turbine is composed of an iron housing in which rotates a wheel covered with curved vanes or blades. These blades fit precisely within the turbine housing. When the turbine housing is mounted to an engine's exhaust manifold, the escaping hot exhaust gases flow through the housing and over the vanes, causing the shaft to spin rapidly. After the exhaust has passed through the turbine, it exits through a large pipe, called a downpipe, to the rest of the car's exhaust system.

Before and after

This typical complete turbocharger kit (GReddy for Civic SI) has all the good stuff, plus a set of performance fuel injectors and a computer upgrade, and . . .

. . . this is what that same kit looks like after fitting on a Civic SI in the real world.

Within the compressor housing is another wheel with vanes. Since both wheels are connected to a common shaft, the intake wheel spins at the same speed as the turbine, so the compressor draws intake air in where the rapidly-spinning wheel blows the air into the engine's intake side. The more load there is on the engine, the more the turbocharger works to give the engine horsepower. As the engine goes faster, it makes more exhaust, which drives the turbocharger faster, which makes the engine produce more power.

The unit in the centre of this turbo "sandwich" has the important function of reliably passing the power between the two housings. What makes this so difficult is the tremendous heat involved and the high speeds the shaft must turn.

Millions of turbochargers have been manufactured using a sleeve-type bearing that relies on a high volume of engine oil to keep it and the shaft cool enough to continue without seizing, but many of today's performance turbochargers feature ball-bearings. The technical name for the centre portion of the turbo is the CHRA, for "centre housing and rotating assembly". Some turbos are fitted with a water-cooled CHRA, where engine coolant is circulated through the bearing housing to carry away extra heat beyond what the oil can do. The CHRA is also sometimes called a "cartridge".

Turbochargers
by the numbers

- You like high engine speeds, like 8000 or 9000 rpm? At speed, a turbocharger is rotating at 100,000 rpm or more!

- Some turbo tuners speak of boost in "inches" instead of psi because it's a finer measurement. If you need to mentally convert, the inches are about double, i.e. 20 inches of boost is about 10 psi.

- A good intercooler will reduce the intake air temperature by at least 50%. If this is a difference of 100°, that translates to a 10% increase in horsepower.

- After a period of "spirited driving", parts of the turbocharger can heat to 1800°F.

Here are two show-winning efforts on the same kind of car, the Toyota Supra inline six-cylinder - this one uses HKS turbo components to blow through an up-front intercooler (not seen here) then into a Veilside "surge-tank" intake plenum with huge 100mm throttle body - there's some serious flow here . . .

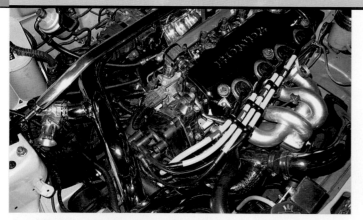

Consider the turbocharger like the six-gun "equaliser" of the old West - the SOHC applications are a good candidate for boost because it allows them to compete in performance with the more-talked-about DOHC motors.

Advantages and

This cycle of the engine driving the turbine is why some say the turbocharger makes "free" horsepower. What they mean is that the engine's exhaust is making the turbo go, unlike a supercharger that's driven mechanically by the engine, through belts/pulleys, a chain or direct gearing to the crankshaft. With a supercharger, driving the blower takes some engine horsepower away because it must operate at all times, from idle on up. A turbocharger imposes very little load until called upon to do some power-making.

The "not at all times" boost of the turbocharger is an advantage for fuel economy, operating noise level and driveability, but in some cases may be a drawback when compared to the mechanical supercharger. Elsewhere in this book, we'll get more into supercharger design, but while a supercharger adds boost in relation to rpm (i.e. the faster the engine goes, the faster the blower pumps),

. . . but look at this setup - two turbochargers, in fact two of almost everything and nitrous oxide for the bottom-end punch until those big turbos start spoolin'. Whoa, baby...

disadvantages of the turbocharger

it runs up against physical limitations eventually and can't pump any more. In order to make any more boost with a supercharger, you have to change the pulleys or gearing that drives it, and there's generally nothing you can do to the internals to make more boost. The good side of the supercharger is that the positive-displacement type blower gives an engine more bottom-end torque because the blower is working right from idle upwards.

The limitation for the blower-equipped car is in top end performance, and this is where the turbocharger has the distinct advantage. The turbocharger is much more customisable, with various wheels and housings available to suit the intended engine or purpose. Boost can be made to come in early, or come in later at a higher boost level. The same basic turbocharger can be used for road use, or modified to make more boost than your engine can live with!

Such customising, called sizing, should be done by an experienced turbo specialist who can select the exact components for your engine size and power requirements. A turbo expert can take your information on the engine modifications, bottom-end strength and projected horsepower goal, figure the airflow required to meet those parameters, and come up with the right-sized turbocharger with the right compressor and turbine. Too big or too small, and you and your engine will be unhappy.

One of the more serious disadvantages of the turbocharger is the heat it will put into the intake air charge. Actually, superchargers also heat up the intake air, but the hot-exhaust-driven turbocharger definitely warms the air charge most, which is why most successful turbo systems utilise an intercooler to combat this. Heat is the enemy of power and of reliability.

While trying to make and keep heat in the exhaust to make boost, you also need to protect other components in the engine compartment from heat - in this very professionally-done turbo Supra installation, the turbine has a heat shield, but also a metal heat dam was placed to protect the ABS brake components from turbo heat.

Turbochargers and heat

Anytime air is compressed and made to move very quickly, it gets hotter. For example, run your hand slowly across the carpeting in your house and you can feel slight friction from the carpet. Now move your hand more rapidly across the carpet at the same hand pressure and you'll feel warmth in your hand - go too fast and you'll have "rug burn". The same thing happens to the air inducted into your engine. Just travelling through your air intake, throttle body and intake manifold in non - turbo mode, air incurs a certain amount of friction between it and the surfaces its touches, especially cast surfaces that aren't perfectly smooth, like the inside of an intake manifold. Now force that air in under the pressure of a turbocharger, and the high-speed air tends to really heat up.

Beyond the frictional heating of the air, the turbocharger itself adds extra heat because it's mounted on the exhaust. If you've ever seen a performance turbo on an engine operating under a load on the dyno, you can turn out the lights and see the turbine housing and exhaust manifold start to glow red-hot! It's making serious power at this point, but obviously the air compressor side of the turbocharger is going to get some of that heat.

This heat is perhaps the biggest downside to turbocharging, but a number of excellent fixes have been developed over the years. First, improper turbo selection can worsen the heat problem. If the chosen turbo is not running at its proper efficiency, it can overspeed (over 100,000 rpm) - here, the air is moving too fast for the capacity of the engine and "backs up" in the pipeline. This hurts the turbocharger and your performance. The proper initial choice of turbocharger and the match of its turbine and compressor to your exact needs should keep you out of that range and make the right amount of boost without excessive shaft speeds.

Next up, everything should be done to keep the turbine's heat isolated from the compressor. It's true that heat on the exhaust side is what makes the turbine work, but that heat should be kept "inside" as much as possible and not transferred to the engine compartment air and the compressor/intake side. This is perhaps more critical on engines that have the exhaust side of the head facing the radiator, like most Hondas. Extra hot air from the radiator is flowing right over your turbo, which is usually mounted very close to the radiator, probably the hottest spot in the engine compartment.

Custom tubular manifolds for turbocharger installations make sense in terms of equal-length flow or if there is no cast manifold available for the application, but they tend to develop weld cracks and don't keep as much heat in, unless it's made of thick stainless steel, or ceramic-coated.

This racer used a cast-iron manifold with wastegate mount, and had the manifold high-temp-coated to retain even more heat in the turbine for more boost - heat is good on the turbine side, bad for the intake side.

An efficiently-designed cast-iron manifold, here with a Turbonetics wastegate directly mounted, is ideal for road-use constant heating and cooling cycles, but regular "high-temp" exhaust paint will come off in no time - temperatures here get into the red-hot range under a full load.

One of the best ways to keep the exhaust heat inside the turbine tract where it's needed is the right manifold. Though it may not look as trick as a custom-fabbed bundle of tubular pipes, a cast-iron turbo exhaust manifold is the most durable choice for the exhaust, especially for road use. It's thick enough to retain the heat inside, and can withstand repeated heating/cooling cycles without cracking, which is a problem with exhausts made from tubing. This heat can be further isolated by having the cast manifold treated to a high-temperature coating. The standard "high-temp" coatings used on manifolds will probably fail on a turbo manifold, but some of the coating companies have a ceramic-based coating that can withstand very high temperatures (up to 2000 °F). The equal-length tubular exhausts seen on the old F1 turbocharged race cars can extract that last little bit of extra horsepower, but a good one's expensive, and if it isn't made of thick-walled tubing, preferably stainless steel, it may not retain all the heat, and all the weld joints along the route may even slow the exhaust gases down.

Further isolation of the exhaust side heat can be achieved by using a shield over the turbine housing. Shields are available that are a formed sandwich of thin stainless steel sheetmetal with a core of high-temperature insulation. Some have an exterior that looks like formed tinfoil, but others have a smooth-shaped stainless exterior that has the added benefit of making the whole installation look as cool as it acts.

Having the exhaust/turbo so close to the radiator led this tuner to have his tubular manifold ceramic-coated. Also fitted is a larger aluminium radiator. Nice.

You say your need for speed exceeds - then top off your turbocharging installation with a full-on nitrous package that pours on the juice until the turbo is pumping - this installation uses four Nitrous Express nozzles and stainless-steel hard line plumbing for both the fuel and N$_2$O.

When you add an intercooler to the mix, you have additional plumbing - here on a turbo installation on a VW Golf (seen here with the front bumper off), the hot, boosted air leaves the compressor on the engine, travels out to the front where it enters the intercooler, exits the intercooler in "refreshed" mode and finally enters the intake manifold.

Intercoolers

The most effective and most common method of dealing with air temperature in the intact tract on a turbocharged car is an intercooler. This is a honeycomb affair much like a radiator, usually mounted out in front in an opening below the bumper, where cooler air is found. The boosted air from the compressor is ducted through pipes and into the intercooler, and then to the intake of the engine. Thus, the cooler is between the compressor and the engine, so it's called an *inter*-cooler.

Most intercoolers for road cars are of the air-to-air type. Intake air flows through the end tanks, through the tubes and fins of the cooler just like engine coolant does through a conventional radiator. The

The Subaru WRX also has its factory intercooler located on top of the engine - when some tuners do a turbo upgrade on the WRX, they fit a much larger aftermarket cooler in place of the standard one.

outside air, especially at vehicle speeds where the turbo is really working, flows over the intercooler and cools off what's passing inside. Although the longer piping of the intercooler system does add more frictional area for the air to pass over, the cooling effect makes enough change in horsepower to more than make up for that. In some cases, a good intercooler is taking out more than half of the intake heat, and for every drop of 10 °F in the intake air fed to your engine, your power goes up about 1%. If the intake air from your compressor is up to 200 to 300 °F (depending on the boost level), the intercooler can drop that to 100 to 140 °F. Work out the figures, and the intercooler's effectiveness is a no-brainer! The same engine and turbocharger combination may make one pound or so more boost without all that piping to travel through, but the temperature improvement is worth more than that slight drop in boost.

Of course, you can run a turbo setup without an intercooler, but you can't make optimal horse-power and the dreaded spectre of detonation will be haunting you unless you're using *high*-octane fuel and a few other tricks. Even factory-built turbocharged cars, like the Subaru WRX and others, have intercoolers designed into the car, both to make more power at a safe level of boost and to cope with the poor quality of fuel available to us at most pumps.

If you want the maximum airflow over the intercooler, and you want everyone to know you're packin' forced induction, the area below the bumper provides the space for a wide intercooler installation.

Boost Controls

The main boost control device on a turbocharger is an exhaust wastegate - the more the turbo system is designed to flow, the bigger the wastegate must be.

As wonderful as boost can be, it's a dangerous animal that needs certain controls to harness its power. Too much boost for the octane rating of your fuel and you have serious detonation. Even without detonation, high boost can and will destroy your engine if it isn't sufficiently reinforced to handle the increased cylinder pressure.

The primary "leash" on the turbo beast is an exhaust wastegate. The wastegate is a device that senses boost pressure in the engine and releases some exhaust to the atmosphere when needed. If the boost is too high, releasing the exhaust pressure built up causes the turbine wheel to slow down, reducing the boost to a safe level. On most production turbocharged cars, the wastegate is integral to the turbocharger, and dumps excess exhaust back into the exhaust system downstream of the turbine. In most of these applications, the system is designed for a relatively-low level of boost to maintain reliability. When the wastegate actuates, the driver never even notices it - the power simply doesn't increase.

If you make more boost than the factory intended, the engine will need more fuel and probably less ignition timing advance. You may be able to do both with an aftermarket electronic "piggyback" controller. There are boost-regulated mechanical fuel pressure regulators that raise the fuel delivery pressure to meet the boost conditions, more fuel for more boost. Depending on the make of your car and turbo, even higher boost levels can be obtained if you're careful. As always, our advice is to make changes in incremental steps up, listening to your engine signs of detonation, and always keep checking your spark plugs for signs impending problems.

The efficiency of your exhaust system has a lot to do with the boost level you can achieve. Sometimes factory engineers design an exhaust with just enough backpressure to keep the turbo from making too much boost. A really free-flowing aftermarket downpipe and larger-diameter cat-back exhaust system will probably increase your boost and still be within acceptable levels.

Really high-performance turbocharging applications will use a wastegate that is not integral to the turbocharger, mounted instead on the exhaust manifold ahead of the turbine. These are generally much larger than the factory type and are adjustable for

boost level with the simple turn of a screw on top of the wastegate. They can also be regulated by dashboard controls that alter the vacuum/boost signal to the wastegate. To operate efficiently, the wastegate must be sized to the horsepower level of the application. Too small a wastegate can't keep up with a powerful turbo, and you could overboost beyond what the wastegate is set to. While factory wastegates dump their excess exhaust downstream into the system, the aftermarket wastegate is usually allowed to vent into the atmosphere, though they all have a mounting flange that can permit a pipe to be installed that routes the gases away from the engine compartment. Most enthusiasts don't put on a pipe, they like the loud "braaakkkkk" noise when the wastegate opens!

A second type of control used in most aftermarket turbo installations is a blow-off (dump) valve. Unlike the wastegate, this type fits on the intake system. When a turbocharger is spinning at high speeds and making boost, it can't stop or even slow very easily or quickly. If you happen to quickly back off the throttle when you've been under boost, the intake system is still filled with pressurised air. The blade in your throttle body is closed, but the turbo's compressor is still packing in air behind it. Since the pressure has no place to go, a pressure wave backs up into the compressor and tries to make the wheel go the other way, causing a pressure surge that is damaging to the compressor. Another negative effect of the pressure backwave is that the compressor starts to slow down, so when you get back on the throttle again it has to work to catch up to the pressure it had before. These two problems can happen any time the throttle is closed, but is a real pain where you're on-off-on the throttle for every gearchange.

The solution is the dump valve. Mounted on the intake pipe, the valve contains a spring-loaded diaphragm or piston that lifts when it senses a surge. As soon as the air is released for a split-second, you've finished changing gear and the boost resumes with hardly a noticeable lapse. Aftermarket dump and bypass valves are available for any turbo application, but the most common is the dump valve because it makes a sharp and loud hiss ("tsssch") when it opens. A must-have noise for any seriously-tuned engine, you'll find you're changing gear just to hear it.

Wastegates mount in the exhaust stream ahead of the turbine. When the boost limit is exceeded, the wastegate releases some exhaust to slow down the turbo - in this installation with a very tall wastegate, an elbow's been used to mount the wastegate for underbonnet clearance - note how they wrapped the downpipe with insulation to prevent heat transfer to the engine's sump.

To be a little more subtle and quiet (why?), this wastegate has a pipe plumbed down to the exhaust system - the pipe's also insulated to keep the heat away from the radiator.

The other type of boost control is a dump valve. Designed to be mounted on the intake side, it prevents pressure surges if you close the throttle quickly, like when gearchanging, while the turbo's working hard.

In this installation, a flange was welded to the intake tube just before the intake manifold to mount the dump valve - as in most setups, the valve's release port is left open to atmosphere rather than plumbed back in ahead of the turbo (don't lose the noise).

If you really want everyone to know you're boosted, get a dump valve like this, with a horn-shaped exit - makes a real blast for every gearshift you make on boost.

Preparing your car for turbocharging

Of all the accessories you can get to go along with a forced induction system, none is more important than the boost gauge.

Although most turbocharging kits have everything you need to actually fit the turbo, there are a number of considerations beyond the supplied parts. Is your engine ready for boost? The kit instructions, if they're good ones, will give you recommendations for other modifications you can make to allow the turbo setup to work even better on your engine.

Perhaps no other "accessory" is more important for a turbo'd car than an accurate boost gauge. Unless you have a way to keep track of actual boost in the engine, you'll never know if the turbo is working at its potential or if the wastegate is adjusted where you want it, and working. The gauge is also helpful to diagnose faults on your system. If you see a lesser amount of boost than normal (under the same conditions of throttle, rpm and load), you should inspect the piping and hoses in your intercooler plumbing to see if there's a minor leak. The best boost gauges are dampened to give steady needle readings and indicate both vacuum (negative side, in inches of mercury) and boost (positive side, in inches of mercury or psi).

A strong aftermarket ignition system will be very helpful to fire the plug gaps in the dense atmosphere in the combustion chamber when the turbo is cramming all that air in. The manufacturer may also recommend different spark plugs to use, or just a different plug gap for the standard plugs you're using.

This "pilot" has the controls and data equipment he needs to watch over his boost-accumulating engine - one is a piggyback fuel controller and the other an electronic boost controller, both from A'PEXi.

Heat is always a critical factor in a turbocharged application. The turbo kit you use should include or recommend what's needed in the way of fuel management and timing controls to prevent detonation, but there's also engine heat. A really good radiator is going to be crucial, and you might consider an aftermarket heavy-duty radiator with more rows of tubes than standard. Aftermarket companies also make some excellent fan/shroud combinations that flow more air through the radiator than a standard fan. If you don't opt for a new radiator or fan, then at least check the Haynes repair manual for your car for info on cleaning and maintaining your standard cooling system.

Oil is a big issue with a turbo because the oil not only lubricates this very precisely machined and balanced assembly, the oil is also the cooling system for a device that gets mega-hot. Keeping the turbo alive and cool means there must be a steady flow of clean, quality oil, in and out. The supply line should be free of sharp bends or kinks, but this is even more critical on the much larger drain hose that comes from the bottom of the CHRA. The hose doesn't carry a great deal of pressure like the supply hose, but it must be capable of carrying away an unrestricted volume of oil back to your sump. Route the drain hose without kinks, and when the drainback hose fitting is welded to your sump, have it come into the sump at a slight downward angle and above the normal oil level. If there is any restriction in this drainback system, oil will back up into the CHRA and slow the cooling/lubricating action.

Most kits don't include this, but you may want to consider a turbo timer as an option. This is an electronic unit that will run your engine for a specified period, say five minutes, after you shut it off with the key. This is a cooling cycle for the turbocharger, and some factory turbo cars have one. The reason for this is a problem called coking, which occurs when you've been running your turbo hard and then shut off the engine. Tremendous heat-soak occurs in the CHRA because oil is no longer flowing through to cool the bearing. The coking happens because the oil that remains sitting in the turbo's bearing area may caramelise into coke, the kind of coal-like material used in steel foundries. These little particles of now-crunchy oil get circulated in the turbo and the rest of your lubrication system. The turbo timer gives the turbo a chance to cool down after a run.

A final entry on your good-idea list for the lubrication system is using an engine oil cooler. Many standard engines have a factory oil cooler sandwiched between the oil filter and the block, with coolant lines connected to the cooling system. If your car doesn't have one, there are a number of aftermarket oil coolers available. An oil cooler is a good thing for any high-revving small engine, but good insurance for a turbocharged one. Keeping the oil cool is one reason not to run uninsulated turbo pipes near the sump.

As we have mentioned in other Chapters, your engine should be thoroughly checked out and in top shape before any mods are undertaken, but especially for a power-adder like a turbocharger. Boost is going to rapidly kill any engine with weak valve springs, worn rings or loose bearings. Depending on the level of boost, there may be other steps to take to give your engine a longer life under pressure. If you're running a 5 to 7 psi setup and you have adequate controls against detonation like high-octane fuel and fuel/timing controls, you should be fine unless your driving style means the engine's on boost for five minutes of every ten-minute trip to the shops. Higher levels of boost require more safeguards, starting with your pistons. New forged pistons with a lower-than-standard compression ratio will help deal with the pressure much better. Once you get to the 8-10 psi range you should lower the static compression to 9:1, and if you venture to higher boost levels, you'll need to get pistons for 8:1 compression. In the higher ranges of boost for serious road or drag racing horsepower, you'll have to do a lot more to strengthen your engine, and these kinds of "insurance" mods are covered elsewhere in this book.

Above - The GReddy "Profec EO-1" is a multi-tasker for the boost-minded - it manages your boost, has several warning functions, can log 3 hours' worth of data, and the LED screen can display boost, rpm and another channel all at once.

Left - In some boosted applications, the fuel pressure is raised under boost, or larger injectors are used to supply extra fuel - using one or more additional injectors that are only used under boost is one way to keep the engine happy without affecting normal driving air/fuel ratios, and a controller for the additional injector(s) makes this possible.

The 300ZX may be old now, but you can't tell by how it runs - the JWT-upgraded twin turbos do their thing, and the engine's never had the heads off for work in 200,000 miles.

Turbo durability

It looks like a plain, white, older Nissan, despite it being in great shape and having a nice set of wheels. The 1990 Nissan 300ZX owned by Alfred Torres is actually a fine-handling sports car that gets driven daily, and turns in dangerously close to 11-second quarter-mile times at the dragstrip.

Alfred bought the car when it was two years old, and has put 200,000 miles on it (under boost most of the time) and it's a great example of what you can do by buying a factory turbo car and upgrading it.

The performance work on the twin-turbo car was done over a period of time, as he could afford the changes, and included a pair of upgraded turbos from the Nissan specialists at Jim Wolf Technology, a computer from that same firm, and a number of aftermarket control devices. The electronics include: a GReddy exhaust gas temperature (EGT) gauge, A'PEXi multi-checker, GReddy boost controller, two boost gauges (one for each turbo bank), and a steering wheel button (remote) that operates the boost controller without Alfred's hands leaving the wheel. The EGT is fitted to No 6 cylinder - it's the one that runs hottest and leanest so it's the one to watch. He uses iridium plugs, one range colder than standard.

The happy owner controls the boost setting depending on the fuel available. In everyday driving, the control is set for 15 to 16 psi for ordinary petrol. When Alfred can get a little high- octane unleaded, he clicks the control and runs 18 psi, and when he's at the track and can get racing fuel, he's got his "phasers on stun" at 23 pounds of boost! That's when he runs right around 12 seconds or less in the quarter.

What's the moral of the story? Just that, contrary to what most people think, you can have a performance daily driver that's smooth, reliable, and you can keep it for years. Do careful research on the right car and the right components for it, learn what you need to know to take care of it (of course, buy a Haynes repair manual for it) and know the car's limits, and yours.

Two boost gauges, several electronic aftermarket control devices, and an ominous-looking pushbutton on the steering wheel all contribute to putting the driver in control of how much power he wants, and when he wants it. Now! Go!

Turbo ultra-performance

There couldn't be a better example of the power potential of turbocharging when dealing with small engines than the car seen here. The Summit mail-order performance company is a familiar name to any American modifying enthusiast, being a similar outfit to Demon Tweeks in the UK. They campaigned this "2002 Chevrolet Cavalier" in the NHRA/Summit Sport Compact drag series, where it won the 2002 Modified Championship. For us Brits, a Chevy Cavalier is a broadly similar car to our Vauxhall Vectra - not the kind of car you'd expect to be doing this sort of thing. At all.

It ran a best of 7.665 seconds at just shy of 180 mph in the quarter-mile, and what makes that a phenomenon is the engine that did it, a 2.2 litre Ecotec four-cylinder. While the car was built by Jerry Haas and driven by Matt Hartford, our real interest here is in the basic GM (Vauxhall/Opel) engine that now runs like a blown hemi V-8.

John Lingenfelter Performance Engineering, famous builders of Chevrolet engines, took a quite basic Ecotec engine that originally squeezed out 130 horsepower, and turned it into a fire-breathing race motor with 1080 horsepower at the wheels!

We don't have all the detailed specs on the engine's internals, but it's safe to say that considerable work was done to make the reciprocating parts stronger and lighter, to reinforce the block to withstand the huge increase in cylinder pressure, and to do everything possible to the cylinder head in port work, valves, and cams to achieve high-rpm flow of the highest order.

Obviously, the star player in the engine compartment has to be the big Garrett ball-bearing turbocharger, and most of the power increase is from the serious amount of boost it pumps. We do know that the engine sucks air in through a large intake duct, and that the compressor output travels through a liquid-to-air intercooler before entering the fabricated Hogan intake manifold with big throttle body. The engine also features an MSD 8 ignition, an Autoverdi dry-sump lubrication system, and a Big Stuff 3 engine management system.

This race car was built by some of the top people in the country, and we're not suggesting that this kind of power level is available to you simply by bolting on a turbocharger, but it is an incredible example of what can be done in small-engine turbocharging. Probably no other technology would have permitted such performance from a couple of litres.

Owners of Vauxhall/Opel Ecotec engines should be very encouraged by the variety of performance equipment offered for these engines by GM Performance Parts Division of General Motors. Their US catalogue includes a 2.2 litre heavy-duty block with steel sleeves, bigger head and main studs, and it's machined for metal O-ring type head gaskets. They also have available billet crankshafts and rods, a fabricated intake manifold and a CNC-ported cylinder head.

These DOHC engines have balance shafts in standard 2.2 litre form, but most engine builders feel these are a limitation in high-rpm race engines, so GM even offers a pair of balance shafts with "neutral" balance for use in performance engines. And don't let's forget, the Ecotec series engine was originally designed to be emissions and environment-friendly. Yeah, right!

If this one pulls up next to you at the lights, let it go...

Superchargers

If you've read Chapter 6, you know that an internal-combustion engine operates like a compressor. It sucks in a combustible mixture of air and fuel, ignites it and uses the resulting pressure to push the piston up and down and make the crankshaft deliver the power to the wheels. For the purposes of this Chapter, the key word in that very simplistic explanation is "sucks". Hmmm.

Your engine relies on the downstroke of the pistons to draw the air/fuel mix through the air filter, intake pipe, throttle body, intake manifold, cylinder and finally, past the valves to the combustion chamber where the action is. That's one very long and tortuous journey when you think about it!

Atmospheric pressure

Or why your car runs better at the beach than in the Rockies

Our atmospheric pressure is 14.7 pounds per square inch (psi) at sea level. At high altitude this pressure is less, of course, because there's that much less atmosphere "stacked up" over us. So 14.7 pounds is all we have to urge a mixture to enter our engine. When the piston goes down and creates a vacuum, the atmospheric pressure is higher than the "negative pressure" of the vacuum, so stuff goes in.

Boost, that intoxicating elixir of performance, is any pressure beyond 14.7. If you have a turbo or supercharger that's making 14.7 psi of boost, then you have effectively added another "atmosphere" of pressure. Twice that amount of boost and you've added two atmospheres, and you command the bridge of a rocket ship!

Many methods have been tried to "help out" the engine so it didn't have to work so hard just to get a breath of freshly-vapourised petrol and air. Forcing air in by some external device has been the project of engineers almost since the car was invented. Superchargers have been used on piston-driven warplanes and racecars since the Twenties, and the technology and marketplace have narrowed this field called "forced induction" down to the two basic devices we're concerned with in this book - turbochargers and superchargers.

This Toyota V6 features a belt-driven, Rootes-type blower. The entire bolt-on kit is available from Toyota Racing Development (TRD).

Our last Chapter dealt exclusively with the turbocharger. It's similar in function to the supercharger, but differs in that the turbo is driven by exhaust gases, rather than by mechanical means. A supercharger is driven by the engine, either with gears, chains or belts, so there is direct correlation between the engine speed and the boost produced by the supercharger. While the turbocharger may have the upper hand when you're talking about all-out high-rpm performance on the track, the supercharger shines at improving road performance almost from idle speed upwards.

Since the supercharger is directly linked to the crankshaft, it starts making its boost right from "the basement". This gives you the kind of low-end power you get to enjoy in most normal driving circumstances without hammering the right pedal to the floor all the time. Driving a supercharged car gives you the sensation that you have a much bigger engine, without the nose-heavy weight and less-acceptable fuel economy.

Low-end torque is what we need and that's what a mechanical supercharger does best. By packing in more air, the engine ingests a denser mixture of air and fuel without the effort of having to suck it in using normal atmospheric pressure.

Boost

You must have a boost gauge to monitor the performance of any forced-induction engine. The best gauges indicate both the full range of vacuum (negative pressure, usually in inches of mercury) on one side of the zero mark, and the positive pressure (boost) side goes from that zero mark to 10, 20, or more psi of boost. In a typical vehicle in good condition, your engine may be idling at 600 to 700 rpm and vacuum is high, maybe 17 to 20 inches unless you have an aftermarket camshaft, which would lower the idle vacuum. This vacuum will drop rapidly when the engine is accelerated quickly, but then smooth out at most speeds; when you're in top gear and cruising, your gauge may again read something like your idle vacuum, indicating that you are driving at good efficiency.

Put a supercharger on that same vehicle and your gauge readings are quite different. The idle might be close to standard, but once you first start to hit the pedal and the revs rise, you'll see the vacuum reading go down and stay down as you increase engine speed. At a certain speed under load, say 1500 to 2500 rpm, you start to go right onto the boost side of the gauge. What many newcomers to boost-gauge watching don't realise is that the section of the vacuum/boost gauge from your idle vacuum reading all the way up to zero on the gauge can't be discounted. Anytime your forced induction system is "taking away" vacuum, it's making performance, so you don't have to be showing 6 pounds of boost to feel like your engine is bigger than it used to be. The more your gauge goes clockwise, the more you have to hang on!

As heady as all this is, we must be realistic about boost levels. As with a turbocharger, fitting a supercharger doesn't mean your engine will get trashed. Nonetheless, there's a limit to the boost your blower can make, and probably a much lower limit of how much boost your engine can take, regardless of how the boost was generated. Most road-use supercharger kits are limited to

Above left - This shot of the JR Focus kit outside the car shows how the long belt arrangement works the blower drive in with all the factory accessories.

Once the kit is installed, the underbonnet view of the finished Focus installation by Jackson Racing looks almost standard, until you spot the Eaton supercharger near the bulkhead.

between 5 and 7 psi, to make some power while working well on a basically standard engine that sips pump fuel. Some kits on the market have optional pulleys that will spin the blower faster for more boost, but, as with any power adder, you can only go so far in increasing cylinder pressure before you have to make serious modifications to strengthen the engine (see Chapter 13 for more on engine durability mods).

Your engine's existing compression ratio has an important effect on the boost level you can hope to use with any forced induction system. The higher the static compression ratio, the less boost you can run without detonation. If your compression ratio is too high, the small amount of boost you can reliably use may not be worth the effort and expense of the supercharger system.

Our modern engines generally have higher compression ratios than other vehicles on the road, which is a good thing for engine efficiency, but not so good for supercharging. If you have a Jap import, or a Jap engine conversion, the compression could be 10:1 or even higher because of Japan's 100-octane fuel and less-stringent emissions laws - in that case, your engine is not a candidate for forced induction unless you change to much lower-compression pistons. Just as a guideline, you should be able to use 5 to 7 psi of boost if your engine's compression ratio is 9:1 or lower. If you're rebuilding your engine before installing the forced induction, it's a good idea to equip it with new forged pistons of 8:1 compression. This should let you run 8 to 12 psi of boost, which is a big difference in performance when your big right Reebok goes down. This is just a general guideline - the design and efficiency of the supercharger you choose will also be a factor.

Most us only dream about riding in a true sports car like the Honda NSX, but if you've got one, the Honda experts at Comptech have this screw-type blower package you'll want - it fits under the standard engine cover and doesn't void your warranty (most of these kits are fitted by Honda dealerships).

With the top cover off the Whipple twin-screw blower used on the Comptech NSX kit, you can see how the two screws squish and compress the incoming air between them for good mechanical efficiency - such precision comes expensive.

Heat and detonation

We discussed the demon that is detonation in the turbocharging Chapter, but it bears repeating here because the problem is the same with all power adders. The octane rating of a fuel is an indication of its anti-knock resistance. In the Sixties, you could buy 100-octane petrol right from the pumps (like you still can in Japan) - those were the glory days for hot rodders, who ran around the streets with 12:1 compression pistons. Once that nasty lead (ethyl) was removed from the gas for environmental reasons, what we're left with at the pumps today is not so suitable to modified engines. Knock, pinking, pre-ignition and detonation are all terms that describe abnormal combustion in an engine. What it boils down to is when the combustion chamber pressure and temperature rise to a certain point, hot spots develop in the chamber and instead of one steady flame front across the mixture, you have more than one fire burning, or burning taking place before it's supposed to.

The two main factors in detonation and its control are heat and timing. Octane is also a factor, but once you've stepped up to using the "super" fuel, there isn't much you can do to get more octane unless you resort to using a can of aftermarket octane booster with every tankful. That can get both annoying and

Intercoolers help make more power and stave off detonation by cooling the incoming air and making it more dense.

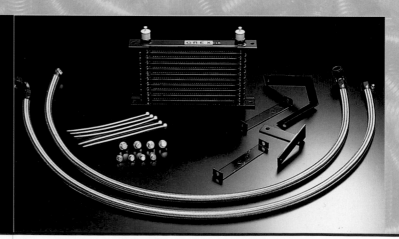

Heat is the enemy of your engine, and the more you can reduce that, the more boost you can run - an oil cooler kit will help keep temperatures down.

expensive. Ignition timing does offer some ways to deal with detonation. Supercharged engines generally "like" more timing, especially initial advance, but once you're making full boost and the car's under load, too much ignition advance can bring on the "death rattle" you don't want to hear. Your computer-controlled engine management system incorporates a knock sensor on the block that signals the ECU to pull back ignition timing if knock begins. However, things happen more rapidly in a boosted car than a normal situation where it's just reacting to a bad tank of fuel. How much advance your application can handle is a trial-error-experience thing, but if you're using a production blower kit from a known manufacturer, these tests have already been made, and some kind of timing control program should be included.

Note: *When you do pull back ignition timing, you're also reducing your power, so there is a point of diminishing return.*

Heat, in the blower and intake tract, has a major effect on detonation control. A boosted application that can take 8 psi on a cool morning may need some kind of controls to counter detonation on a hot afternoon. Although a supercharger doesn't put as much heat into the intake tract as does an exhaust-driven turbocharger, plenty of heat we don't want is still added to the intake tract. When you compress air and force it through the whole intake tract, the friction of these parts against the airflow heats the air. Hot air is less dense, and remember that the reason for using a supercharger is to make the intake charge denser. A mechanical supercharger may add 100 to 200 °F to whatever the ambient air is, so on a 70-degree day, the intake air could be nearly 300 degrees!

As we discussed in the turbocharging chapter, one really effective way to lower the temperature of the intake side is with an intercooler. This is a heat exchanger, usually an air-to-air cooler, which mounts in the intake tract. When boosted air is forced to travel through a cooler (like a small radiator) that's exposed to outside air, the intake charge temperature drops and power goes up. That's the beauty of intercooling; it not only helps avoid detonation, it makes more power. With normally-aspirated or forced-induction, for every 10 °F you drop the intake temperature, you gain 1% in power. Drop the temperature by 100 degrees and you gain 10%, which is substantial when we're talking about already-efficient small engines.

The bad news is that most bolt-on supercharger kits don't include an intercooler. In some cases, small mechanical superchargers don't make high levels of boost, and plumbing the whole thing through more pipes and an intercooler may slow down the air enough to almost wipe out the positive effect of the cooling.

Blower kits

There are several types of small superchargers used in kits designed for modern engines. Of course, each manufacturer will tell you their design is the best, but you should do plenty of research on your own before making a decision to buy a kit that may cost £2000 or more. The two main types of supercharger design you'll see are the Rootes type or "positive displacement", and the centrifugal design.

The Rootes-type mechanical blower uses a pair of rotors that turn inside a housing. Some may have straight rotors with two or three lobes, and as the rotors turn, they capture a certain amount of air and propel it to the inner circumference of the case and out to the intake manifold. Each time they turn around, they capture air, hence the "positive" description. The benefit of this type is that it starts making boost at very low rpm, but some Rootes-type blowers are noisier than other designs, induce more heat into the intake tract, and take a little more crankshaft horsepower to drive. Most of the smaller blowers used on kits have very proven designs that have been around for years, and in the case of the Eaton blower, have been used by major car manufacturers on factory-supercharged installations.

A variation of this type of blower is the screw-type. These have two rotors with helically-wound vanes that, as the name implies, look like two giant screws. When the two

Packaging a supercharger kit for an already "compact" engine compartment can be a challenge - this kit puts the blower right where it needs to be by using a (very) long-belt drive system.

This well-engineered Civic SI kit from Vortech includes a shaft that is belt-driven at the drivebelt end of the engine, and places the centrifugal blower at the gearbox end where there's room - the kit includes a dump valve and a liquid-to-air intercooler not often seen on road car installations.

This very complete package includes wiring, hoses, fuel pump, FMU, supercharger and drive, and the compete water system for the Maxiflow Power Cooler.

screws mesh together (there is a male and a female rotor), the air is actually compressed between the screws.

The other major type of bolt-on supercharger is the centrifugal design. From a quick examination, the centrifugal blower looks just like the compressor half of a turbocharger, being a multi-vaned wheel within a scroll-type housing. Unlike a turbocharger, this type of blower isn't driven by exhaust but by a mechanical drive from the engine, usually a belt. On the back of the compressor is a gearbox that speeds the compressor wheel up compared to engine rpm. Now you have some of the boost potential of a turbocharger without the added intake heat from the exhaust-driven turbine. These types of blowers are not "positive-displacement", and thus do not necessarily make their boost down on the low end, but have plenty of air-movement potential when they're spinning rapidly. The centrifugals also don't take as much horsepower to drive as some other mechanical blowers that are positive-displacement. In general, centrifugal superchargers will make more power than a positive displacement type, but the power will come at higher rpm. You have to decide what your own performance needs are to decide on the right kit for your application.

Unlike a turbocharger kit, a supercharger kit for most cars includes a whole new intake manifold, since the intake must match the outlet configuration of the blower. On most centrifugal blower kits, however, a new intake manifold isn't needed, because the boost can be plumbed to your existing intake as is done with a turbo install.

This Honda is equipped with an Eaton blower from Jackson Racing - note how neatly the blower drive tucks in under the standard power steering pump, like it grew there.

The well-thought out installation that takes maximum advantage of the supercharger will include other modifications - in addition to the JR blower, this showy Honda has an induction kit, manifold, high-output ignition and a revamped fuel system with custom fuel rail, FMU, fuel pressure gauge and big fuel filter.

Most reputable blower kits have everything you need to install the system and use it reliably. Contents include the blower, intake manifold (if needed), belt, mounting hardware, instructions and some type of electronic gear to control fuel delivery and/or ignition timing. Some kits use a larger-than-standard fuel pump that replaces your in-tank pump, and a special fuel-pressure regulator that may be boost-sensitive. Other components could be hoses, wire harnesses, air intake, an intercooler, and parts that relocate items in the engine compartment to provide room for the blower. Some installations may include an oil filter relocation kit that allows for easier oil changes after the supercharger kit is installed. These kinds of extras are installation-specific, but well worth seeking out, for making installation easier, and living with the blower afterwards less of a problem.

Most kits can be fitted by a competent mechanic, provided he reads the manufacturer's instructions before ripping out the standard parts and slapping new parts in. The quality of the instructions varies among manufacturers, but all companies have tech lines to answer your questions about fitting or tuning, as well as websites that explain the typical FAQs (frequently-asked questions). A Haynes repair manual for your specific vehicle will be a big help, especially when dealing with "where did this gasket go or what wire went here?". If you're new at this kind of engine work, you may want to have a tuner do the install for you, or at least have a friend who has more experience provide a helping hand. Most manufacturers claim their kits can be installed in around 8 to 10 hours, but some installations are more complicated because of engine compartment and engine layout, and you may need to spend the weekend working on it. Just take your time and you'll have a successful conversion to forced induction. As with any other kind of car modifying, it always pays not to rush it.

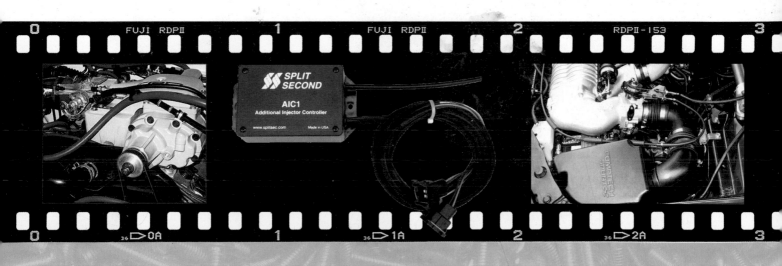

Good for any forced-induction application, Holley makes this boost-compensating adjustable fuel pressure regulator - adjustment range is from 20 to 75 psi, and it will raise fuel pressure 4 psi for each psi of boost the engine sees.

Making your engine suit the supercharger

The manufacturer of your kit has done their homework to make their blower right for your car, but it's your responsibility to see that your engine's ready for the blower. At the relatively-low boost levels of most kits, a standard engine in good condition should work fine. The supercharger should not have any serious effect on the engine's longevity, but of course that assumes your engine's in perfect condition to start with. There's an extra load on the crankshaft to drive a mechanical blower, and the boost is not going to be all that effective if your valves are leaky and piston rings really worn. Leaking valve guides or rings can let engine oil into the combustion chamber, and this is an invitation to detonation under boost, even if everything else in your installation is done right.

Start your "boost-suitability-check" by giving the engine a thorough service, then check the engine's compression and take vacuum readings. Both these important diagnostic checks are covered in the Haynes manual for your car. Your car's most

If you need to have a stronger head gasket to handle boost, this GReddy metal-reinforced piece is what your need - some are available in a thick version to reduce static compression so you can apply more boost

In race applications with lots of boost, you may need an extra injector to provide enough fuel - bosses like this GReddy can be welded to an intake tube and accept stock or aftermarket injectors

likely computer-controlled, which means that the engine management system stores diagnostic information in the form of fault codes. If you experience idling or driveability problems that your service didn't fix, you may want to visit a good garage with the diagnostic equipment extract any fault codes from your car (see Chapter 4 of this book to read more about code readers and fault codes).

Check your Haynes manual to learn more about diagnosing faults on your fuel system, and perform all basic maintenance, such as changing fuel filters and checking fuel pressure. In Chapter 7 of this book, you'll find more information about aftermarket improvements to your fuel system that ensure a steady supply of clean fuel so you aren't going to "lean out" under boost.

By now you're aware of the effect of high temperatures on your engine, and adding a forced induction system will tax your cooling system further than most other mods. You must make sure your radiator and water pump are in perfect order. At the very least, you should have the radiator professionally cleaned and tested at a radiator specialist. If you plan on running under boost a lot, or want to upgrade to higher boost levels, you may need a larger aftermarket radiator to keep temperatures under control.

We have discussed earlier in this Chapter how big a role is played by your existing static compression ratio, and how switching to low-compression pistons (like 8:1) will help you make better use of a supercharger by allowing more boost to be used. Aftermarket steel head gaskets are available that are thicker-than-standard, to reduce the compression ratio for power-adder applications. Even if you have a relatively low compression ratio engine already, use of

Split Second makes several types of programmable electronic controls and software for modified engines - this Additional Injector Controller does just what the name suggests - it can control up to four extra injectors and is usually calibrated by forced-induction kit installers.

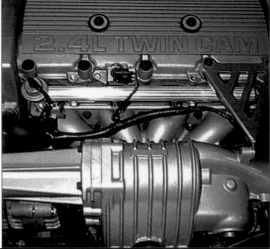

GM Performance Parts is there for the forced induction needs of GM owners in the US, with neatly-done kits like this even having full 12-month warranties if fitted by an approved dealer.

If your car's of the German persuasion, Neuspeed has this nicely-packaged blower kit for several Vee Dubs.

more than 8 psi of boost can compromise engine internals if you learn to love the sensation of boost and are constantly on the throttle. In such a case, you may want to switch pistons anyway, fitting forged aftermarket pistons that can better take the stress. After all, the first components to feel the bad effects of detonation will be the tops of your pistons, and forged pistons can take abuse longer than your cast standard pistons. Hopefully, you won't experience detonation, but the forged pistons are good insurance. When you get into double-digit boost, further engine mods may be required.

Boost and detonation both put increased loads on pistons, rods, bearings and crankshaft. For applications where you'll be drag racing or running high boost on the road, you might consider aftermarket internals such as improved connecting rods and a high-strength crankshaft if one is available for your engine. At least, if you're stripping the engine anyway, have a machine shop go over the con-rods by Magnafluxing them for flaws, smoothing the beams, shot-peening, restoring the rod bores, balancing, and fitting them with aftermarket rod bolts.

As with turbocharging, if you're running high levels of boost, you may want to give your cylinder head the treatment by fitting stainless steel valves, a three-angle valve job, and even machining the head for metal O-rings to better seal the cylinder bores. Unless you're racing, you don't need to spend money on porting and polishing the cylinder head. While we're talking about the cylinder head, camshaft choice can make a difference in your boosted engine. What works best for an "all-motor" (no nitrous/turbo/blower) engine isn't going to be productive for a supercharged engine. Check with the manufacturer of the kit you're fitting. to see what they recommend, cam-wise. Even if you leave the standard cams in place, at least fit high-

performance valve springs and lightweight retainers (Chapter 8).

The two most important engine modifications that can complement your forced induction (other than a low-restriction air intake, which we'll consider a given) are the exhaust and ignition system. The supercharger is designed to pack more air into the engine, and your standard exhaust system is going to stifle all that from getting out of the engine. A good manifold and cat-back exhaust will help reduce backpressure, allowing the supercharger to do a better job.

The ignition system will be important because of the extra-dense mixture that the plugs are trying to ignite. All that boost pressure makes it harder for the spark to jump the plug gaps, so an aftermarket coil and HT leads should be considered a minimum investment here. Any of the good CD ignition boxes will also be helpful (see Chapter 5 of this book).

If you've done your homework and picked a good kit, set your engine up properly to take advantage of all the supercharger can provide, installed a good boost gauge on your dash and loaded your fuel tank with super, then buckle up your belts and get out there and rock 'n' roll! You will love the feeling of boost, and for your first month of driving you'll be using it all the time, but you may eventually settle down to where you only use the boost 5 to 10% of your driving time, and your fuel economy will come back to something near standard. While a supercharger does have some mechanical noise to it, it's more "stealthy" than a turbocharger, without the sound effects from a dump valve or wastegate. You can expect to gain anywhere from 50 to 100 horsepower with a blower, depending on the type of kit and your application, but whatever the improvement, you can bet it will outweigh quite a few other 5 to 10hp mods, and it can all be fitted in a weekend!

Fitting a supercharger

The staff at Comptech deal with precision work and demanding customers all the time. They have a range of intake and exhaust components for most Honda applications, including the common-man models you and I drive, but their greatest involvement has been with the higher-end cars from Honda, like the NSX, the new S2000 and the Legend Coupes. The following is an installation on the V6 Legend Coupe. Okay, so it's not a car often seen in the UK, but at least it'll give you an idea what's involved in a supercharger install.

Comptech's kits have very detailed photo-filled instructions, but they still like to see their kits fitted by professional mechanics. They include an ESM (electronic signal modifier) with every kit, but they need to know your exact year and model to include the right calibration. The ESM interrupts and modifies the signal between the MAP sensor and the ECU, to allow the ECU to handle boost.

Certainly each supercharger installation will be unique to the make, model and model year of the car and engine. Before attempting the installation at home, thoroughly research every step of the job.

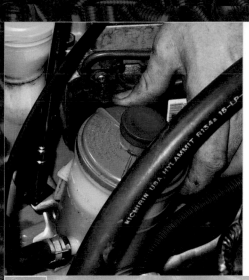

01 The first order of business (after disconnect the battery negative lead) is to relocate the power steering pump's fluid reservoir with a new bracket supplied in the kit - the drive end of the supercharger system has to squeeze in at this end of the engine - also relieve the fuel system pressure (follow your Haynes manual).

02 The alternator is unbolted, and the alternator pulley swapped for a pulley with new grooved section to power the blower - you can remove/refit a pulley with two spanners, but an impact gun makes the job way easier.

03 When the alternator is refitted, the upper bracket is replaced by this billet mount that will secure one end of the supercharger drive - the wiring harness has to be relocated slightly where it runs by the alternator.

04 Once you have the extra air coming into an engine that a forced induction system can supply, manifolds are highly recommended to allow the engine to exhale better as well.

>

05 Drain the cooling system - clearance is tight between the engine and the radiator, but that's where the blower will live, so a new radiator hose is supplied (fitted here) that has a tighter radius on the upper bend. It's all about making room for the new kit.

06 The fan shroud on the left (standard one on the right) has been modified (it's an exchange item) to give clearance to the new radiator hose (notice the cut-down area at the front here) - two ribs are removed also.

07 In addition to the shroud modification, the fan motor is moved to the radiator side of the shroud, and mounted using these spacers between the motor and the shroud, effectively giving more clearance from the fan to the blower and new radiator hose.

08 The standard battery and battery tray (big ones at the left) are taken out and replaced with a new battery tray, new "slenderised" coolant overflow bottle and more compact 51R battery.
Big kid's toys are just like little kid's toys . . . the battery isn't included!

09 Comptech calls their induction kit the "Icebox", and this V6 Icebox is included with each supercharger package.

10 After the standard air cleaner box and hose is removed from the engine compartment, the lower pipe of the Icebox is worked through this opening in the left inner wing - the radiused entry to the pipe is good for airflow, but hard to angle in here (this will be clamped from below once the airbox is mounted).

11 The two-piece air filter box is bolted down into the inner wing, after unclipping and relocating one wire loom - note the room for the blower provided by the smaller battery, lower-mounted battery box and smaller coolant overflow bottle.

12 After removing the standard EGR valve (where studs are located here), remove the two bolts and the rear camshaft cover at the back of the front cylinder head - this is where the blower mounting will go.

13 The aluminum blower mounting is fitted with an O-ring and pushed into the camshaft hole (provided for camshaft removal). Lube the O-ring with clean oil and work the mounting into the hole slowly so the O-ring isn't pinched.

14 The blower mount is bolted to the cam cover holes, and the EGR valve is refitted with a new gasket - for further blower support, a third bolt is threaded into the cylinder head, but because of the casting variations in the heads, a threaded collar is adjusted to take up space between the bracket and the head before the bolt is tightened.

15 There are two throttle bodies on automatic cars - here the first TB (for the traction-control system) is unbolted and set aside.

16 This cast-aluminum elbow will take the place of the main throttle body (at right) - mark and disconnect all the hoses and electrical connectors at the throttle body, then mount this block-off plate with O-ring to the original MAP sensor locationon the throttle body - the MAP sensor is relocated to top of this cast-aluminum elbow which will take the place of the throttle body at the intake manifold.

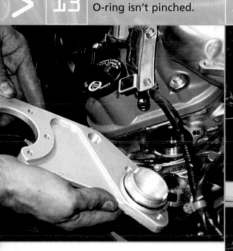

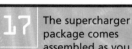

17 The supercharger package comes assembled as you see it here, with the Eaton blower, the drive and the cast intake and outlet housings in place.

18 Tim carefully lowers the package into place onto the two mountings at the engine, making sure there's no interference with wiring harnesses or coolant hoses.

19 At the belt-drive end, the air conditioning hose is moved until it fits between the mounting bracket and the pulley - fit the two bolts through the mounting and into the alternator bracket, but don't tighten them yet.

20 The lower four bolts where the drive meets the blower are removed (do NOT loosen the top bolts, or the blower's internal oil reservoir could leak) - when the longer Allen bolts are inserted through the mounting on the engine to the blower and started, you can tighten the pulley-end mounting bolts to spec, then tighten the four Allen bolts at this end.

21 Before mounting the rest of the intake system components, a brace is mounted from the supercharger body to the gearbox - note that the studs from the top of the throttle body mount at the intake manifold were removed (use double-nuts to remove) and fitted at the blower intake flange, along with a new gasket.

22 Hoses that were attached to the throttle body in its standard location are replaced with longer hoses (mark the end locations before removing the standard hoses, so there's no mix-up) and several wire groups that went to the throttle body sensors (idle air control, MAP, throttle position sensor) must be separated from the corrugated plastic looms, and run to the new locations. Any unprotected wires should be covered with loom material or electrical tape.

23 Slide the silicone hose and clamps over the intake elbow, bolt the elbow to the intake manifold with a new gasket, then centre the hose over the joint and tighten the hose clamps.

24 The fuel pressure regulator mounts to the edge of the cowl (you work through a hole in the cowl once a small access panel is removed) and is plumbed according to the instructions - it's specifically sized for this application with a large diaphragm to respond better than the small standard regulator.

25 The standard fuel pressure regulator (FPR) is replaced with an AN fitting whose braided lines goes to the "IN" fitting on the new regulator, and a new vacuum hose runs from the intake manifold to the FPR - the other fuel side of the FPR connects with a hose to the standard steel fuel return line.

26 The main throttle body is rotated until the cables are up and there are no kinks, then it's bolted to the intake elbow of the blower, and the coolant hose and IAC and TPS connectors are hooked up. This elbow being clamped in place is to mount the other throttle body for the traction-control system.

27 The bottom of the elbow (shown here with traction-control throttle body attached) has two fittings for vapour lines, one from the valve cover and one to the air-assist valve for emissions - it's easier to attach the hoses here before mounting the elbow or throttle body - they hook up just as they did before, but here with longer hoses.

28 Here both throttle bodies are fitted and all linkages, hoses and wires connected.

29 Remove the top from the air filter housing, and mount the new air filter and its rubber elbow in place, clamping the elbow to the traction-control throttle body, then refit the airbox cover.

30 At the belt end of the installation, you can see how the new belt goes around the blower drive and the alternator pulley, while the supplied tensioner keeps it tight - you can also see here how the air-con line is routed and why the steering pump reservoir had to be relocated.

The last step before the car goes back to an anxious owner is a thorough check of everything on the rolling road - a calibration of the electronic signal modifier between the ECU and the MAP sensor and the V6 was running factory-smooth, but with extra horsepower to use - the test car made 40 more bhp, but they're looking to greatly improve that with a piggyback **31** fuel/spark controller.

Just for comparison to our subject car, here's the intake end of the package on a six-speed manual car, where there's only one **32** throttle body.

This is an overall view of the six-speed installation - in both manual and automatic applications, there's some minor trimming of the plastic engine covers where they meet the blower and drive - the six-speed cars gain up to 70 bhp with the Comptech conversion. **33**

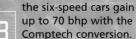

Exhaust systems

It's not all about the sound.
You can gain some horsepower too!

Whether you're a real performance nut or just content to pose and profile, you car's sound is still important. Lucky for us a good performance exhaust system can satisfy both needs. When you put together the right package of exhaust components that allow your engine to really breathe, the car's going to sound as good as it performs. It bears repeating here that the exhaust system is one of the few aspects of the car you can modify that gives you the performance you want without any of the drawbacks or compromises that usually come with engine mods. Exhaust work should have no effect on your idling or smooth driveability, and your fuel economy will actually go up, not down! The cool sound is a bonus, too.

Production car exhaust system designers are saddled with a bucketload of considerations, such as emissions testing, vehicle floorpan configuration, bean-counting accountants who want the least expensive part that does the job, and achieving sound levels down to that suitable for the average library. Unfortunately, none of these restrictions contribute to the production of a highly-effective performance exhaust but, luckily for us, the aftermarket has been filling that void almost since the car was invented.

Backpressure and flow

Even a standard engine that operates mostly at lower speeds has to get rid of the byproducts of combustion. If it takes fuel and air in, it has to expel those gases after the reciprocating components have turned the cylinder pressures into work. The exhaust system needs to allow swift exit of those gases, and any delay or obstruction to that flow can cause engine efficiency to suffer. If there is an exhaust flow problem somewhere in the system, the pressure waves coming out with the gases can "back up", which can cause the cylinders to work harder to complete their four-stroke cycle. In exhaust terms, this is called backpressure, and getting rid of it is the chief aim of performance exhaust system designers. An old prank kids used to pull was to take a raw potato and stick it into the end of a car's exhaust pipe. While the kids watched, the owner would start the car and it might run for a second or two, but then quit and not start again. A silly thing, but it demonstrates the important role played by the exhaust.

Almost every type of system has some backpressure. Even a straight length of open pipe adds some frictional delay to the flow. The biggest compromise to having the least backpressure is the muffling of the sound.

The two main sections of the performance exhaust system are the tubular manifold that lets the exhaust out freely and may even draw it out . . .

. . . and the remainder of the exhaust system, including the back box and exhaust pipe(s) – even the catalytic converter you choose can be a performance factor.

Any road car is going to have some kind of exhaust system that quiets down the engine to an acceptable level. Almost anything you can do to muffle the sound of an exhaust system will create some backpressure, so the trick of performance tuning the exhaust is to have the best compromise. For instance, there may be dozens of silencer designs that will reduce sound to the desired level in any one application, but the trick is finding the design that accomplishes this with the least backpressure. If a potato created maximum back-pressure and caused the engine to quit, what would be the effect of say, half a potato? The engine would run, but its efficiency would be drastically reduced, especially as engine speed went up. A sharp old mechanic we used to know would check many things on the car when a customer came in with a complaint of a sudden power loss when accelerating or on the motorway. He always checked the full length of the exhaust system on a hoist, because he knew from experience that a kink or crush in the exhaust pipe from road debris or driving over a kerb could cause this sluggishness on an otherwise perfectly-tuned engine.

It seems that if you improved components to the point where you had no restriction at all, you could do no more for the exhaust, but there's another element of gas flow dynamics we haven't talked about. It's possible for an exhaust to perhaps flow better than a straight piece of pipe, or at least to make more horsepower. Why does an aftermarket induction kit make more power than just having the throttle body open to the air with no filter or entry pipe? Part of it's due to cooler air coming in, but also because the long shiny intake pipe helps build an intake momentum, what used to be called a "ram" effect. Instead of letting air come in, the intake pipe helps the air come in better.

The same type of improved flow is what aftermarket exhaust engineers have been focused on for decades. There are many theories and lots of experiments have been tried, but one thing we know for sure, the right parts can almost suck the exhaust out of the engine. In other words, instead of releasing the gases, the right system can draw them out. On a multi-cylinder engine, a combination of the right size and shape of pipes, connected in the right order, can take advantage of the engine's timing of its exhaust pulses. Let's say your engine's firing order is 1-3-4-2. If you arranged the manifold pipes in a way that the pipe carrying the exhaust pulse from cylinder one was meeting the pipe from cylinder four at the right time, it could conceivably create a slight negative pressure that helped the pulse from cylinder four come out faster. If you follow the idea, it's possible for a manifold to be designed where each cylinder's exhaust pulse helped the next one, in a process called cylinder "scavenging".

Manifolds

The first major component of your performance exhaust system is the manifold, a tubular replacement for your standard cast-iron exhaust manifold. In most modern cars, the original manifold isn't too bad, at least for the needs of your standard economy engine. The exhaust flow needs of an engine go up exponentially with the state of performance "tune". The flow and backpressure needs of a standard engine aren't excessive, especially when the engine spends the bulk of its driving life under 4000 rpm. But what happens when you modify the engine and then take advantage of those modifications by using the high end of the rpm scale? The exhaust system that was once adequate is now restrictive to a great degree.

How much power you make with just the manifold depends on several factors. On a car with a really restrictive standard exhaust system, particularly an exhaust manifold full of tight bends and twists, the manifold will make a bigger improvement than on a car with a decent system to start with. What's behind the manifold can make a big difference as well.

If the standard exhaust system includes restrictive converter and silencer box designs, small-diameter exhaust pipes and lots of "wrinkle bends" to boot, the manifold isn't going to have much chance of making a big improvement in performance. A good manifold on a typical engine with few other modifications can be expected to make only 3-5 horsepower, depending on how good or bad the standard manifold had been. That's with a standard exhaust system from the manifold back.

That sounds disappointing, but if we take a case where the engine has numerous modifications yet still has a standard exhaust manifold, the same aftermarket manifold could gain 10 horsepower. Any of the big "power-adder" modifications, including nitrous oxide and supercharging virtually "require" a manifold and free-flowing exhaust system to take advantage of their power potential.

Manifold design is an inexact science, most of what we know is through trial and error, but basically the idea is to have the right size and length pipes, and arrange them so each pipe complements the others in terms of timing.

One of the popular manifold designs is the 4-2-1, or "four-branch", in which four pipes merge into two pipes which travel back and finally merge into the one collector pipe.

Fitting a performance manifold is quite easy. Most aftermarket manifolds are made to use all the factory mounting points and braces. In fact, beware of one that doesn't, because the manifold may sound "tinny" when fitted if the proper braces aren't connected. Make sure before buying a manifold that you give your exact year, model and engine. On cat models, the location of the oxygen sensor varies, too - that's if you're keeping the cat.

Other factors to consider when manifold shopping would be looking for thick flanges that aren't going to warp and leak, and thick-walled tubing that won't rot out (and sounds better than thin tubes). Ground clearance is another issue.

When shopping for a manifold, look for clean complete welds and thick, flat flange plates for a good seal – note the pairing of cylinders 1 and 4 and 2 and 3 in the four-tube section.

This four-to-one racing manifold design keeps all four pipes long, for good torque – a four-to-one design may provide less ground clearance for road use than a 4-2-1 – note that this racer has wrapped all the pipes to keep heat in.

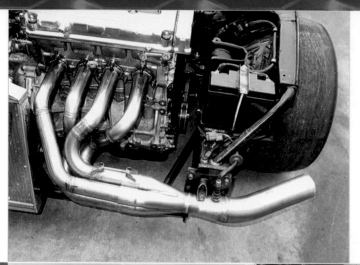

If your ride is standard height and going to stay that way, any manifold design is going to work for you, but on a seriously lowered car, you may want to stick with a 4-2-1 manifold, because the two pipes under the car are side-by-side and take up less room under there than the four tubes on a 4-1 manifold.

Manifold finish is a consideration. There are usually a few choices, even within one brand of manifold. The least expensive finish would be plain steel, which you would paint yourself with spray cans of manifold paint (lots of colours available). Next would be factory-painted manifolds, followed by high-temp-coated manifolds and manifolds made of stainless-steel. The high-temp coatings and stainless pipes are the longest lasting, and the polished stainless pipes are arguably the coolest looking. Some manifolds are also available in chrome-plated steel, which is pretty trick, too.

In a race-only application, there's room to build an exhaust without compromises – most designs use larger tubes because they're only concerned with high-rpm operation, and equal-length pipes and collector length are also important when the header is all there is to the exhaust system.

Some manifolds have unusual requirements to satisfy in the application – this Focus manifold has to work with the existing cat location and flange, so to get some primary-tube length, the tubes have to curve around like this.

Racing improves the breed they say – Shad Huntley of Comptech poses with his company's stainless-steel four-cylinder Honda header and a pair for a V6 engine.

Some sports hatches models have tubular performance manifolds as factory equipment (left) . . .

. . . compared to a typical aftermarket 4-2-1 manifold like this.

This 4-2-1 has gone a little further in trying to get all four primary pipes to be of equal length - the outside pipes have to be longer, so the inside pipes snake around just a little before joining the others.

Keeping the heat in the manifolds makes the exhaust flow faster, which is what we want – this high-temperature insulating "wrap" may not look exciting, but it could help you a little on exhaust scavenging.

All about exhaust flow

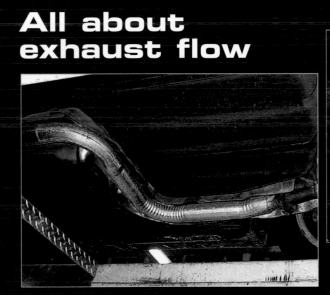

STANDARD - "Wrinkle bends" often seen in OEM and mass-produced aftermarket pipes will give some restriction as the exhaust exits.

BETTER - A second type of bend, the "crush" bend, is normally seen on pipes bent on hydraulic benders – it's smoother inside than a wrinkle bend, but not ideal. Note how the section at the bend is a smaller diameter.

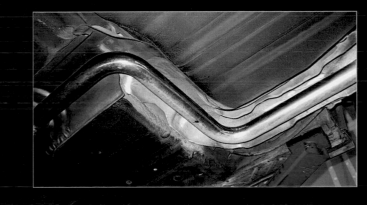

BEST - Good aftermarket performance exhausts have less bends than standard, and where there have to be bends, "mandrel" bends are used that are smooth and as consistent in diameter as the straight sections of pipe.

Standard silencers often have an indirect route for the exhaust, through a "maze" that scrubs off some of the harsh tones (as well as some of your power).

A classic performance silencer/back box is a straight-through design, in which there's a perforated core surrounded by fibreglass sound-dampening material. This is the classic 'cherry-bomb' design.

Depending on the level of modifications, the exhaust pipe in the cat-back system should be sized for the engine capacity and state-of-tune – this system features two-inch pipes, which should be good for road-use.

The converter and beyond

Once the exhaust gases leave your efficient new manifold, they travel a long way to get out from under your car, and our goal is to make it more of a motorway than a labyrinth. First off, there's the catalytic converter, usually bolted right there to the downpipe. For most of us, this is not an optional component because we have to have it. That's fine, because the converter does do a great job of cleaning up engine emissions, and the designs of current converters are more free-flowing for legal road use than the older ones, so the converter isn't something to whine about too much. If you have to replace yours due to its age, by all means shop around and try to find as free-flowing a replacement cat as you can. There are a number of "performance" cats on the market that have a stainless-steel shell, which is long-lasting and looks good. If your engine is going to eventually get forced-induction, you might even think about using a slightly larger cat, or at least one with larger inlet and outlet pipes than your original.

If your standard converter is going to stay for the time being, at least have it checked out to make sure it isn't clogged. A clogged converter can choke your engine down like the half-a-potato we talked about earlier. The biggest causes of a clogged catalytic converter is using non-approved fuels or additives, or a worn engine whose rings allow too much oil in the exhaust (you'll be able to tell because people driving behind you will always be coughing).

Polished stainless-steel exhaust parts will probably last the lifetime of the vehicle, besides looking the nuts - you can't go wrong.

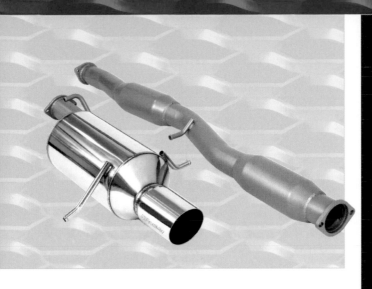

Most of the aftermarket exhaust systems on the market are called "cat-back", because they include everything from the converter back. The system may come in several pieces (see our how-to procedure on fitting one) to simplify packaging, shipping and installation, but it should bolt right up to the back flange of your converter and include whatever silencer(s) are needed. Many of the cat-back systems include the back box, which is a part of the car that's very visible, especially when it's a really big one mounted right at the rear bumper. If you find the systems out there don't offer the kind of back box action you're after, choose a system minus a box and add whatever kind you want.

Changing the exhaust of your vehicle for a performance system is one of the modifications with more perks than almost any other. You get increased power, improved fuel economy, the sound that will complement your performance profile, and parts that make your ride look better, too. All that, and there's no real downside or sacrifice as with most engine mods!

If you have lowered your car quite a bit, you might consider using a system with an oval-shaped muffler rather than round – the oval muffler and oval tip doesn't hang down as low as a large round muffler, giving you some additional ground clearance at this critical spot.

WHAT IF . . . rusted exhaust bolts and nuts

Exhaust system fasteners can be REALLY tough to remove, especially from older vehicles. The high heat coupled with the exposure to the elements can "weld" the bolts and nuts in place. Do yourself (and your knuckles) a favour and buy the best penetrating oil you can. Spray it on all the fasteners you need to remove - and don't be shy, use a lot of it. Then let it soak in for a good long time.

When it comes time to remove the fasteners, you may need a long breaker bar to gain some extra leverage. In some cases (like exhaust pipe or hanger bolts) if things go snap, it's not a problem since you'll be using new replacement fasteners anyway. But when it comes to exhaust manifold bolts or studs on the engine, be very careful. How 'bout another shot of that penetrating oil!

If the fasteners are rusty, get out the penetrating oil and give them a good soak first. Hopefully, once the clamp nuts are unscrewed, the clamp can be persuaded off, and the joint itself will separate - removing a section like this isn't as bad as a "sleeved" joint, like you get on the back box.

Hold the bolt heads with one spanner, and loosen the nuts with another. If the bolts break, that's okay. If the nuts have rusted away to nothing, you're in trouble - locking pliers or a nut splitter will be needed.

After unscrewing the manifold nuts, inspect the studs - if they're really rusty or damaged, replace them.

Cat-back installation

01 Use a long ratchet and six-point socket to loosen the nuts/bolts at the rear of the catalytic converter.

For the performance enthusiast, the exhaust system consists of two main ingredients: the exhaust manifold and cat, and everything else. The latter makes up much of the system, and on today's cars with emission controls, we call them "cat-back" exhausts because we have to keep the catalytic converter to pass emissions tests. The modern catalytic converter poses less of a restriction than older ones; just make sure yours is not clogged up before you add high-performance exhaust components, or you won't get the gains you expect.

The installation of a quality-built cat-back system like this one isn't difficult, and while the use of someone's hoist would be great, it can be done with the car on axle stands if you need to. Just follow common sense with the jack and four sturdy axle stands. New performance and the sound to go with it can be yours in one to two hours!

This Honda has another bolted joint at the rear of the system, just ahead of the rear suspension – take **02** these fasteners off.

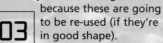

Use a crowbar to get the rubber exhaust hanger "doughnuts" off the body mounts – be gentle because these are going **03** to be re-used (if they're in good shape).

There's also a doughnut near the rear system joint, and another holding **04** up the silencer.

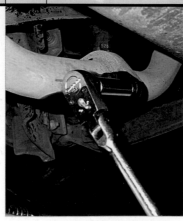

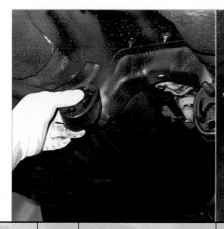

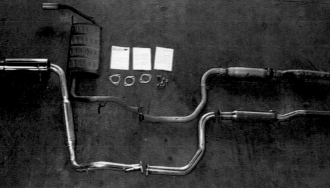

05 Clean the exhaust doughnuts of grime, then refit them on the car – any broken ones must be replaced.

06 Here laid out on the floor, you can see how the shiny new stainless-steel system compares to the standard exhaust (upper in photo) just removed – it fits just the same but is much more free-flowing.

07 Before putting the new components on the car, apply a little white grease to the holes where the exhaust hangers have to squeeze in.

>

Clean the threads on the studs at the converter flange, then put the new gasket in place.
08

09 The exhaust came with stainless-steel fasteners, so stainless nuts were put on at the cat, with a little anti-seize on the threads, so they'll come off easier if needed in the future.

10 The rear section of the exhaust includes the large rear section and back box – hang this section on the rubber doughnuts at the front and rear – this holds the pipes so you can bolt them up.

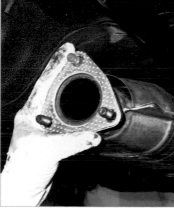

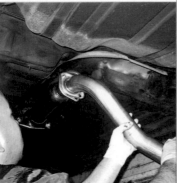

11 The system is in three pieces and we have the front and rear hanging there, so now position the middle pipe to the back of the front section, using the new gasket, and start the nuts in place by hand – you still have to support the rear of this piece while doing the front, so you may want a helper.

12 When you bolt up the rear of the middle section with a new gasket and bolts, the whole system starts to line up and become more solid – tighten the bolts at both ends of the middle section now.

A little tip for your stainless steel

Go over all that polished stainless with alcohol, because any fingerprints or smudges you may have made may stay forever if you heat the new stainless without cleaning it first.

The back box has a "coffee-can" size tip, but it comes with this bolt-in insert – this system has a great sound, not raspy, but with the insert bolted in (one bolt) it becomes more **13** civilised.

Manifold fitting

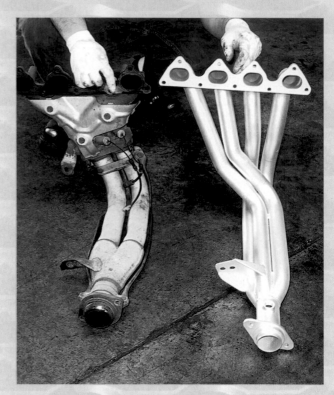

For comparison, you can see the restrictive standard manifold (left) and the new 4-1 manifold – the new manifold is much lighter and maintains good exhaust velocity all the way.

Almost everyone with a modified motor has at least two modifications: a long shiny intake pipe with an aftermarket air filter, and an exhaust manifold. When people see your engine compartment, they expect at least that, but a good exhaust system is important for more than just cool looks. The right manifold for the application, a good cat-back system and a few tuning tweaks at the dyno and you have the feel and sound of performance along with the looks.

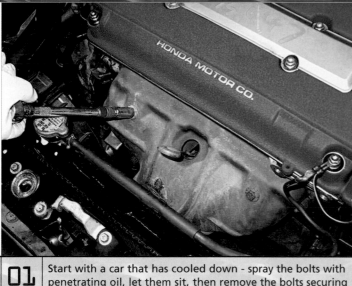

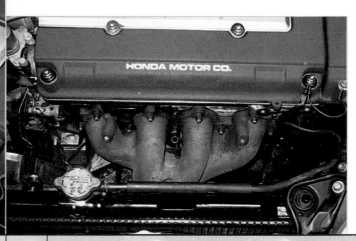

01 Start with a car that has cooled down - spray the bolts with penetrating oil, let them sit, then remove the bolts securing the factory heat shield over the exhaust manifold.

02 Soak all of the exhaust manifold retaining nuts with penetrating oil, then remove them.

Depending on the application, the oxygen sensor may be in the manifold, the collector or the catalytic converter – if it's in the way, disconnect the electrical connector and **03** remove the sensor.

04 Remove the converter flange nuts/bolts.

Remove the remaining bolts and brackets securing the **05** forward pipe and manifold.

Slowly work the exhaust down and out of the car (take care not to damage the radiator in the process). On some cars, the front crossmember **06** may have to be removed.

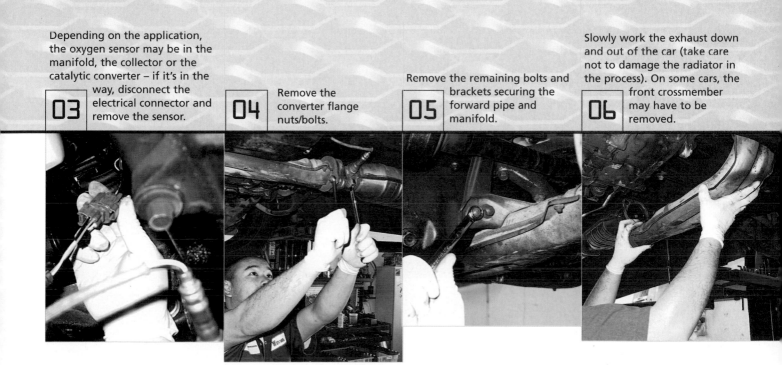

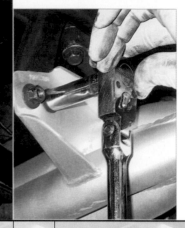

 07 Remove the hard gasket ring and fit it on the end of the new manifold.

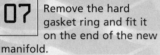 **08** With the old crossmember removed, there's plenty of room to install the new high-temp-coated manifold.

09 Attach the fasteners, but leave them loose at this time.

10 If your application uses a manifold gasket, fit a new one and bolt the manifold to the cylinder head with all of the original nuts.

11 Tighten the bolts at the manifold collector-to-converter flange and the manifold is completely installed. Don't forget to reinstall the oxygen sensor!

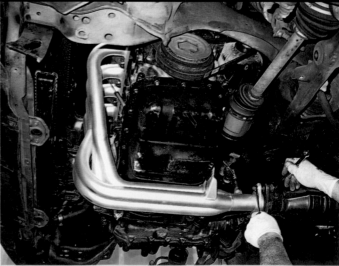

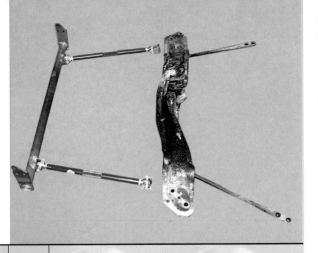

 12 Such is the power of Honda that several companies make special crossmembers for sports manifolds – compare the cool-looking high-strength steel tubing crossmember and racy anodised radius rods to the ugly standard crossmember.

The tubular crossmember bolts into the Honda to the same bolt holes where the original towing bracket used to hang down. The new radius rods bolt to the crossmember and lower control arms with spherical joints at each end, and its length can be adjusted by holding the knurled center, threading one of the joints in or out, then tightening the large locknuts – **13** the final adjustment should be made at a garage (it affects the front wheel alignment).

? WHAT IF . . . flanges don't line up?

One problem you may encounter, especially with engine swaps or when parts had been previously replaced, is that the "clocking" or arrangement of the flange bolts may be different.

We just removed the cat, cut the front flange off with a bandsaw, put the cat back onto the car and moved the flange (now free to rotate) in front where it would line up with the manifold flange.

A minute or two with the MIG-welder and both the manifold and cat flanges align perfectly.

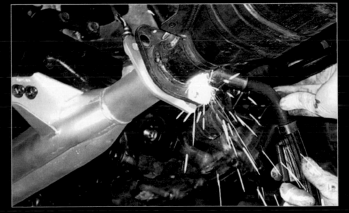

Engine durability

Why is there always money waiting for *go-faster* parts, but none for *keep-alive longer* parts? That big ol' tow truck could be right around the corner waiting for you.

Most engine damage comes about from detonation during the tuner's "learning curve" – here are the results, a piece of block, half a mangled connecting rod, and a piston with a valve-head embedded. No, it's not some art student's project - this really is what the engine internals will look like if it all goes Pete.

Once you put on the slicks and head for action at the track, that's when any potential weakness is exposed, even on a combination that has worked fine on the street.

It's a testament to the car designers and engineers that lots of power can be extracted from what are meant to be little more than efficient powerplants for economy cars. Our engines are lightweight, have good valvetrain dynamics, like to rev, and have amazing longevity in standard or mildly-modified form. However, when extracting maximum power from any engine not designed for this, durability begins to suffer as components are stressed beyond their design limits.

High-horsepower engines are built by teams that have learned through experience what it takes to make the engine live. When pressed had enough, most tuners will reach under their bench and pull out a boxful of melted pistons and bent connecting rods accumulated along the way in the search for power and knowledge.

The wiser tuners with that box of parts under the bench will tell you it's better to spend some money now on beefing up the engine, than later on new parts *plus* the beefing up.

The average modern engine can handle a power increase in the neighbourhood of 50% before you start needing to invest in "engine insurance". That covers most road-use engines with standard modifications. Where the real trouble starts is with either dragstrip action or the use of a power-adder.

Perhaps the modifications that result in the most stress on an engine are the ones that really increase cylinder pressure: high-compressions pistons; nitrous oxide; supercharging; and turbocharging.

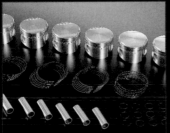

Pistons

The top of the piston usually takes the brunt of damage caused by increased cylinder pressure and detonation. The head gasket and the top of the cylinder walls are also affected by high pressures.

The standard cast-aluminum pistons in your engine now are perfect for what they do. They last a long time, run quietly and withstand all the normal pressures, even with some modifications. Different pistons, however, are required for more serious work.

In some cases the standard compression ratio may be too high for a big shot of nitrous or forced-induction boost, and you just need a replacement piston with lower compression to take advantage of the power-adder's potential. As long as you're replacing the pistons for a lower compression, it only makes sense to get stronger ones while you're at it.

Forged pistons are definitely stronger than your standard pistons, and most have many other subtle tricks to make them live under harsh conditions. Among these other factors are: lighter and stronger pins; full-floating pins that reduce friction losses; smooth edges on the crowns to prevent hot spots; uniform dome thickness for consistent strength; precise machining; heat-treating; and relocated and/or different size ring grooves.

If there's a downside to forged pistons, it's their expansion rate. They tend to expand more than cast pistons as the engine warms up, sometimes resulting in clatter when the engine is cold. Most of today's forged pistons make a little noise only at idle.

Today, the top piston manufacturers have several levels of forged pistons, with a variance in the exact alloy of aluminum used. For instance, for road use with normal power-adder levels, piston manufacturers use a 4032 heat-treated aluminum alloy that has 12% silicon content to limit thermal expansion, and these pistons can be fitted with close-to-standard clearances. For racing applications with higher power levels, they make their pistons from a 2618 alloy that is very low in silicon, but has other elements that contribute to a high-strength piston suited for elevated levels of heat and pressure in the cylinders. The low-silicon forgings do require more clearance.

Like a chain, the engine is only as strong as its weakest link, and once you have a stout piston that can take some punishment, the stress is going to be on the con-rod and its fasteners.

Aftermarket con-rods are very popular with racers, and a wide variety are available. The basic process of making a "forged" connecting rod goes like this: A red-hot chunk of metal is put into a machine that has dies that slam together to force it into something that resembles the desired finished part. These "blanks" are then machined and treated to produce the final product. The benefit of the forging process is that grains of the metal are packed together and aligned into the desired shape, making a very strong, dense part that has less inherent tendency to fracture.

Connecting rods and aftermarket crankshafts

Aftermarket rods are available in a number of types of steel, and in various cross-sectional shapes. Many have names that describe the shape, like the H-beam, A-beam, I-beam, etc. While all of the manufacturers have their own features, they will all offer superior strength to any standard or race-prepped standard rod. They come with high-strength fasteners, are precision balanced, and in addition to being strong, are often lighter than the original standard rods!

There are a few companies making forged cranks for other modern engines. They are much stronger than a standard cast (standard crankshafts on Hondas are forged) crankshaft, and for racing use can even be made lighter than a standard crank, so the engine revs up quicker and has less reciprocating loads.

On Honda blocks the cylinders sit in the middle of the water jacket area, without connection to the deck – when your cylinder pressures are distorting them, you may want to try a block-guard like this one - it taps in between the top of the cylinders and the block, and has holes for water passage connection.

The block

Most engines have a lightweight block designed for efficiency, and with little extra material where it isn't needed. Basic high-performance machining techniques will assure you of a bottom-end that will stay together in all but extreme conditions. Among the blueprinting procedures that are useful is precisely "decking" the top surface of the block so that it is flat and perfectly square to the crankshaft centreline. Align-boring the crankshaft saddles assure you that the crankshaft will run true with minimal friction and you can achieve an exact fit of the bearings.

If you're putting in new pistons, then you're putting in new rings and the cylinder walls need to be honed for a surface the new rings can seat against and "wear in". If your cylinder walls have any scores or deep scratches from a broken piston ring, then you'll have to bore the engine first to get rid of that and order oversize pistons.

For those eight and seven-second Honda-powered racecars, the ultimate solution to block problems could be this new block from Dart with a "conventional" deck, available in two bore sizes and complete with main caps and replaceable ductile-iron sleeves.

GM (Vauxhall/Opel) Ecotec racers also have a race block available, Part#88958630, which is this steel-liner'ed aluminum block machined for stainless O-rings to contain serious boost.

Regular maintenance could be your most important job

Let's assume that you're not running 20 psi of boost or a 200hp shot of nitrous, but you still want to do something within your budget to make your modified engine last longer. Good maintenance habits are always the first line of defence, modified engine or not. Your cooling system, fuel system and lubrication system must be kept up at all times. Don't miss any oil changes (every 3,000 miles) and change the filter with every oil change. The Haynes repair manual for your car will have maintenance information specific to your make and model, plus a recommended maintenance schedule to follow.

Multi-valve engines

Most older car engines have one intake valve and one exhaust valve per cylinder - ie, two valves per cylinder. Many modern engines have three, four, or in a few cases even five valves per cylinder, although the most common configuration is four valves per cylinder. Such an engine has two inlet valves and two exhaust valves for each cylinder (so a four-cylinder engine would be a "16-valve" engine).

Using multiple valves gives improved efficiency, because they allow the fuel/air mixture to enter the cylinder, and the exhaust gases to leave, more easily.

Double-overhead-camshaft engines

Double-overhead-camshaft engines (or "twin-cam") engines have two camshafts, one operating the exhaust valves, and one operating the inlet valves. Multi-valve engines are almost always double-overhead-camshaft engines.

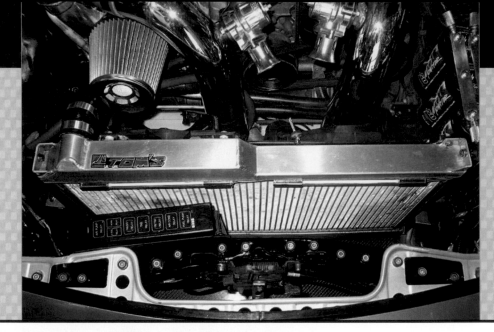

Cooling and Lubrication

The power in fuel is the heat generated when you light it, and a performance engine is going to make more heat. Worse yet, a turbocharger jammed between the engine and the radiator can really raise the underbonnet temperature.

Many modern cars have factory oil coolers, usually in a sandwich between the oil filter and the block, and connected to coolant pipes. In standard form this is fine, but when you already have a big load on your cooling system with a modified engine, you don't want to add more heat to the cooling system by passing coolant through a container of hot oil.

The answer, for cars with or without a factory oil cooler, may be to mount a radiator-type liquid-air cooler out in the car's airstream, although hopefully where it doesn't compete with the coolant radiator for airflow. The extra plumbing and the addition of the cooler to the system also increases the oil capacity of the engine.

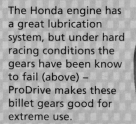

The Honda engine has a great lubrication system, but under hard racing conditions the gears have been know to fail (above) – ProDrive makes these billet gears good for extreme use.

This oil cooler kit, when mounted in the right place to get cool outside air, can keep engine temps down, even on a turbo application where engine oil must pass through "lubricant hell" to get back to the sump.

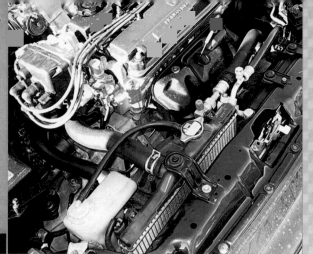

Aftermarket cooling fans keep the air moving faster than a standard fan, and the aftermarket fan/shroud packages are generally slimmer - this is an FAL (Flexalite) setup for a Civic.

A small radiator is light and handles normal loads, but doesn't have a lot of coolant capacity and is usually a one-row style.

The radiator in most small cars is, well, *small*. Luckily, the aftermarket companies have a wide variety of radiators with extra cooling capacity. Even in the conventional-construction category, your local radiator specialist can supply you with a radiator just like your standard one, but with extra rows of tubes in it. Yours may be a one-row now, and you can replace it with a two-row for peace of mind.

Compare this Honda with the previous photo - this tuner has added an aluminum radiator – it's roughly the same size as the original but cools better – you can even get racing radiators that incorporate an electric water pump, which saves engine horsepower.

Aftermarket aluminum radiators are rugged and available in sizes to fit almost any car.

Engine swapping
Why swap?

When done with patience and care, the swap will not only give you better performance, but also a great new look.

Sometimes it just makes sense to make a change

There are a few basic truths to creating horsepower. When all other factors are equal, the larger the engine capacity, the more power it will make ("there ain't no substitute for cubes"). And the same modification made to a larger-capacity engine will generally gain more power over a smaller engine. For example, if you replace the 1.5 litre engine in your Honda Civic with a 2.2 litre Prelude engine, you'll automatically get a substantial power increase, largely because the engine's nearly 50% bigger.

How tough will the job be?
Do your research!

In a typical swap, you'll need to change the engine compartment wiring harness, engine mountings, radiator hoses, exhaust pipe and component mounting brackets. In some cases you may also need to change the gearbox (or linkage), driveshafts, clutch, radiator and front springs (to alow for a heavier engine). Every swap is a little different, so it's important to study up before you get the spanners out.

In all probability, you're not the first person to try the swap you're planning. And why make the same mistakes the others made? Go to car shows and events. Find a car club. Go on the Internet. Basically, locate people who have already done the swap you're thinking about, and pick their brains . . . see their car . . . find out what worked and what didn't.

Now let's say you want to add a manifold, cat-back exhaust system and induction kit. On the 1.5 litre engine, these mods might have netted you 20 extra horsepower. The same mods on the 2.2 litre engine would likely get you closer to 30 extra brake, or about 50 % more. This is the simple, yet powerful argument for extra cc's.

Another reason for engine swapping is to obtain the latest technology and tuning potential. For example, swapping your tired Single OverHead Cam (SOHC) engine for a later-model Double OverHead Cam (DOHC) engine will get you some extra power, even though the engine capacity may be the same. The additional benefit is that the DOHC engine will respond better to tuning, since the cylinder head design is less restrictive and will allow better airflow when other modifications are made. And don't forget about other interesting standard later-model features, like turbos!

Engine numbers

All engines have an ID number that uniquely identifies that particular engine. That number appears on the vehicle registration document, so you ought to notify the DVLA when swapping. It's likely that they won't ask too many questions, but they usually want an invoice to prove the work's been done, and to indicate what vehicle it came from. Remember, engine size now determines how much road tax you pay to the DVLA.

Putting in a new engine without having your car's paperwork updated means your "numbers don't match", and this makes your car look well-dodgy when you come to sell it. For this reason, don't buy an engine without numbers on it - it could be stolen.

Engine ID numbers can be difficult to find on the engine block. Buy a Haynes manual to help.

Keep it legal -
engine swaps and insurance

Insurance companies are just out to spoil your fun, basically, aren't they? All you want to do is modify your motor for maximum stand-out appeal, style and performance, and there they are, holding you back.

Trouble is, you do an engine swap and don't tell them, and they won't pay out if you stack it. Which gets to be rather inconvenient if you end up hurting anyone other than you, thanks to all those personal injury claims specialists which seem to have sprung from the American culture of suing people. If your insurance company finds out your humble 1.2 litre Nova's actually a fire-breathing 2.0 litre monster, they'll void your insurance, This might firstly be of interest to the police, of course. Driving without insurance is an offence, after all. But the real stinger is all those thousands of pounds you'll be paying any other accident victims when they claim off you. That's thousands. And you'll be paying. Because your insurance company won't. Think about it.

Okay, you're convinced - what's the secret to keeping your insurance company happy? The secret is having no secrets, and telling them everything. In the case of a new engine, they'll probably want an engineer's report on the car. These can be arranged through any garage doing vehicle inspections - look in the Yellow Pages. Don't put your car in for one until all the work's been done, and not just on the engine. A vehicle inspector's looking to see not just that the engine's been put in properly (not likely to fall out, rip away from its mountings, or spring fuel, oil and coolant leaks) - he's looking for appropriately-modified brakes, suspension, wheels and tyres. He has to approve your re-engined car to be safe to handle its new level of power, essentially. Which means no bodges. So a bit like the MoT test then - a bit of a pain, but good for safety and peace of mind.

Who will do it?

Probably the most important question is who will actually do the work. Usually, the safest option is to have a tuning specialist that specialises in your type of car do the work for you. Often, this is the most costly option. But the advantage is that the work will be warrantied and done by people who are familiar with all the special considerations for your vehicle. If you also buy the engine from them, you may get a warranty on the engine, as well. So if anything goes wrong, there won't be any finger-pointing.

If you want to save some money, buy the engine separately and take it to a garage to have it fitted. Many people choose this option and save the mark-up that a specialist is likely to add onto the engine price. But remember - you can't blame the garage if you purchase a bad engine. So if you're not sure of the quality of the engine, it's usually best to let an expert select the engine for you.

If you're a hands-on person who's pretty handy with tools, you may be able to handle the job yourself, with the guidance of someone who's done it before. The advantages to doing the job yourself are:

1) You'll save money.
2) You'll know exactly what was done, so, if you have repair issues later, you'll be able to knowledgeably explain to the technician what was done.
3) You can do the job the way you want to do it. There's a bit of art to this, as well, and since a pro will be doing the job quickly, they may not pay attention to the details the way you would. You may want to take some extra time to add artistic flair to your wiring, or paint your engine differently. When you do it yourself, you can take the extra time.

A reconditioned or remanufactured engine provides your best assurance of quality - most have a warranty, too.

Finding your engine

Remanufactured engines

Your best chance of getting a quality engine is to purchase it remanufactured (reconditioned) from an engine rebuilder. As you may have guessed, this is the most expensive option. But getting a warranty and being assured that the internals of the engine are "like-new" is usually worth the extra cost. Another advantage of a recon engine is that you can sometimes specify upgrades for internal parts. For example, if you'll be putting nitrous oxide to the engine, you should pay extra for forged pistons and high-strength connecting rod bolts.

Used engines

Used engines provide a more cost-effective option if you're on a budget. Since you probably won't be looking inside the engine, it will be difficult to know its condition. The best indicator of quality is the reputation of the seller. Find other people who are happy with their replacement engines and find out where they got theirs. Again, try to find a reputable seller who will provide a warranty on the engine. We've seen quite a few people who were told they were getting a good engine, but, when the engine was actually fitted, they found it was in poor mechanical condition. Don't be caught like this without a warranty! The best answer, of course, is to hear it running.

Engine retailers

As mentioned earlier, if you're not sure how to check the quality of a used engine, it's best to let the garage who's doing the work select the engine for you. The next best approach is to locate a source that warranties the engines they sell. There are many sources for used engines, especially in larger cities - check in Exchange & Mart. If you're not lucky enough to have inexpensive used engines close by, check the Internet. Often, you can find prices so low they're still a bargain, even after adding the postage cost. But be sure you're dealing with a reputable company that will warranty the engine.

Used engines are a more economical solution. Secondhand engines are available from many sources and often have very low mileage. Check low-mileage engines for signs of accident damage.

Top tips for scouring the scrapyard

Check it out!

Checking out an engine at a scrapyard can be difficult, since you're working in relatively primitive conditions. But if you know what to look for, you can do a pretty good job:

• If the engine is still fitted in a vehicle, check the mileage.

• Aside from obvious body damage, look at the overall condition of the car. Chances are, the owner who polished the paint and vacuumed the carpets also changed the engine oil and replaced worn engine parts.

• Remove the oil cap and check for a "mayonnaise" look under the cap and in the oil itself. This is evidence that the cylinder head is cracked or the head gasket has blown – look for another engine if you see this. Also check the dipstick for the same evidence. Remember, cars end up in scrapyards for other reasons than a huge accident - expensive engine repairs could be why this one's here.

• Carefully look inside the valve cover (a small torch helps). Look for signs of carbon or sludge build-up, which indicate an abused engine (overheating and/or irregular oil changes).

• Compare the spark plugs to the condition chart in the Ignition Chapter to get a clue about the inside of the engine.

Gauges and monitoring engine performance

Having the right gauges provides you with an early warning system to help you spot problems before they can cause major engine damage. On a standard road car, the engine is so reliable that these situations are pretty rare. But when you start modifying your engine, stuff happens, which is why you'd better keep tabs on things.

Where do I put the gauges?

When cars were bigger, so were the dashboards. There was always room for extra gauges. On modern cars, however, there's not a lot of unused space for extra gauges. The one really flat space for gauges is of course the existing instrument "cluster" (the one-piece unit that houses the speedometer, tachometer and a few other gauges such as the fuel level and coolant temperature gauges). So, if you're swapping the old instrument cluster for a new unit, it should be a very straightforward procedure. But if you're planning to install additional gauges, then you'll have to be creative.

Gauge "cups" are the traditional strategy for housing gauges that can't be installed in the instrument cluster area. A cup is usually a black metal, chrome or plastic enclosure designed to house one gauge or a series of gauges. These are often simply mounted at the bottom edge of the dashboard. One drawback is that the wires between the gauge and the sender, voltage source, ground, etc. are exposed between the back of the cup and where they disappear into the dash.

All of the gauge manufacturers offer finished mounting plates, pre-cut to fit into storage recesses or ashtray receptacles in the dashboards of most modern cars. These empty spaces, which are usually located in the centre of the dash, were intended for storing small sundries such as sunglasses, cell phones and other small items. If your car's dash is equipped with one of these storage areas, consider yourself lucky, because this is an easy way to add some gauges and make it look "factory."

There are gauge plates designed to fit into the ashtray receptacle of many makes and models. One neat thing about the ashtray is that the electrical lead to the cigarette lighter means that a convenient battery voltage source is already available.

Most of the gauge manufacturers also offer a wide range of "gauge pods," which are plastic housings designed to accept various sizes of gauges. There are pods for just about every vacant area on the dash: above the instrument cluster, to the left or right of the cluster, in the centre of the dash, etc. Gauge pods usually have a black pebble-grain finish that blends nicely with most dashes.

One popular variation of the gauge pod is known as a "pillar pod." Pillar pods, which are designed to fit the driver's side A-pillar (the windscreen pillar), are manufactured to accept one, two or three small gauges. A pillar pod is easy to install and looks as if it were installed at the factory, but be ready to do some drilling in the body and/or the dash to hide all the wires.

Gauge speak

Typical gauges

Air/fuel ratio gauge - The air/fuel ratio gauge indicates whether your air/fuel mixture ratio is rich or lean. It's a particularly helpful tuning tool if your engine is carburetted instead of fuel injected. Most air/fuel ratio gauges work with the existing oxygen sensor, according to the manufacturers, but how old is the existing oxygen sensor? Oxygen sensors become "lazy" before they actually fail. A lazy O_2 sensor might still work, but if its signal is intermittent, irregular or slow (which it probably is if it's the original unit on a 10-year-old car), replace it. Or fit another O_2 sensor that's dedicated to the air/fuel ratio gauge.

Ammeter - An ammeter tells you how much current your alternator is putting out. Ammeters are not as popular as they once were (most people fit a voltmeter instead).

Boost gauge - A boost gauge indicates the boost pressure on a supercharged or turbocharged engine. This is not an option on these vehicles. An overboost condition caused by a stuck wastegate can cause serious damage.

Coolant temperature gauge - The coolant temperature gauge indicates the temperature of the engine coolant. You might already have a coolant temperature gauge; if you're going to replace it, you'll need to consult the manufacturer to determine whether your new gauge will work with the existing sender for the old gauge. If you want to add a coolant temperature gauge - and you don't already have one - you'll need to fit a coolant temperature sending unit. Also keep in mind that on many modern vehicles, a single Engine Coolant Temperature (ECT) sensor, which is the information sensor for the Powertrain Control Module (PCM), also functions as the coolant temperature sending unit for the coolant temperature gauge. On these models, you might want to fit another sender dedicated to your new coolant temperature gauge.

Cylinder head temperature gauge - A cylinder head temperature gauge tells you the temperature of the cylinder head (obviously!), but its real value is that it can provide you with a general idea of the engine's operating temperature. For example, it can indicate whether an engine overheats under full power, or whether it has a tendency to run too cold, just right or too hot over a longer period. You will need to fit a new sender for a cylinder head temperature gauge because this type of gauge is rarely found on cars as original equipment.

Exhaust gas temperature (EGT) gauge - An exhaust gas temperature gauge tells you the temperature of the exhaust gases as they're exiting the combustion chamber. An exhaust gas temperature of 1100 to 1200 degrees F should result in nice tan-coloured spark plug electrodes. A lower reading should produce darker coloured plugs, and higher readings should give you grey or white plugs. Once you've identified the "normal" temperature range that produces tan plugs, all you have to do is monitor the EGT gauge(s) and watch for any deviation from normal. An EGT gauge is a valuable tuning tool when you're trying to set up the correct mixture ratio. A lean mixture will run hotter than normal, while a rich mixture will run cooler than normal (and will actually make increasingly less horsepower as it gets richer). An EGT can also help you identify "hot spots" which can occur when chopping the throttle from a full-throttle situation.

Fuel pressure gauge - A normally-aspirated high performance engine, or an engine with nitrous oxide, supercharger or turbo makes big demands on the fuel delivery system under acceleration, so you need a heavy-duty fuel pump capable of supplying sufficient fuel. And you need a fuel pressure gauge to make sure that the fuel pressure is adequate under all conditions. A fuel system that fails to deliver sufficient fuel under acceleration or high speed running leans out the air/fuel mixture ratio, which leads to detonation and/or preignition conditions, and it can ruin a motor in seconds! The fuel pressure gauge is primarily used for tuning. One reason for this is that you can't fit it inside the car; you wouldn't want high-pressure fuel spraying the inside of the car if a compression fitting came loose!

Nitrous gauge - If you're running nitrous oxide, you need to know how much nitrous is in the tank. Running out of nitrous in the middle of a drag race will cause your air/fuel mixture to turn really rich in a hurry, which could cause big trouble. If you're going to fit

a nitrous kit, make sure you have a gauge to monitor the level in the tank.

Oil pressure gauge - The oil pressure gauge tells you the pressure of the engine oil. If you don't have an oil pressure gauge, this is one of the first gauges you should consider fitting. An oil pressure gauge can save your engine from some expensive damage. If the engine loses oil pressure because of oil pump failure or a blocked oil passage, oil pressure will drop suddenly; without an oil pressure gauge, you might very well run the engine until it destroys itself. Many aftermarket oil pressure gauges can work with the existing oil pressure sending unit.

Oil temperature gauge - The oil temperature gauge tells you the temperature of the engine oil, which is generally considered a more accurate way of monitoring engine temperature.

Shift light - A shift light is a large, bright LED that can be programmed to come on at a specific, predetermined rpm level. You don't have to take your eyes off the road to watch a shift light; because of its intensity, a shift light can be seen out of the corner of your eye. A shift light can be located on the face of a special aftermarket racing tachometer, or housed in a separate enclosure mounted on top of the dash.

Tachometer - The tachometer tells you the engine speed in revolutions-per-minute, or rpm. Some aftermarket tachos are also equipped with shift lights, which can be programmed to come on at the desired rpm. And some of the top-of-the-line units even make a recording of each run (or even multiple runs) so that you can analyse the data afterwards.

Voltmeter - The voltmeter tells you the voltage output of your alternator.

How much horsepower?
How fast?

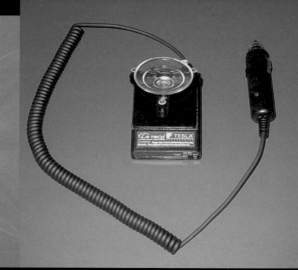

G-TECH/Pro tuning tools

One interesting and very helpful product in aftermarket instrumentation is the G-TECH/Pro, from America. The G-TECH/Pro uses a silicon accelerometer, which is a sensor that can measure acceleration, or G-force. The G-TECH/Pro measures the speed and distance travelled by integrating acceleration over time. It's all very complicated exactly how it works, but, bottom line, it does work. If you want to know how much power you really gained with that new induction kit, hook up the G-TECH before and after. Want to know 1/4-mile times without going to the drag strip? Plug in the G-TECH.

The G-TECH/Pro is ridiculously easy to fit. Simply position the G-TECH/Pro in the middle of the dash (below the rear view mirror), push the rubber suction cup against the inside surface of the windscreen, and plug it into your cigarette lighter. That's all there is to it. You're ready to go!

The G-TECH/Pro COMPETITION model can measure:

1/4-mile elapsed time and top speed
1/8-mile elapsed time and top speed
1000-foot time
Accelerating and braking Gs
Braking distance
Engine rpm
Engine rpm vs. time graph
Gs vs. time graph
Handling Gs
Horsepower
Horsepower and torque vs. rpm graph
Reaction time
Speed vs. distance graph
Speed vs. time graph
Torque
Zero-to-100 mph
Zero-to-330 feet
Zero-to-60 feet
Zero-to-60 mph

Another advantage is its portability. You can remove it from its mounting bracket to study your tuning data more closely. You can review the results, store logged runs that you want to save and even change the settings before putting the unit back in the car. Or in another car: Specific vehicle data such as weight and shift light settings can be stored and recalled for up to four vehicles.

Scan tools:
Spend some quality time
with your car's computer

All modern cars are equipped with sophisticated engine management systems run by a powerful computer. You don't have to be a dealer mechanic or specialist with expensive equipment in order to tap into your car's computer.

Hand-held scan tools are the most powerful and versatile tools for diagnosing the engine management systems on modern cars. Think of the scan tool as a way to peek inside your engine's brain. First, some terminology. OBD stands for On-Board Diagnostics; essentially a load of sensors feeding information to a computer. OBD cars started appearing in the early 1990s. OBD-II is a much more sophisticated system that was introduced in the mid-1990s.

On some pre-OBD-II cars, if the dashboard Check Engine Light or Service Engine Soon light comes on, you might be able to extract stored diagnostic codes with a simple and inexpensive "code reader" which displays the code(s) when you plug it into the car's diagnostic connector. Or you might be able to put the computer into a diagnostic output mode in which it displays the code(s) by flashing the Check Engine light on and off. Refer to a Haynes repair manual for your vehicle for more information, but on all 1996 and later cars, you'll need a scan tool to extract and identify the code(s). And even

on earlier vehicles, a scan tool will tell you a lot more information than the diagnostic code number.

Little engine modifications like upgraded HT leads or a free-flowing air filter will have little if any effect on the serial data being exchanged between the information sensors, the computer and the actuators. But as the number and complexity of your engine mods increases, you will sooner or later do something that causes a sensor or its circuit to go out of range. A scan tool can help you understand how a recent modification affects the overall operation of your engine because you can "look" at the data.

A high-end scan tool can also help you diagnose the most maddening intermittent driveability problems by allowing you to retrieve freeze frame data from the memory of the computer. Freeze frame data is a digital recording for the interval during which a problem was detected.

Aftermarket scan tools are now widely available at automotive retailers. These tools, which are designed for the do-it-yourselfer, are not as powerful or versatile as pro units, but they can display all codes, and some of the better units can tell you a little about each code and can indicate whether a circuit is operating inside or outside its intended operating range. These are best used in conjuction with a Haynes repair manual.

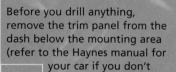

Fitting a tachometer

It's recommended to mount the tacho where it's easy to see without taking your eyes off the road. Make sure that the dash material is substantial enough to support the tacho. Once you've settled on the perfect spot for your tacho, **01** mark the position of the mounting bracket.

Remove the tacho from the mounting bracket, and mark the position of the **02** bracket holes for drilling.

∧

Before you drill anything, remove the trim panel from the dash below the mounting area (refer to the Haynes manual for your car if you don't **03** know how to remove the trim panel) . . .

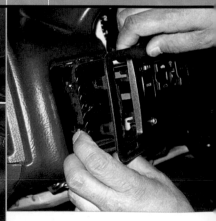

> **04** . . . and verify that your drill bit (and mounting screws) won't hit anything important like electrical wiring.

05 Carefully drill the mounting bracket holes. If you've got a fancy right-angled drill adaptor, this job's a lot easier. Most of us will have to struggle just a bit.

06 Place the tacho mounting bracket in position, align it with your marks, fit the bracket screws and tighten them securely, but don't overdo it or you'll strip the dash material.

>

07 Fit the tacho in its mounting clamp, then bolt the clamp to the mounting bracket. Before tightening the mounting bolt and nut, hop in, adjust the seat to your regular driving position and adjust the angle of the tacho so that it's facing directly at you.

08 Most electric tachos have four wires: power, earth, illumination and signal. To route the wires so they're hidden from view, we ran them through a gap between the left end of the dash and the A-pillar trim. Then we covered the short exposed section of wiring between the tacho and the pillar with some split loom tubing.

09 Pull the wires down to the interior fuse panel (usually located on the kick panel or tucked up under the end of the dash) and cut off the excess, but leave enough so there's plenty of room to add connectors to the ends. If you're new to wiring, it's a good idea to label the wires so that you don't mix them up.

10 Now you're ready to start hooking up the wires. First, using a test light or continuity tester, find a pair of vacant 12-volt terminals on the fuse panel for your power (red) and illumination (white) wires. You want a switched 12-volt terminal for the power wire, which means that it's open-circuit when the car is turned off, but live when the ignition key is switched to ON. You'll also need a switched 12-volt terminal for the illumination wire that's only live when the sidelights are switched on.

11 Strip off a little insulation from each wire, crimp a connector the same size as the spade terminals you're going to hook up to and connect the power and illumination wires to the fuse panel. Those of you with sharp eyes will notice that these wires are oversize. That's because we plan to use these same wires for the illumination and power leads to the pillar pod gauges and the air/fuel ratio meter we'll be fitting later.

12 Look for a close and convenient fastener to connect the earth wire. Make sure that it earths the wire to metal, not plastic. We attached the earth wire to the body at this crossmember brace bolt. If you can't find a fastener nearby, drill a hole into the body and attach the earth wire with a self-tapper.

13 Unlike the other three wires, the signal wire must be routed through the bulkhead to the engine compartment. Look for a convenient cable grommet (throttle, clutch, bonnet release, etc.) in the bulkhead and make a hole in it with a bradawl. We used the clutch cable grommet because it's big and because it's easy to get to.

14 Insert the signal wire through the plastic tube from under the dash and pull it through from the engine compartment side. Crimp on a suitable connector and connect the signal wire to the negative primary terminal on the ignition coil (standard-type coil) or to the auxiliary terminal meant for a tacho wire (aftermarket, high-performance coil). That's it! You're done. Now set the telltale needle to the desired redline and be sure to not let the red needle go past it!

Fitting pillar pod gauges

01 Unpack the oil pressure gauge kit and make sure you have everything you'll need to fit it. If you're fitting a mechanical type oil pressure gauge like this one, you will need to tap into the hole in the engine block or cylinder head for the oil pressure sender. So make sure that the kit includes all the adapter fittings you'll need to tee into the existing hole for the oil pressure sender.

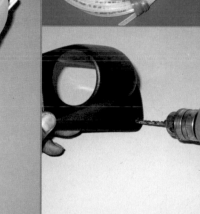

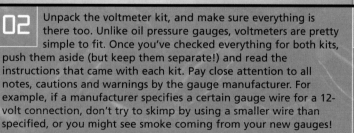

02 Unpack the voltmeter kit, and make sure everything is there too. Unlike oil pressure gauges, voltmeters are pretty simple to fit. Once you've checked everything for both kits, push them aside (but keep them separate!) and read the instructions that came with each kit. Pay close attention to all notes, cautions and warnings by the gauge manufacturer. For example, if a manufacturer specifies a certain gauge wire for a 12-volt connection, don't try to skimp by using a smaller wire than specified, or you might see smoke coming from your new gauges!

03 Okay, let's get started. Get your pillar pod and dummy it up exactly where you want to put it. Make sure it's a good fit before proceeding. Then drill a hole at each corner of the pod as shown.

04 Place the pod in position on the pillar, and mark the locations of the four holes you're going to drill. Make sure the holes aren't going to be too close to the edges of the pillar.

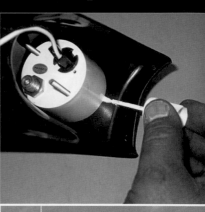

05 Using the same drill bit, drill the holes in the pillar trim.

06 Insert the gauges into the pillar pod, place the pod in position on the pillar, then rotate the gauges so the "OIL" and "VOLTS" on the gauge faces are horizontal and parallel to each other.

07 Carefully turn the pillar pod upside down and mark the position of each gauge in relation to the pod (we're using typing correction fluid to make the marks).

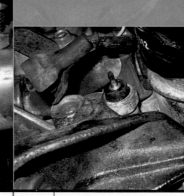

12 We spliced the power, illumination and earth leads from all three pillar pod gauges into the same leads we used for the illumination and earth wires for the tachometer. Then we routed the oil line for the oil pressure gauge through the bulkhead to the engine compartment.

13 Find the oil pressure sending unit and disconnect the electrical connector. The sender is usually - but not always - located somewhere near the oil filter. Refer to your Haynes manual if you have difficulty finding it. Be prepared to catch any oil that runs out when you remove the sender - the lower the sensor location on the head or block, the more oil you'll lose when you remove it.

14 Here's our setup for tee-ing into the standard sending unit on our project vehicle. Before assembling, be sure to wrap the threads of the sender, the adapter fitting and the compression fitting with PTFE tape to prevent leaks.

08 Okay, remove the gauges from the pillar pod and connect the wires for power, earth and illumination . . .

09 . . . and on the oil pressure gauge, the tube that will carry oil from the oil pressure sender to the gauge.

10 Refit the gauges in the pillar pod, and clamp them into place with the clamps provided by the manufacturer. Note how we spliced the two illumination bulb wires and the two earth wires together.

11 Route the wires and the oil line for the oil pressure gauge through the gap between the end of the dash and the A-pillar, then fit the pillar pod/gauge assembly on the pillar, and attach it with the four mounting screws. Don't overtighten the screws or you'll strip out the holes. When you're done with this phase, hide the wires with some split-loom tubing.

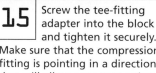

15 Screw the tee-fitting adapter into the block and tighten it securely. Make sure that the compression fitting is pointing in a direction that will allow easy connection of the oil pressure gauge line.

16 Insert the line into the compression fitting, slide the olive down the line until it seats inside the open end of the fitting, thread the nut on and tighten it securely.

17 Screw on the oil pressure sending unit, tighten it securely, reconnect the electrical connector to the sender and you're done!

Fitting an air/fuel ratio gauge

Most gauge manufacturers offer a wide variety of mounting solutions for any gauge installation. We bought this gauge bracket, which was designed for under-dash installations, but works just fine for this job.

01

06 Using a hole saw bit, drill a hole in the exhaust, then clean up the edge around the hole with a small grinding tool until it's smooth and clean.

07 Once you've drilled the hole and cleaned it up, place the weld-in boss over the hole, centre it with a socket or an extension to keep it exactly in place.

08 Tack-weld the boss into place.

09 With the boss tacked into position, remove the socket/extension, then weld the boss to the exhaust pipe.

02 You'll also need to buy an oxygen sensor and a weld-in boss from the manufacturer of the gauge. Don't buy a sensor from the manufacturer of your car. It will cost more money, and it won't include a weld-in boss, which you're going to need in order to screw the new sensor into the exhaust pipe.

03 After removing the entire ashtray assembly, we discovered a couple of mounting holes that we could use for our under-dash mounting bracket. (If you need help removing the ashtray, refer to your Haynes manual.) We also discovered a big hole behind the ashtray receptacle through which we could route the wires (another reason why the ashtray receptacle is a good location for this or any other gauge which you might wish to fit in this spot).

04 For our installation, we removed the gauge and fitted the bracket first, then fitted the gauge in the bracket. Then we routed the power (red), earth (black) and illumination (white) wires over to the fuse panel and spliced them into the same connections that we created for the tachometer install.

05 Now for the fun part! There's no place to fit your new oxygen sensor, so you're going to have to make one. First, mark the spot with a punch where you want to fit the new sensor. For the best accuracy, it should be very near the oxygen sensor for the engine management computer (but be sure to offset it enough so the sensor tips don't touch each other).

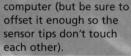

10 Inspect your work and make sure the weld completely surrounds the boss, with no holes. Any holes will allow air into the exhaust system and will cause false readings.

11 Apply a film of anti-seize compound to the threads of the new sensor . . .

12 . . . then screw the sensor securely into the boss (a special sensor socket is being used here).

13 Finally, attach the sensor wire to the gauge wire; we used a bullet connector here. Now lower the car and test the gauge. Keep in mind that the gauge won't give you an accurate reading until the sensor has warmed up fully.

Smokin' those tyres looks cool, but to get your power to the tarmac, you'd better take a hard look at that driveline.

Drivetrain upgrades

Once you've started modifying your machine, you can't go back to a standard clutch, or the combination of an aggressive driving style and an aggressive engine will fry a new standard clutch in short order. If you've "done" your clutch once already, you know much trouble it can be to get the car safely jacked up enough to be able to drop the gearbox out on the driveway. You don't want to have to do that too often. If you're having a pro do the installation, there's even more reason to do it once and do it right, since it can get expensive to re-clutch professionally. With an investment either way, in knuckle-busting labour or hard-earned cash, you need to choose your new clutch wisely.

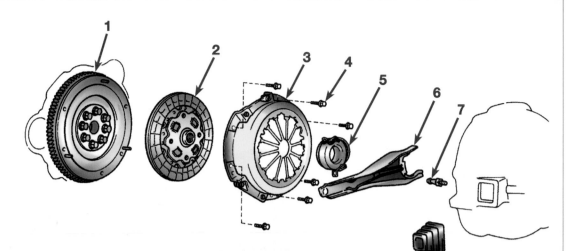

Clutch and flywheel

When we say "clutch", we really mean the assembly that connects the engine to the gearbox and transfers power. It consists of four basic components: flywheel; clutch disc; pressure plate or cover; and the clutch release mechanism. The flywheel is a large metal disc bolted to the back of the crankshaft. The clutch cover or pressure plate is bolted to the flywheel, and sandwiched between the flywheel and pressure plate is the clutch disc. The disc is held tightly between the pressure plate and flywheel and power is transferred to the gearbox because the disc is splined in the centre and rides on the splines of the gearbox's input shaft. When you need to "release the clutch", like to

A typical clutch system for performance use would include an aluminium flywheel, organic-faced clutch disc and higher-pressure clutch cover – this set is from Advanced Clutch Technology.

Clutch disc friction materials run from like-stock to the exotic, but most street clutches use organic or Kevlar material for holding power with long life and good clutch "feel"– note the springs around the center of each disc hub; you've got to have these for a smooth street clutch engagement

change gear, pushing the clutch pedal with your foot puts leverage against the pressure plate to let the disc spin independently of the flywheel. Let the pedal out and the power is again connected to the gearbox. This is a simplified explanation and there are a few smaller components to the system, but that's how it works.

For performance purposes, what we need to look at is the holding power and durability of a clutch system. From here on, by the way, we're going to use the term "clutch" to refer to the combination of clutch disc and pressure plate, because they normally are sold as a set, and it isn't recommended to intermix components of different brands. When you make more power, and tend to drive with race-style quick-shifting, the frictional load on the clutch is greatly increased, to the point where a standard clutch won't last.

While we may chuckle at "standard" and want a "manly" clutch, you can go too far. A really stiff racing clutch is OK for a dragstrip run, since you only need to go through the gears once, but on the road, you'll need Arnie's left leg for everyday driving. Fortunately, the aftermarket clutch companies have

divided their products into "stages" to make your choice easier. As you go up in stages, the clutches get stronger and stiffer; you basically match the clutch stage to your driving needs and horsepower level (or expected future level).

When you get into the clutches that have holding power for racing, things get expensive. There are disc designs with small metal or ceramic pucks instead of a full circle of friction material, discs without centre springs (too harsh for road cars), an even multiple-disc designs. In the latter case, there would be studs on the flywheel, one disc goes against the flywheel then a "floater" plate slides over the studs, another disc is added and then the clutch cover. Essentially there's the frictional "grab" area of two complete clutches, and usually the discs are smaller than normal, so rotating weight is reduced.

When choosing your clutch components, ask clutch manufacturers, tuning specialists and your friends about the clutches they have used. What you're concerned about is the amount of

Most clutches are of the diaphragm style, in which a multi-fingered plate leverages against the pressure plate to clamp down on the clutch disc - most aftermarket clutch covers are similar, but with altered leverage to increase clamping power without a big increase in pedal pressure.

Not all aftermarket flywheels are aluminium - this Comptech flywheel is made of CNC-machined chrome-moly steel, yet still weighs only 8.75 pounds.

Safety . . .
Shrapnel and scattershields

If you plan on racing at the dragstrip, you'd also be wise to check that the clutch is of an approved type. At many events, you must have an approved clutch and flywheel if you go quicker than 12 seconds.

Under extreme racing use, an original-type clutch and flywheel combination can literally explode in the car. The continued heat from hard gear changes can crack a flywheel or clutch pressure plate to the point where the component eventually comes apart. Flying pieces of clutch/flywheel shrapnel can injure the driver or cut a fuel line and cause a disastrous fire. This we don't want, so invest in a quality approved lightweight flywheel. Even with the right clutch and flywheel, there are some events and classes in which you will also have to have a "scattershield" which is a 1/4 -inch-thick steel shield that goes around your bellhousing to contain shrapnel if anything happens. We should also mention that when fitting a performance clutch and or flywheel, you should use only top-quality, new, high-strength bolts to secure them. Go fast, but be safe.

pedal pressure, how the clutch engages (or its "feel"), and how long a particular clutch can be expected to handle performance use.

Flywheels are an important part of the clutch system as well, but the choices are fewer. A lighter flywheel allows an engine to rev quicker. For road use and only occasional racing with a mildly upgraded engine, the standard flywheel should be fine. As your driveline needs get more demanding, consider a performance flywheel at the same time your upgraded clutch is fitted. And aftermarket companies have been making lightweight aluminium flywheels for performance use for years.

Racing clutches have solid hubs (no springs) and usually have exotic materials for the friction surfaces, like ceramic or metallic pads, either in a full circle or in pucks like these.

36 ▷ 1A   2   36 ▷ 2A   3   36 ▷ 3A

There aren't a lot of gear ratio choices for modern cars, and a new ring and pinion set like this is expensive, but if you're racing and determine that you need the extra gearing because you're running much bigger tyres (slicks) these could be just what you need.

Drivetrain
improvements

Once you have a decent clutch that can handle your engine's new output, you will probably never have a driveline problem on the road. It's possible, of course, but the major limit to your car's take-off is "where the rubber meets the road". Road tyres will just go up in smoke when you apply too much throttle on a high-horsepower car; this could cause an engine problem if you over-rev during the wheel spin, but the driveline shouldn't break. Once you put on a pair of slicks or a wider, softer tyre that really bites, that's when things can snap!

If you have a standard differential in your car, most of your engine load is going to wind up going to one driveshaft when you're burning away from the lights. This increases the chances of breaking that driveshaft. One solution that can take the extra burden off is a limited-slip differential (LSD). This differential has a type of clutch in it that "locks up" under acceleration, providing more equal distribution of power to the two driveshafts, giving you more traction and each shaft has less load on it . This sounds perfect but there are catches, of course. An LSD is expensive, and most DIYers have someone experienced do the fitting, which adds to the cost.

How the LSD bites is the other consideration. Such differentials differ in style of clutches but also in how much percentage of lockup, or "hook" they offer. Units with a higher percentage of lockup are less fun to drive around corners on the road, making ratcheting or clunking sounds because one shaft (on the outside of the corner) is trying to turn faster than the other. The LSDs that are better for the road have less hook, but they are still a major improvement in traction for road or dragstrip.

For serious *dragstrip-only* use, the complete answer is a spool. This is a solid unit that takes the place of the differential, and absolutely provides half the power to each axle. The disadvantage is that it doesn't like to go around corners at all, not really practical for the road.

A limited-slip differential works great on the street for providing increased traction, but for track-only use, a nearly-unbreakable spool like this Pro Drive gives equal torque to each axle

Since all your new power is getting transferred very suddenly to your new slicks, you may need to upgrade your hub assembly to one with a billet flange and stronger wheel studs – this one is from Pro Drive

With plenty of power and plenty of traction, the only thing missing in the equation is plenty of driveshaft strength. Your driveshafts typically have a CV joint on the outside, a middle shaft, and a tripod-type joint at the inner end. One or all of these components will fail with enough force against them on the start line. Once you've upgraded your driveline, you'll be fine until the tyre companies come out with a stickier or bigger slick, then you'll have to upgrade to the next level of shafts.

If you've been reading our book up to this point, and you're making enough new power and torque to start worrying about driveline breakage, that makes us feel good. Not that you're breaking parts, but that our advice in the power-making department has served you well!

As engine builders keep finding more power and use bigger slicks, for extreme drag use you need a completely-new drivetrain – this package from Moore Performance includes big shafts, billet joint components, billet spool, and chrome-moly knuckles with hubs, bearings and lightweight disc brakes.

Stronger driveshafts and bigger CV joints will handle the extra loads imposed by running slicks – once you upgrade, you won't have to carry spare standard driveshafts to the track with you.

17

Safety and tools

Safety

We all know that working on your car can be dangerous - and we're not talking about the danger of losing your street cred by fitting naff alloys or furry dice! Okay, so you'd be hard-pushed to injure yourself fitting some cool floor mats or a tax disc holder, but tackle more-serious mods, and you could be treading dangerous ground. Let's be honest - we have to put this safety section in to cover ourselves, but now it's in, it would be nice if you read it…

Burning/scalding

The only way you'll really burn yourself is if your car's just been running - avoid this, and you won't get burned. Easy, eh? Otherwise, you risk burns from any hot parts of the engine (and especially the exhaust - if you've got one, the cat runs very hot), or from spilling hot coolant if you undo the radiator hoses or filler cap, as you might when you're braiding hoses.

Fire

Sadly, there's several ways your car could catch fire, when you think about it. You've got a big tank full of fuel (and other flammable liquids about, like brake fluid), together with electrics - some of which run to very high voltages. If you smoke too, this could be even worse for your health than you thought.

a Liquid fuel is flammable. Fuel vapour can explode - don't smoke, or create any kind of spark, if there's fuel vapour (fuel smell) about.

b Letting fuel spill onto a hot engine is dangerous, but brake fluid spills go up even more readily. Respect is due with brake fluid, which also attacks paintwork and plastics - wash off with water.

c Fires can also be started by careless modding involving the electrical system. It's possible to overload (and overheat) existing wiring by tapping off too many times for new live feeds. Not insulating bare wires or connections can lead to short-circuits, and the sparks or overheated wiring which results can start a fire. Always investigate any newly-wired-in kit which stops working, or which keeps blowing fuses - those wires could already be smouldering…

Crushing

Having your car land on top of you is no laughing matter, and it's a nasty accident waiting to happen if you risk using dodgy old jacks, bricks, and other means of lifting/supporting your car. Please don't.

Your standard vehicle jack is for emergency roadside use only - a proper trolley jack and a set of axle stands won't break the overdraft, and might save broken bones. Don't buy a cheap trolley jack, and don't expect a well-used secondhand one to be perfect, either - when the hydraulic seals start to fail, a trolley jack will drop very fast; this is why you should always have decent stands in place under the car as well.

Steering, suspension & brakes

Screwing up any one of these on your car, through badly-fitted mods, could land you and others in hospital or worse. Nuff said? It's always worth getting a mate, or a friendly garage, to check over what you've just fitted (or even what you've just had fitted, in some cases - not all "pro" fitters are perfect!). Pay attention to tightening vital nuts and bolts properly - buy or borrow a torque wrench.

To be absolutely sure, take your newly-modded machine to a friendly MOT tester (if there is such a thing) - this man's your ultimate authority on safety, after all. Even if he's normally a pain once a year, he could save your life. Think it over.

Even properly-fitted mods can radically alter the car's handling - and not always for the better. Take a few days getting used to how the car feels before showing off.

Wheels

Don't take liberties fitting wheels. Make sure the wheels have the right stud/bolt hole pattern for your car, and that the wheel nuts/bolts are doing their job. Bolts which are too long might catch on your brakes (especially rear drums) - too short, and, well, the wheels are just waiting to fall off. Not nice. Also pay attention to the bolt heads or wheel nuts - some are supposed to have large tapered washers fitted, to locate properly in the wheel. If the nuts/bolts "pull through" the wheel when tightened, the wheel's gonna fall off, isn't it?

Asbestos

Only likely to be a major worry when working on, or near, your brakes. That black dust that gets all over your alloys comes from your brake pads, and it may contain asbestos. Breathing in asbestos dust can lead to a disease called asbestosis (inflammation of the lungs - very nasty indeed), so try not to inhale brake dust when you're changing your pads or discs.

Airbags

Unless you run into something at high speed, the only time an airbag will enter your life is when you change your steering wheel for something more sexy, and have to disable the airbag in the process. Pay attention to all the precautionary advice given in our text, and you'll have no problems.

One more thing - don't tap into the airbag wiring to run any extra electrical kit. Any mods to the airbag circuit could set it off unexpectedly.

Exhaust gases

Even on cars with cats, exhaust fumes are still potentially lethal. Don't work in an unventilated garage with the engine running. When fitting new exhaust bits, be sure that there's no gas leakage from the joints. When modifying in the tailgate area, note that exhaust gas can get sucked into the car through badly-fitting tailgate seals/joints (or even through your rear arches, if they've been trimmed so much there's holes into the car).

Tools

In writing this book, we've assumed you already have a selection of basic tools - screwdrivers, socket set, spanners, hammer, sharp knife, power drill. Any unusual extra tools you might need are mentioned in the relevant text. Torx and Allen screws are often found on trim panels, so a set of keys of each type is a wise purchase.

From a safety angle, always buy the best tools you can afford - or if you must use cheap ones, remember that they can break under stress or unusual usage (and we've all got the busted screwdrivers to prove it!).

DO Wear goggles when using power tools.

DO Keep loose clothing/long hair away from moving engine parts.

DO Take off watches and jewellery when working on electrics.

DO Keep the work area tidy - stops accidents and losing parts.

DON'T Rush a job, or take stupid short-cuts.

DON'T Use the wrong tools for the job, or ones which don't fit.

DON'T Let kids or pets play around your car when you're working.

DON'T Work entirely alone under a car that's been jacked up.

Legal modding?
No such thing!!

The harsh & painful truth

The minute you start down the road to a modified motor, you stand a good chance of being in trouble with the Man. It seems like there's almost nothing worthwhile you can do to your car, without breaking some sort of law. So the answer's not to do it at all, then? Well, no, but let's keep it real.

There's this bunch of vehicle-related regulations called Construction & Use. It's a huge set of books, used by the car manufacturers and the Department of Transport among others, and it sets out in black and white all the legal issues that could land you in trouble. It's the ultimate authority for modifying, in theory. But few people (and even fewer policemen) know all of it inside-out, and it's forever being updated and revised, so it's not often enforced to the letter at the roadside - just in court. Despite the existence of C & U, in trying to put together any guide to the law and modifying, it quickly becomes clear that almost everything's a "grey area", with no-one prepared to go on record and say what is okay to modify and what's not. Well, brilliant. So if there's no fixed rules (in the real world), how are you meant to live by them? In the circumstances, all we can promise to do is help to make sense of nonsense…

Avoiding roadside interviews

Why do some people get pulled all the time, and others hardly ever? It's often all about attitude. We'd all like to be free to drive around "in yer face", windows down, system full up, loud exhaust bellowing, sparks striking, tyres squealing - but - nothing is a bigger "come-on" to the boys in blue than "irresponsible" driving like this. Rest assured,

if your motor's anywhere near fully sorted, the coppers will find something they can nick you for, when they pull you over - it's a dead cert. Trying not to wind them up too much before this happens (and certainly not once you're stopped) will make for an easier life. There's showing off, and then there's taking the pee. Save it for the next cruise.

The worst thing from your point of view is that, once you've been stopped, it's down to that particular copper's judgement as to whether your car's illegal. If he/she's having a bad day anyway, smart-mouthing-off isn't gonna help your case at all. If you can persuade him/her that you're at least taking on board what's being said, you might be let off with a warning. If it goes further, you'll be reported for an offence - while this doesn't mean you'll end up being prosecuted for it, it ain't good. Some defects (like worn tyres) will result in a so-called "seven-day wonder", which usually means you have to fix whatever's deemed wrong, maybe get the car inspected, and present yourself with the proof at a police station, inside seven days, or face prosecution.

If you can manage to drive reasonably sensibly when the law's about, and can ideally show that you've tried to keep your car legal when you get questioned, you stand a much better chance of enjoying your relationship with your modded beast. This guide is intended to help you steer clear of the more obvious things you could get pulled for. By reading it, you might even be able to have an informed, well-mannered discussion about things legal with the next officer of the law you meet at the side of the road. As in: "Oh really, officer? I was not aware of that. Thank you for pointing it out." Just don't argue with them, that's all...

Documents

The first thing you'll be asked to produce. If you're driving around without tax, MOT or insurance, we might as well stop now, as you won't be doing much more driving of anything after just one pull.

Okay, so you don't normally carry all your car-related documents with you - for safety, you've got them stashed carefully at home, haven't you? But carrying photocopies of your licence, MOT and insurance certificate is a good idea. While they're not legally-binding absolute proof, producing these in a roadside check might mean you don't have to produce the real things at a copshop later in the week. Shows a certain responsibility, and confidence in your own legality on the road, too. In some parts of the country, it's even said to be a good idea to carry copies of any receipts for your stereo gear - if there's any suspicion about it being stolen (surely not), some coppers have been known to confiscate it (or the car it's in) on the spot!

Number plates

One of the simplest mods, and one of the easiest to spot (and prove) if you're a copper. Nowadays, any changes made to the standard approved character font (such as italics or fancy type), spacing, or size of the plate constitutes an offence. Remember too that if you've moved the rear plate from its original spot (like from the tailgate recess, during smoothing) it still has to be properly lit at night. You're unlikely to even buy an illegal plate now, as the companies making them are also liable for prosecution if you get stopped. It's all just something else to blame on speed cameras - plates have to be easy for them to shoot, and modding yours suggests you're trying to escape a speeding conviction (well, who isn't?).

Getting pulled for an illegal plate is for suckers - you're making it too easy for them. While this offence only entails a small fine and confiscation of the plates, you're drawing unwelcome police attention to the rest of your car. Not smart. At all.

Lights

Lights of all kinds have to be one of the single biggest problem areas in modifying, and the police are depressingly well-informed. Light mods are a priority for any modder - so if they fit properly, and work, what's the problem?

First off, don't bother with any lights which aren't fully UK-legal - it's too much hassle. Being "E-marked" only makes them legal in Europe, and most of our Euro-chums drive on the right. One of our project cars ended up with left-hand-drive rear clusters, and as a result, had no rear reflectors and a rear foglight on the wrong side (should be on the right). Getting stopped for not having rear reflectors would be a bit harsh, but why risk it, to save a few quid?

Once you've had any headlight mods done (other than light brows) always have the beam alignment checked - it's part of the MOT, after all. The same applies to any front fogs or spots you've fitted (the various points of law involved here are too many to mention - light colour, height, spacing, operation with main/dipped headlights - ask at an MOT centre before fitting, and have them checked out after fitting).

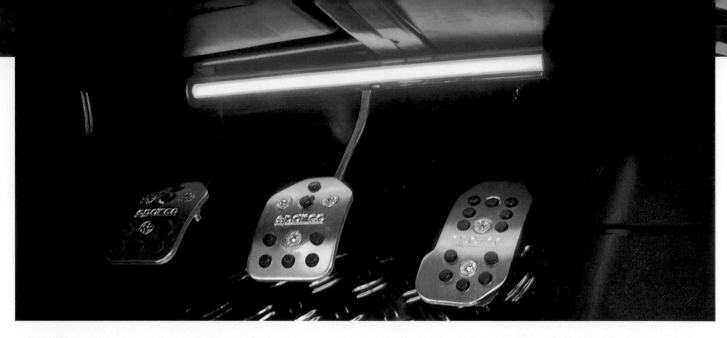

If Plod's really having a bad day, he might even question the legality of your new blue headlight bulbs - are they too powerful? Keeping the bulb packaging in the glovebox might be a neat solution here (60/55W max).

Many modders favour spraying rear light clusters to make them look trick, as opposed to replacing them - but there's trouble in store here, too. One of the greyest of grey areas is - how much light tinting is too much? The much-talked-about but not-often-seen "common sense" comes into play here. Making your lights so dim that they're reduced to a feeble red/orange glow is pretty dim itself. If you're spraying, only use proper light-tinting spray, and not too many coats of that. Colour-coding lights with ordinary spray paint is best left to a pro sprayer or bodyshop (it can be done by mixing lots of lacquer with not much paint, for instance). Tinted lights are actually more of a problem in daylight than at night, so check yours while the sun's out.

Lastly, two words about neons. Oh, dear. It seems that neons of all kinds have now been deemed illegal for road use (and that's interior ones as well as exteriors, which have pretty much always been a no-no). If you fit neons inside, make sure you rig in a switch so you can easily turn them off when the law arrives - or don't drive around with them on (save it for when you're parked up). Distracts other road users, apparently.

Big alloys/tyres

One of the first things to go on any lad's car, sexy alloys are right at the heart of car modifying. So what'll interest the law?

Well, the first thing every copper's going to wonder is - are the wheels nicked? He'd need a good reason to accuse you, but this is another instance where having copies of receipts might prove useful.

Otherwise, the wheels mustn't rub on, or stick out from, the arches - either of these will prove to be a problem if you get stopped. And you don't need to drive a modded motor to get done for having bald tyres...

Lowered suspension

Of course you have to lower your car, to have any hope of street cred. But did you know it's actually an offence to cause damage to the road surface, if your car's so low (or your mates so lardy) that it grounds out? Apparently so! Never mind what damage it might be doing to your exhaust, or the brake/fuel lines under the car - you can actually get done for risking damage to the road. Well, great. What's the answer? Once you've lowered the car, load it up with your biggest mates, and test it over roads you normally use - or else find

a route into town that avoids all speed bumps. If you've got coilovers, you'll have an easier time tuning out the scraping noises.

Remember that your new big-bore exhaust or backbox must be hung up well enough that it doesn't hit the deck, even if you haven't absolutely slammed your car on the floor. At night, leaving a trail of sparks behind is a bit of a giveaway...

Exhausts

One of the easiest-to-fit performance upgrades, and another essential item if you want to be taken seriously on the street. Unless your chosen pipe/system is just too damn loud, you'd be very unlucky to get stopped for it, but if you will draw attention this way, you could be kicking yourself later.

For instance - have you in fact fitted a home-made straight-through pipe, to a car which used to have a "cat"? By drawing Plod's attention with that extra-loud system, he could then ask you to get the car's emissions tested - worse, you could get pulled for a "random" roadside emissions check. Fail this (and you surely will), and you could be right in the brown stuff. Even if you re-convert the car back to stock for the MOT, you'll be illegal on the road (and therefore without insurance) whenever your loud pipe's on. Still sound like fun, or would you be happier with just a back box?

It's also worth mentioning that your tailpipe mustn't stick out beyond the very back of the car, or in any other way which might be dangerous to pedestrians. Come on - you were a ped once!

Bodykits

The popular bodykits for the UK market have all passed the relevant tests, and are fully-approved for use on the specific vehicles they're intended for. As long as you haven't messed up fitting a standard kit, you should be fine, legally-speaking. The trouble starts when you do your own little mods and tweaks, such as bodging on that huge whale-tail spoiler or front air dam/splitter - it can be argued in some cases that these aren't appropriate on safety grounds, and you can get prosecuted. If any bodywork is fitted so it obscured your lights, or so badly attached that a strong breeze might blow it off, you can see their point. At least there's no such thing as Style Police. Not yet, anyway.

Other mods

Anything else we didn't think of - is probably illegal too. Sorry. Any questions? Try the MOT Helpline (0845 6005977). Yes, really.

Thanks to Andrew Dare of the Vehicle Inspectorate, Exeter, for his help in steering us through this minefield!

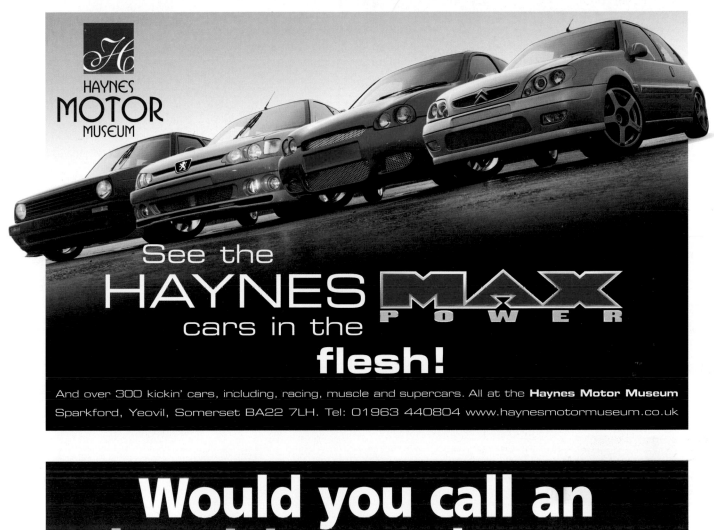

Haynes Car Manuals

Title	Code
Alfa Romeo Alfasud/Sprint (74 - 88	0292
Alfa Romeo Alfetta (73 - 87	0531
Audi 80, 90 (79 - Oct 86 & Coupe (81 - Nov 88	0605
Audi 80, 90 (Oct 86 - 90 & Coupe (Nov 88 - 90)	1491
Audi 100 (Oct 82 - 90 & 200 (Feb 84 - Oct 89)	0907
Audi 100 & A6 Petrol & Diesel (May 91 - May 97)	3504
Audi A4 (95 - Feb 00	3575
Austin A35 & A40 (56 - 67) *	0118
Austin Allegro 1100, 1300, 1.0, 1.1 & 1.3 (73 - 82) *	0164
Austin/MG/Rover Maestro 1.3 & 1.6 (83 - 95)	0922
Austin/MG Metro (80 - May 90)	0718
Austin/Rover Montego 1.3 & 1.6 (84 - 94)	1066
Austin/MG/Rover Montego 2.0 (84 - 95)	1067
Mini (59 - 69)	0527
Mini (69 - 01)	0646
Austin/Rover 2.0 litre Diesel Engine (86 - 93)	1857
Austin Healey 100/6 & 3000 (56 - 68) *	0049
Bedford CF (69 - 87)	0163
Bedford/Vauxhall Rascal & Suzuki Supercarry (86 - Oct 94)	3015
BMW 316, 320 & 320i (4-cyl) (75 - Feb 83)	0276
BMW 320, 320i, 323i & 325i (6-cyl) (Oct 77 - Sept 87)	0815
BMW 3-Series (Apr 91 - 96)	3210
BMW 3- & 5-Series (sohc) (81 - 91)	1948
BMW 520i & 525e (Oct 81 - June 88)	1560
BMW 1500, 1502, 1600, 1602, 2000 & 2002 (59 - 77) *	0240
Chrysler PT Cruiser (00 - 03)	4058
Citroën 2CV, Ami & Dyane (67 - 90)	0196
Citroën AX Petrol & Diesel (87 - 97)	3014
Citroën BX (83 - 94) A to L	0908
Citroën C15 Van Petrol & Diesel (89 - Oct 98)	3509
Citroën CX (75 - 88)	0528
Citroën Saxo Petrol & Diesel (96 - 01)	3506
Citroën Visa (79 - 88)	0620
Citroën Xantia Petrol & Diesel (93 - 98)	3082
Citroën XM Petrol & Diesel (89 - 00)	3451
Citroën Xsara Petrol & Diesel (97 - Sept 00)	3751
Citroën Xsara Picasso Petrol & Diesel (00 - 02)	3944
Citroën ZX Diesel (91 - 98)	1922
Citroën ZX Petrol (91 - 98)	1881
Citroën 1.7 & 1.9 litre Diesel Engine (84 - 96)	1379
Fiat 126 (73 - 87) *	0305
Fiat 500 (57 - 73)	0090
Fiat Bravo & Brava (95 - 00)	3572
Fiat Cinquecento (93 - 98)	3501
Fiat Panda (81 - 95)	0793
Fiat Punto Petrol & Diesel (94 - Oct 99)	3251
Fiat Regata (84 - 88)	1167
Fiat Tipo (88 - 91)	1625
Fiat Uno (83 - 95)	0923
Fiat X1/9 (74 - 89)	0273
Ford Anglia (59 - 68) *	0001
Ford Capri II (& III) 1.6 & 2.0 (74 - 87)	0283
Ford Capri II (& III) 2.8 & 3.0 (74 - 87)	1309
Ford Cortina Mk III 1300 & 1600 (70 - 76) *	0070
Ford Cortina Mk IV (& V) 1.6 & 2.0 (76 - 83) *	0343
Ford Cortina Mk IV (& V) 2.3 V6 (77 - 83) *	0426
Ford Escort Mk I 1100 & 1300 (68 - 74) *	0171
Ford Escort Mk I Mexico, RS 1600 & RS 2000 (70 - 74) *	0139
Ford Escort Mk II Mexico, RS 1800 & RS 2000 (75 - 80) *	0735
Ford Escort (75 - Aug 80) *	0280
Ford Escort (Sept 80 - Sept 90)	0686
Ford Escort & Orion (Sept 90 - 00)	1737
Ford Fiesta (76 - Aug 83)	0334
Ford Fiesta (Aug 83 - Feb 89)	1030
Ford Fiesta (Feb 89 - Oct 95)	1595
Ford Fiesta (Oct 95 - 01)	3397
Ford Focus (98 - 01)	3759
Ford Galaxy Petrol & Diesel (95 - Aug 00)	3984
Ford Granada (Sept 77 - Feb 85)	0481
Ford Granada & Scorpio (Mar 85 - 94)	1245
Ford Ka (96 - 02)	3570
Ford Mondeo Petrol (93 - 99)	1923
Ford Mondeo Diesel (93 - 96)	3465
Ford Orion (83 - Sept 90)	1009
Ford Sierra 4 cyl. (82 - 93)	0903
Ford Sierra V6 (82 - 91)	0904
Ford Transit Petrol (Mk 2) (78 - Jan 86)	0719
Ford Transit Petrol (Mk 3) (Feb 86 - 89)	1468
Ford Transit Diesel (Feb 86 - 99)	3019
Ford 1.6 & 1.8 litre Diesel Engine (84 - 96)	1172
Ford 2.1, 2.3 & 2.5 litre Diesel Engine (77 - 90)	1606
Freight Rover Sherpa (74 - 87)	0463
Hillman Avenger (70 - 82)	0037
Hillman Imp (63 - 76) *	0022
Honda Accord (76 - Feb 84)	0351
Honda Civic (Feb 84 - Oct 87)	1226
Honda Civic (Nov 91 - 96)	3199
Hyundai Pony (85 - 94)	3398
Jaguar E Type (61 - 72)	0140
Jaguar MkI & II, 240 & 340 (55 - 69) *	0098
Jaguar XJ6, XJ & Sovereign; Daimler Sovereign (68 - Oct 86)	0242
Jaguar XJ6 & Sovereign (Oct 86 - Sept 94)	3261
Jaguar XJ12, XJS & Sovereign; Daimler Double Six (72 - 88)	0478
Jeep Cherokee Petrol (93 - 96)	1943
Lada 1200, 1300, 1500 & 1600 (74 - 91)	0413
Lada Samara (87 - 91)	1610
Land Rover 90, 110 & Defender Diesel (83 - 95)	3017
Land Rover Discovery Petrol & Diesel (89 - 98)	3016
Land Rover Freelander (97 - 02)	3929
Land Rover Series IIA & III Diesel (58 - 85)	0529
Land Rover Series II, IIA & III Petrol (58 - 85)	0314
Mazda 323 (Mar 81 - Oct 89)	1608
Mazda 323 (Oct 89 - 98)	3455
Mazda 626 (May 83 - Sept 87)	0929
Mazda B-1600, B-1800 & B-2000 Pick-up (72 - 88)	0267
Mazda RX-7 (79 - 85) *	0460
Mercedes-Benz 190, 190E & 190D Petrol & Diesel (83 - 93)	3450
Mercedes-Benz 200, 240, 300 Diesel (Oct 76 - 85)	1114
Mercedes-Benz 250 & 280 (68 - 72)	0346
Mercedes-Benz 250 & 280 (123 Series) (Oct 76 - 84)	0677
Mercedes-Benz 124 Series (85 - Aug 93)	3253
Mercedes-Benz C-Class Petrol & Diesel (93 - Aug 00)	3511
MGA (55 - 62) *	0475
MGB (62 - 80)	0111
MG Midget & AH Sprite (58 - 80)	0265
Mitsubishi Shogun & L200 Pick-Ups (83 - 94)	1944
Morris Ital 1.3 (80 - 84)	0705
Morris Minor 1000 (56 - 71)	0024
Nissan Bluebird (May 84 - Mar 86)	1223
Nissan Bluebird (Mar 86 - 90)	1473
Nissan Cherry (Sept 82 - 86)	1031
Nissan Micra (83 - Jan 93)	0931
Nissan Micra (93 - 99)	3254
Nissan Primera (90 - Aug 99)	1851
Nissan Stanza (82 - 86)	0824
Nissan Sunny (May 82 - Oct 86)	0895
Nissan Sunny (Oct 86 - Mar 91)	1378
Nissan Sunny (Apr 91 - 95)	3219
Opel Ascona & Manta (B Series) (Sept 75 - 88)	0316
Opel Kadett (Nov 79 - Oct 84)	0634
Opel Rekord (Feb 78 - Oct 86)	0543
Peugeot 106 Petrol & Diesel (91 - 02)	1882
Peugeot 205 Petrol & Diesel (83 - 97)	0932
Peugeot 206 Petrol and Diesel (98 - 01)	3757
Peugeot 305 (78 - 89)*	0538
Peugeot 306 Petrol & Diesel (93 - 99)	3073
Peugeot 309 (86 - 93)	1266
Peugeot 405 Petrol (88 - 97)	1559
Peugeot 405 Diesel (88 - 97)	3198
Peugeot 406 Petrol & Diesel (96 - 97)	3394
Peugeot 406 Petrol & Diesel (99 - 02)	3982
Peugeot 505 (79 - 89)	0762
Peugeot 1.7/1.8 & 1.9 litre Diesel Engine (82 - 96)	0950
Peugeot 2.0, 2.1, 2.3 & 2.5 litre Diesel Engines (74 - 90)	1607
Porsche 911 (65 - 85)	0264
Porsche 924 & 924 Turbo (76 - 85)	0397
Proton (89 - 97)	3255
Range Rover V8 (70 - Oct 92)	0606
Reliant Robin & Kitten (73 - 83)	0436
Renault 4 (61 - 86) *	0072
Renault 5 (Feb 85 - 96)	1219
Renault 9 & 11 (82 - 89)	0822
Renault 18 (79 - 86)	0598
Renault 19 Petrol (89 - 94)	1646
Renault 19 Diesel (89 - 96)	1946
Renault 21 (86 - 94)	1397
Renault 25 (84 - 92)	1228
Renault Clio Petrol (91 - May 98)	1853
Renault Clio Diesel (91 - June 96)	3031
Renault Clio Petrol & Diesel (May 98 - May 01)	3906
Renault Espace Petrol & Diesel (85 - 96)	3197
Renault Fuego (80 - 86) *	0764
Renault Laguna Petrol & Diesel (94 - 00)	3252
Renault Mégane & Scénic Petrol & Diesel (96 - 98)	3395
Renault Mégane & Scénic Petrol & Diesel (Apr 99 - 02)	3916
Rover 213 & 216 (84 - 89)	1116
Rover 214 & 414 (89 - 96)	1689
Rover 216 & 416 (89 - 96)	1830
Rover 211, 214, 216, 218 & 220 Petrol & Diesel (Dec 95 - 98)	3399
Rover 414, 416 & 420 Petrol & Diesel (May 95 - 98)	3453
Rover 618, 620 & 623 (93 - 97)	3257
Rover 820, 825 & 827 (86 - 95)	1380
Rover 3500 (76 - 87)	0365
Rover Metro, 111 & 114 (May 90 - 98)	1711
Saab 95 & 96 (66 - 76) *	0198
Saab 99 (69 - 79) *	0247
Saab 90, 99 & 900 (79 - Oct 93)	0765
Saab 900 (Oct 93 - 98)	3512
Saab 9000 (4-cyl) (85 - 98)	1686
Seat Ibiza & Cordoba Petrol & Diesel (Oct 93 - Oct 99)	3571
Seat Ibiza & Malaga (85 - 92)	1609
Skoda Estelle (77 - 89)	0604
Skoda Favorit (89 - 96)	1801
Skoda Felicia Petrol & Diesel (95 - 01)	3505
Subaru 1600 & 1800 (Nov 79 - 90)	0995
Sunbeam Alpine, Rapier & H120 (67 - 76) *	0051
Suzuki Supercarry & Bedford/Vauxhall Rascal (86 - Oct 94)	3015
Suzuki SJ Series, Samurai & Vitara (4-cyl) (82 - 97)	1942
Talbot Alpine, Solara, Minx & Rapier (75 - 86)	0337
Talbot Horizon (78 - 86)	0473
Talbot Samba (82 - 86)	0823
Toyota Carina E (May 92 - 97)	3256
Toyota Corolla (Sept 83 - Sept 87)	1024
Toyota Corolla (80 - 85)	0683
Toyota Corolla (Sept 87 - Aug 92)	1683
Toyota Corolla (Aug 92 - 97)	3259
Toyota Hi-Ace & Hi-Lux (69 - Oct 83)	0304
Triumph Acclaim (81 - 84) *	0792
Triumph GT6 & Vitesse (62 - 74) *	0112
Triumph Herald (59 - 71) *	0010
Triumph Spitfire (62 - 81)	0113
Triumph Stag (70 - 78)	0441
Triumph TR2, TR3, TR3A, TR4 & TR4A (52 - 67) *	0028
Triumph TR5 & 6 (67 - 75) *	0031
Triumph TR7 (75 - 82) *	0322
Vauxhall Astra (80 - Oct 84)	0635
Vauxhall Astra & Belmont (Oct 84 - Oct 91)	1136
Vauxhall Astra (Oct 91 - Feb 98)	1832
Vauxhall/Opel Astra & Zafira Diesel (Feb 98 - Sept 00)	3797
Vauxhall/Opel Astra & Zafira Petrol (Feb 98 - Sept 00)	3758
Vauxhall/Opel Calibra (90 - 98)	3502
Vauxhall Carlton (Oct 78 - Oct 86)	0480
Vauxhall Carlton & Senator (Nov 86 - 94)	1469
Vauxhall Cavalier 1300 (77 - July 81) *	0461
Vauxhall Cavalier 1600, 1900 & 2000 (75 - July 81)	0315
Vauxhall Cavalier (81 - Oct 88)	0812
Vauxhall Cavalier (Oct 88 - 95)	1570
Vauxhall Chevette (75 - 84)	0285
Vauxhall Corsa (Mar 93 - 97)	1985
Vauxhall/Opel Corsa (Apr 97 - Oct 00)	3921
Vauxhall/Opel Frontera Petrol & Diesel (91 - Sept 98)	3454
Vauxhall Nova (83 - 93)	0909
Vauxhall/Opel Omega (94 - 99)	3510
Vauxhall Vectra Petrol & Diesel (95 - 98)	3396
Vauxhall/Opel Vectra (Mar 99 - May 02)	3930
Vauxhall/Opel 1.5, 1.6 & 1.7 litre Diesel Engine (82 - 96)	1222
Volkswagen 411 & 412 (68 - 75) *	0091
Volkswagen Beetle 1200 (54 - 77)	0036
Volkswagen Beetle 1300 & 1500 (65 - 75)	0039
Volkswagen Beetle 1302 & 1302S (70 - 72)	0110
Volkswagen Beetle 1303, 1303S & GT (72 - 75)	0159
Volkswagen Beetle Petrol & Diesel (Apr 99 - 01)	3798
Volkswagen Golf & Bora Petrol & Diesel (April 98 - 00)	3727
Volkswagen Golf & Jetta Mk 1 1.1 & 1.3 (74 - 84)	0716
Volkswagen Golf, Jetta & Scirocco Mk 1 1.5, 1.6 & 1.8 (74 - 84)	0726
Volkswagen Golf & Jetta Mk 1 Diesel (78 - 84)	0451
Volkswagen Golf & Jetta Mk 2 (Mar 84 - Feb 92)	1081
Volkswagen Golf & Vento Petrol & Diesel (Feb 92 - 96)	3097
Volkswagen LT vans & light trucks (76 - 87)	0637
Volkswagen Passat & Santana (Sept 81 - May 88)	0814
Volkswagen Passat Petrol & Diesel (May 88 - 96)	3498
Volkswagen Passat 4-cyl Petrol & Diesel (Dec 96 - Nov 00)	3917
Volkswagen Polo & Derby (76 - Jan 82)	0335
Volkswagen Polo (82 - Oct 90)	0813
Volkswagen Polo (Nov 90 - Aug 94)	3245
Volkswagen Polo Hatchback Petrol & Diesel (94 - 99)	3500
Volkswagen Scirocco (82 - 90)	1224
Volkswagen Transporter 1600 (68 - 79)	0082
Volkswagen Transporter 1700, 1800 & 2000 (72 - 79)	0226
Volkswagen Transporter (air-cooled) (79 - 82)	0638
Volkswagen Transporter (water-cooled) (82 - 90)	3452
Volkswagen Type 3 (63 - 73) *	0084
Volvo 120 & 130 Series (& P1800) (61 - 73) *	97010
Volvo 142, 144 & 145 (66 - 74)	0129
Volvo 240 Series (74 - 93)	0270
Volvo 262, 264 & 260/265 (75 - 85) *	0400
Volvo 340, 343, 345 & 360 (76 - 91)	0715
Volvo 440, 460 & 480 (87 - 97)	1691
Volvo 740 & 760 (82 - 91)	1258
Volvo 850 (92 - 96)	3260
Volvo 940 (90 - 96)	3249
Volvo S40 & V40 (96 - 99)	3569
Volvo S70, V70 & C70 (96 - 99)	3573

* = Classic Reprints